UNEQUAL EDUCATIONAL PROVISION
IN ENGLAND AND WALES

WITHDRAWN

UNEQUAL EDUCATIONAL PROVISION IN ENGLAND AND WALES: THE NINETEENTH-CENTURY ROOTS

W. E. MARSDEN

Reader in Education
University of Liverpool

'*Everywhere was found disparity, irregularity*'
(*Hansard*, 3rd Series, vol. 109 (1850), col. 32)

THE WOBURN PRESS

First published 1987 in Great Britain by
THE WOBURN PRESS
Gainsborough House, Gainsborough Road,
London, E11 1RS, England

and in the United States of America by
THE WOBURN PRESS
c/o Biblio Distribution Centre
81 Adams Drive, P.O. Box 327, Totowa, N.J. 07511

British Library Cataloguing in Publication Data

Marsden, W.E.
 Unequal educational provision in England and
 Wales : the nineteenthl-century roots.
 1. Education — Great Britain — History
 — 19th century
 I. Title
 370'.941   LA631.7

ISBN 0-7130-0178-X

Library of Congress Cataloging-in-Publication Data

Marsden, W.E. (William Edward)
 Unequal educational provision in England and Wales.

 Includes index.
 1. Educational equalization—England—History—
19th century.   2. Educational equalization—Wales—
History—19th century.   I. Title
LC213.3.G72E546   1987   370.19'092   86-26755
ISBN 0-7130-0178-X

Printed and bound in Great Britain by
A. Wheaton & Co. Ltd, Exeter

Contents

List of Figures

Unequal Educational Provision in England and Wales

List of Photographs

Acknowledgements

This book comprises extensively revised and reordered material which has appeared in other publications together with a considerable amount of new material. I am pleased to acknowledge the following publications in which the earlier material has appeared.

The introductory chapter draws on two methodological articles: 'Historical Geography and the History of Education', *History of Education* (1977), and 'Ecology and Nineteenth-Century Urban Education', *History of Education Quarterly* (1983).

Chapter 2 is in large part an article of a similar title in *History of Education* (1982) with some additional material drawn from 'Historical Geography and the History of Education'. Chapter 3 is a revised version of an essay 'Education and Urbanisation in Nineteenth-century Britain', to be published in *Paedagogica Historica* (1986–7).

Chapter 4 is a revision of 'Social Stratification and Nineteenth-century English Urban Education' which appears in R. K. Goodenow and W. E. Marsden (eds.), *Urban Educational History in Four Nations: the United States, the United Kingdom, Australia and Canada* (Holmes and Meier, 1986); while Chapter 5 is a significantly extended version of 'Schools for the Urban Lower Middle Class: 3rd Grade or Higher Grade?' in P. Searby (ed.), *Educating the Victorian Middle Class* (History of Education Society, 1982).

Chapter 6 is taken in part from 'Variations in Educational Provision in Lancashire during the School Board Period', *Journal of Educational Administration and History* (1982), but contains a considerable amount of new material. Chapter 7 is largely new but draws on material found in 'Education and the Social Geography of Nineteenth Century Towns and Cities' in D. A. Reeder (ed.), *Urban Education in the Nineteenth Century* (Taylor and Francis, 1977), and in 'Travelling to School: Aspects of Nineteenth-century Catchment Areas', *Geography* (1980). It is also complementary to a paper read at the American Educational Research Association (Montreal, 1983) entitled 'Residential Segregation and the Hierarchy of Elementary Schooling from Charles Booth's London Surveys', in *The London Journal* (1986).

Chapter 8 is new but is based on sections of 'Social Environment, School Attendance and Educational Achievement in a Merseyside Town, 1870–1900' in P. McCann (ed.), *Popular Education and Socialization in the Nineteenth Century* (Methuen, 1977); 'Census Enumerators' Returns, Schooling and Social Areas in the Late Victorian Town: a Case Study of Bootle' in R. Lowe (ed.), *New Approaches to the Study of Popular Education, 1851–1902* (History of Education Society, 1979); and the previously cited 'Variations in Educational Provision in Lancashire during the School Board Period' (Chapter 6), and 'Travelling to School' (Chapter 7). Chapter 9 is also largely new but contains some material from the essay in the McCann volume (Chapter 8) and more particularly from the case study material included in 'Ecology and Nineteenth-Century Urban Education' (Chapter 1).

Chapter 10 is new but draws heavily on the work of H. J. Foster, some of which appears in 'Private, Proprietary and Public Elementary Schools in a Lancashire Residential Town: a Contest for the Patronage of the Lower Middle Classes 1870–1900' in the previously cited Searby volume (Chapter 5), and some in a forthcoming University of Liverpool Ph.D. thesis. I am particularly grateful for his permission to use the maps forming Figs. 10.1, 10.3, 10.5, and 10.6.

Among other people to whom I am indebted either for general or specific reasons I must mention John Vaughan, Tutor Librarian of the Education Library at the University of Liverpool, whose wide-ranging knowledge of educational history and its sources is a tremendous support; Bob Hunt, for drawing many of the maps; the University's photographic service for prints of some of the photographs of Southport and Birkdale; the editors of the volumes and journals in which some of these articles have appeared; Mr. A. J. Usher, for information on and photographs of Brighthelmston School; and, not least, and while not directly implicated, to Harry Armytage, who started it all off by making the history of education for one student many years ago so stimulating a part of a P.G.C.E. course.

More formally I wish to acknowledge the permission of the following for the reproduction of photographs: G.L.C. Record Office for Plates 1, 2, 3, 4 and 5; and Sefton Libraries for 6, 7, 8, 11, 12, 13 and 14; and for the reproduction of old Ordnance Survey maps (Figs. 9.3 and 10.3), the British Library.

Financial support for much of the research which has gone into this book has been supplied by the University of Liverpool Research Fund for which I have long been grateful. Similarly I am grateful for the help given both recently and formerly by the staffs of Southport and Bootle Public Libraries (now amalgamated under Sefton), the British Library, the British Newspaper Library, the Public Record Office, the G.L.C. Record Office, the National Society, and the libraries of the University of Liverpool and the London School of Economics.

Finally, I should like to register my warmest appreciation for the support and pertinent comments of the editor of this series, Peter Gordon.

W. E. Marsden

Preface

A number of experiences and preoccupations have influenced the ten years or so of research from which this book has emerged. The first is an academic training which has included a first degree in geography and a higher degree in educational history. The combination has provided the impulse and hopefully also the capacity to work comfortably in the disciplinary borderlands.

The second has been the experience in school-teaching, teacher education, research, and as a parent, of the importance of 'placing' in affecting the well-being of children, whether at the micro-level, in terms of the differentially experienced quality of teaching; at the meso-level, in respect of the sustaining or alienating effect of the climate of the particular school; or at the macro-level, the one most relevant to this book, in relation to not only situation in time, but also the pervasive disparities in provision which continue to advance or retard the chances of pupils according to the local authority in which they reside. Thus recent figures of the Chartered Institute of Public Finance and Accountancy (for 1982–3) show at the extremes one authority with a pupil–teacher ratio of 13.8 and another with 20.6; one authority spending £1144 per primary school pupil and another £601; and similarly £1633 and £864 per secondary pupil. And from the Educational Publishers Council we find extremes in per capita book spending in secondary schools from £5.89 in one county to £18.22 in another, with an average of £10.15. Far more publicity has been given to variations arising from home background, than to the variations which have also long existed in provision.

The third influence has been a widely felt impatience, which is in fact gradually being redressed, with much of the content of the existing historiography of education. This is manifest in the concentration on the great events; the great figures; the great confrontations; the great social polarities; the great historical forces and ideological imperatives. Again, in the social history of education, so much relatively has been written about the top and bottom ten per cents of the population, and so little about the much larger groups in the middle; and so much about the aggregates and so little about idiosyncratic group and individual reactions to educational provision.

Turning to family educational history, how few of the readers of this book will have forebears who experienced the extremes of social control of the public school or truant school? But how many will have had contact with the respectable elementary, higher grade and proprietary schools that were emerging in the later decades of the nineteenth century? How few will have been aware of the great confrontations and aggregate forces; but how many personally involved in interplay between individual school and community?

As John Hurt implies, in recounting some of his own family history in the Preface to his *Elementary Schooling and the Working Classes*, parents in the broad middle sector of late nineteenth-century society were faced with anxiety-provoking choices of schools without quite the background they needed to be sure of what was best for their children. Should they select the small but protective private school which was, however, able to offer only a limited range of subjects? Should they opt for the voluntary school and the religious training it offered, and not worry too much about the ageing facilities? Should they choose the new board school, with its impressive buildings, better qualified staff and more wide-ranging curriculum, but run the risk of their children being infected or corrupted by classmates drawn from less fortunate groups? Should they take advantage of the convenience of the nearby school or use the urban transport system and the hazards that entailed to enrol their children at a more prestigious school? At what point should they shift their children from one school to another in the face of social decline in an area, or the alienating influence of an unsympathetic teacher? Should they favour some rather than others of their children in letting them stay longer at school to gain the qualifications needed for an office position, while insisting on the rest leaving early to go into the family business or help with running the home?

This is a book about the urban history, the social history and the local history of education. It is hoped that the framework and the apparatus employed have helped to establish connections, at the appropriate scale, between urban development *and* education; social change *and* education, and community *and* schooling, rather than treating these aspects as a backcloth to educational development. It is also a book about disparities of access to education, and how these were rooted into the developing mass system of schooling in

England and Wales in the nineteenth century, and were characterised and experienced at different social and geographical levels of resolution, at different times, by different groups and individuals, whether providers or recipients of educational facilities.

CHAPTER ONE

Introduction
Approaches to the Study of
Nineteenth-century Educational
Disparities

There might be equality in the aggregate, and the work of popular
education be not more than half-accomplished, from the want of
equality in the distribution. In judging of school accommodation, we
must look to three things respecting it – its *amount*, its *character* and its
distribution.[1] (Anon., 1846)

INTRODUCTION

The degree of discrimination that is evident in this comment on
unequal access to schooling by an anonymous mid-nineteenth-century
columnist has often been lacking in subsequent appraisals. The issues
embedded in the critique remain relevant nearly a century and a
half later, and changes over time would seem to have been of degree
rather than of kind. Extreme variations in educational provision were
endemic in nineteenth century England and Wales. Their nature is,
however, inexactly represented by the polarised distinctions between
schooling for the rich and schooling for the poor which reflect much of
the literature on the subject. While it is obviously the case that in gross
terms the well-to-do enjoyed immeasurably better educational opportunities than less fortunate groups, more finely-tuned appraisals make
it equally clear that unequal access, both quantitative and qualitative,
existed within each social grade.

In approaching nineteenth-century educational disparities it is
necessary to place schooling in a trinity of contexts: of time, of place
and of society. Making the connections involves crossing boundaries
in the network of knowledge,[2] taking a comprehensive and eclectic

view of the field to be covered, and assembling from diverse sources materials which might contribute to an explanatory synthesis.

In this book, therefore, many of the issues that have been central in much of the historiography of education, such as the role of church and state in school provision, policy-making in Whitehall, education and the industrial revolution, and education and the labour movement, and other aspects which reflect largely the view from the centre, are skirted. It explores rather interactions between schooling and the shifting socio-economic and status groupings and the increasing territorial segregation that were integral parts of the dominating nineteenth-century process of urbanisation. While clearly industrialisation and urbanisation cannot sensibly be separated, the emphasis is on the latter rather than the former. The concentration is on the period in which a secondary (industrial) revolution was merging into a tertiary (services, mostly urban) revolution, rather than one in which the main change was from an agricultural to an industrial society. The differences between the two in terms of educational responses are considerable.

The book also focuses on problems of spatial variation and of scale. It explores the tensions between national and local levels of decision-making, and the educational disparities that resulted. The view from Whitehall was different from that from the Town Hall, and that from the School Board Office not necessarily in tune with feelings in the local community. The attempt is made to uncover group and personal experience of education at this detailed level, and to identify the conflicting and confusing pressures which impinged on individual schools and families in urban areas in the second half of the nineteenth century.

Placing schooling in the contexts of time, space and society suggests the need for a broad conceptual framework, and to this end appropriate apparatus from the urban historian, the historical geographer and the urban sociologist is identified and deployed.

URBAN HISTORY

The extent to which educational historians have neglected the process of urbanisation as central to late nineteenth-century educational development is matched only by the extent to which urban historians have neglected education as a social component. The study of urban history in Britain was spearheaded at the University of Leicester by the late Professor H. J. Dyos, but of his group only David Reeder has given any priority to the investigation of the schools and the children that were such burgeoning features of Victorian city life. Reeder has drawn attention to the 'taken-for-granted' attitude of educational historians towards the urban context of schooling,[3] and the emphasis on schooling *in* the city rather than on schooling *and* the city. It is surprising that the pursuit of urban history, so evidently an academic by-product of the anxieties of the 1960s and 1970s about social conflict and the city, has been so little applied to educational development. Anxieties about urban schooling still loom large. There is a self-evident need for a historical perspective on 'the problems of the urban present'.[4]

As a framework for an interactive study of education and urbanisation, the American urban historian Eric Lampard's identification of three basic and overlapping concepts is a useful starting point.[5] These are *demography*, the concentration of population; *structure*, which can be taken to include occupational grouping, social stratification and the social and spatial patterning of the urban habitat; and the *urban experience*, as expressed in modes of behaviour and thought which might justifiably be characterised as 'urban'. Such a framework forms the basis of Chapter 3 of this book.

An equally important component in historical interdisciplinary study is the linkage of a wide range of source materials, and in this respect urban historians and historical geographers have found common ground. In any study which purports to establish relationships between the aggregate and the particular; the official line and the hidden agenda; the bureaucratic accuracy of a minuted agreement and the possibly emotive responses of those it affects; or national policy and local experience – it is not enough to be content with a limited range of sources, however good, perhaps as part of a self-denying ordinance to accept only those which were comprehensively and bureaucratically collected, and can therefore be defined as reliable. It may be that the well-tilled nature of the field of literacy studies, for example, reflects the ready availability of marriage registers as sources of data. It has produced some successful work, but inevitably tells us little about the development of schooling. Similarly, the census enumerators' returns for the mid-nineteenth century contain valuable information on scholar–non-scholar ratios, to be used in Chapter 9, but are by definition less valuable in discussing attendance issues than, for example, school admissions registers. On the other hand, these more pertinent sources are often sadly interrupted and even random in their preservation. It is therefore of some moment when the possibility presents itself of linking the social data contained in the enumerators' returns and information about schooling in admissions registers, and matching them for particular families, providing the possibility of establishing a detailed relationship between parental background and school attendance and achievement, a type of research underpinning some of the conclusions in Chapter 8.

In conventional histories a chronological signposting has often been provided by major pieces of educational legislation. The impact of such events as the provision of parliamentary grants for educational purposes, of the Newcastle Commission and 'payment by results', and above all of the 1870 Act, cannot be ignored. An alternative framework, and one closely though not solely related to urbanisation, is to explore the process of educational development in terms of the increasing rigour of the criteria used in appraising the achievement at successive stages, bearing in mind the inevitable overlap of these criteria as between areas. Thus in the incipient phase of development the mere fact of official and wide acceptance of the notion that mass day schooling was desirable and practicable was a first step in the ladder of progress. This was followed by the actual building of accommodation. The number of places provided could be counted, apportioned by religious body or by geographical spread, and compared. Such enumeration initially revealed the gaps in the highly urbanised counties (Chapter 2). Once the places were provided, however, they might remain only partially filled. The next criterion was enrolment. How many children were there on the books? It was this measure that came nearest to the scholar–non-scholar ratios which can be drawn from the census enumerators' returns, as it might be presumed that children who were categorised by their parents as 'scholars' were on the books of schools.

Many more were enrolled than regularly attended, however, and by the middle of the century there was considerable dissatisfaction over general levels of attendance. Average attendance became an important element in the earning of grant. The streets of towns and cities swarmed with truants, a major source of school anxiety. An associated problem was the length of stay at school. The Taunton Commission used this as a means of grading schools (Chapters 4 and 5). Equally, when compulsory attendance was established in the School Board period, different local authorities accepted different levels of exemption from attendance (Chapter 6), which could be achieved at an earlier age if a particular 'standard' was reached. Thus average attendance and length of stay became important indices of the success of educational development in the second half of the century.

The concept of 'standard reached' was a further and perhaps the most significant criterion of achievement, in being to an extent qualitative. While the Codes changed over the years, the rigidity of the 'payment by results' system ensured some uniformity over time and also across areas, to make comparisons relatively straight-forward. At a gross level, there was a qualitative distinction between the inspected and uninspected school. Then within the inspected category, distinctions could be made according to the 'results' achieved. Appraisals of schools in Inspectors' reports were, if favour-able, widely publicised.

Crucial to the relationship between educational development in the public sector and the process of urbanisation was the emergence of a graduated elementary system of schooling (Chapter 4). In this a match was established between the differentiated nature of social intakes and a typology of schools based on graded fees. During the School Board period, in the major towns and cities in particular, this process was reinforced as a scholarship ladder developed, and the schools could be measured by the number of scholarships achieved. Equally prestigious were the schools which extended both the age limits and curricular conceptions of elementary provision. These became 'higher grade' schools (Chapter 5).

Whatever the criticisms that might be made of nineteenth-century elementary schooling, there can be no doubt that over the period an educational revolution had taken place, from a situation at the beginning where the very notion of mass education of the 'poorer orders' was contested, to one at the end where schooling was uni-versal, compulsory and free, and some children from humble homes were being placed on the ladder to secondary education. The stages of educational development which occurred and overlapped between these two temporal limits provide one of the frameworks which make up this text, and are explored primarily in the urban context.

HISTORICAL GEOGRAPHY

Spatial factors provide another kind of framework.[6] Educational phenomena are distributed in space, and by definition enter the sphere of interest of the geographer. The approach of the historical geographer is through cross-sectional studies at selected points in time, linked by investigations of significant intervening change. An important element in geographical methodology is obviously the mapping of data. Maps were a popular means of presenting information in the Victorian period, and have become highly sophisticated display instruments. They can serve as efficient storage devices for spatial information; as analogue models of reality, helping us to find our way around a place without actually having been there; as vivid, often aesthetically pleasing, and lucid means of portraying spatial information (in contrast, for example, to often indigestible numerical tabulations of data); and in highlighting otherwise obscure and unsuspected relationships. But using maps for correlation in a cause and effect sense is hazardous. It is much safer to regard them as question-posing rather than question-answering agencies. Four concepts that are of general interest to the geographer are explored in this book in the educational context: scale, social distance, sphere of influence (catchment area), and diffusion.

Geographers are by definition concerned with problems of scale. In gross terms, so far as the scope of this book is concerned, we can think of three levels of resolution: the national, regional and local. Differences in scale form the basis of the division of this text into two sections, in which national/regional variations, then in turn local disparities, are explored. The desire to make use not only of quantitative studies of aggregate populations but also of individual constructions of reality prescribes notice being taken of the differential operation of social processes at different scales. The level of resolution is thus fined down from the national, studying variations between regions (the subject of Chapter 2); to that of variations at intra-regional or intra-metropolitan levels (as in Chapters 6 and to some extent 7); and finally to the local level (Chapters 8, 9 and 10).

Further refinement is necessary for local studies, according to whether the concentration is at the inter-community level, enabling comparisons to be made of one community with others; or intra-community, investigating individual streets, groups of families or households. Such detailed grassroots study is an important restraint on determinism and stereotyping, and gives due credence to the complexity, variability and idiosyncracy of human decision-making (Chapters 9 and 10). It defuses some of the criticisms of traditional ecological approaches which will be considered below.

One of the critical connecting concepts is social distance, which links the domestic level of personally perceived status and aspirations with the aggregate level of social grouping, spatial segregation, and external perceptions and stereotyping of particular neighbourhoods. Selection of houses and choice of schools are, in this context, revealing examples of social decision-making. Among under-privileged groups the characteristic experience is restricted choice. A wider choice exists for the 'middling groups'. Here the more complex decisions are animated by personal aspirations and qualitative judgements about particular social areas, yet are at the same time constrained by family size and budget.[7] An accumulation of individual family decisions in an area in the same direction can have an aggregate effect. An influx of young families with a considerable number of young children into a well-established suburb with old people, for example, can lead to a build-up of decisions among the latter to move out, changing the social nature of the area.

It is important therefore to leaven both the aggregate approaches considered above and the ecological approaches to be discussed later in this chapter with an individualised perspective to produce a less splintered and less deterministic vision of people in their social spaces.[8]

For each social group, a network of preferred places, interaction spaces, safe and dangerous locales, and frequented and avoided paths could be mapped ... Such socio-spatial reference systems can be viewed as filters through which the physical environment is known, evaluated and used ... Shops, schools and churches stand out as focuses in the mental maps of their clientele.[9]

The school is obviously the work-place of children and through the nineteenth century increasing numbers of them journeyed thither daily.[10] The catchment area of the school is a feature of considerable interest to the geographer. It is the school's sphere of influence, and provides a framework within which interaction between the built forms and patterns of the environment, the social structure, people's attitudes and behaviours, and the educational system, can be investigated. The size of the catchment area is variously related to factors of physical geography, the extent and population density of the built-up area, the age grouping of children, the nature of the administrative control, the prestige of the particular school, and the existence of competing provision. In general, the more spatially compact, physically flat and densely populated the area, the younger the age group, the lower the prestige of the school, and the more heavily endowed the district is with schools, the smaller will be the catchment zone.

In the Victorian period, a particular area might be surfeited with schools because of competing provision between the church providers. Following the 1870 Act, school boards looking for cost-effective solutions tried to use this spare capacity rather than build new board schools. But Nonconformists declined to send their children to Catholic or Anglican schools, and implacably refused to compromise purely for financial reasons (Chapter 8). In older towns and cities, the traditional parochial system often found itself mismatched with evolving social structures. A fundamental principle of the National Society was the maintenance of religious instruction by the parish clergyman: 'the limits of the benefice properly determine the school area'. Canon Trevor illustrated the consequential problems from the situation in York, where a plethora of city centre churches existed, but where the limited resources and small size of parish units made non-viable the establishment of full elementary provision. He proposed that this should be attempted only in wealthy parishes. Poorer ones would have to combine, perhaps one to support a boys', another a girls' and a third an infants' school.[11]

However small the catchment area, a number of hazards perennially faced children on their journeys through the urban environment to school. Unplanned growth of traffic, with streets crowded with horse-drawn vehicles, trams and, in dockland areas, railways, made travel to school a potential danger, to young children especially. One of the London HMIs, S. N. Stokes, appealed to the London School Board to distinguish infants from juniors and to establish more and smaller infant units to give more restricted catchments. Exemplifying from his Southwark district, Stokes argued that the 'topographical character' of a place had an 'educational bearing', and reminded the Board of the wide thoroughfares and other busy streets, canals and dock entrances in the vicinity of the Thames.[12] Failure to take account of this factor had resulted in some infants' departments being short of clients:

an infants' school draws its scholars from a narrower area than a boys' or girls' school on the same spot, and the infants living at a distance from the school will be more than commonly irregular.[13]

Catchment areas are but one of the topics of study inviting a convergence of historical, geographical and social science interests. For example, investigation of diffusion processes is similarly common to all three fields, for the spread of ideas and innovations takes place in three dimensions: temporal, spatial and social. The diffusion of one of the most important of nineteenth century innovations, mass elementary education, is the subject of Chapter 2.

URBAN SOCIOLOGY: AN ECOLOGICAL APPROACH

The urban arena is the one in which have been fought out burning issues impinging on education, such as class, bureaucracy, racism and social control.[14] The third methodological strand is therefore drawn from the social sciences. The most pertinent field in the present context is urban sociology, and particularly the ecological thinking which derives from British empirical studies of the nineteenth century, but was formalised in the work of the Chicago School in the inter-war years. Less attention is paid here to macro-, structuralist modes of analysis. The main objective is related not so much to an overall predictive political critique of nineteenth-century urban educational policy, as to an 'on the floor' investigation of how urban educational problems and policies evolved. This is not to say that structuralist and ecological approaches are incompatible, and indeed it has been persuasively argued that these and other theoretical perspectives should be brought together.[15]

Formal ecological studies date back to the post-'Origin of Species' years of the middle of the nineteenth century.[16] The German biologist, Ernest Haeckel, introduced the concept of ecology as the natural science dealing with the relations of living organisms with each other and with their environment in 1869, ten years after the appearance of Darwin's great work. Quick to see the social applications of the ecological process of 'natural selection', the anthropologist Francis Galton published *Hereditary Genius*, also in 1869. This was the precursor of Social Darwinism and a new science, eugenics, which advocated improving racial stock by encouraging the reproductive capacities of the fit and restraining those of the unfit.

The popularity of Social Darwinism reflected concern over an urban crisis[17] in which the health of the racial stock was perceived to be at risk. In truth, such unease had been expressed well before the time of the eugenicists. Health, crime and education (see Chapter 2) had represented three long-standing anxieties of nineteenth-century social reformers and generated a 'moral statistical' movement which from the 1830s had appraised the problems created by rapid urban population increase and the resources available to address the problems. The impulses behind this movement were, in characteristic nineteenth-century fashion, two-faced. On the one hand there was a genuine scientific desire to provide a more objective information base on which to promote reform, and a humanitarian wish to ease the dire condition of the urban masses.[18] On the other, there developed a strongly coercive and moralistic 'ideology of improvement'[19] which apportioned the urban masses into deserving (susceptible to improvement) and undeserving (not susceptible to improvement) sections, and defined the former as being in urgent need of protection from the latter. A social residuum was established which became a potent factor in ecological thinking. This was apparent in discussions about educational provision for the lower orders, seen as a necessary means of social control. The cost of building schools would be compensated by the emptying of jails. The thinking was, however, in part built on the false premise that the residuum constituted a dangerously large proportion of the urban population.

Booth's surveys of the *Life and Labour of the People of London*,[20] which form the basis for the discussion of schooling and community in the metropolis in Chapter 7,[21] were an important influence on social thinking in a number of ways. They defused some of the fears that the larger proportion of the urban population comprised a potentially explosive revolutionary mass, by demonstrating empirically that the very poor constituted approximately 10% only of the people of London, and by isolating this minority from the much larger body of poor but relatively respectable working population, and the even larger body of the working classes that lived 'in comfort'.[22] About 30% of London was in poverty, a distressing problem, but one that afflicted the minority none the less.

Booth's work also influenced the growth of an ecologically-based urban sociological theory, developed at the University of Chicago in the 1920s, by a team led by R. E. Park. This theory drew sustenance not only from empirical social work in both the United States and England (Booth and Rowntree),[23] but also from Social Darwinist concepts. Thus Park viewed the human community in systems terms, as

more than mere congeries of peoples and institutions. On the contrary its component elements, institutions and persons are so intimately bound up that the whole tends to assume the character of an organism, or to use Herbert Spencer's term, a super-organism.[24]

This organism contained a territorially organised population rooted in its urban environment with individual units in the first place existing in a symbiotic rather than a societal relationship. In the former, competition acted as a mechanism, regulating numbers, preserving the balance between components, and restoring the communal equilibrium when disturbed. But when competition declined and was superseded by cooperation, the 'kind of order which we call society may be said to exist'. Human ecology's sphere was confined (somewhat arbitrarily) to the biotic level, leaving aside 'society', in which the struggle for existence had assumed higher and more sublimated forms.[25]

The dynamics of the process of urban community development were outlined in Darwinist terms, making vigorous use of concepts such as competition (most stressed of all), invasion, dominance, succession and assimilation. Emphasis was placed on temporal change and territorial pattern rather than on, for example, economic and political structure. The organisation of the urban community was viewed hierarchically, with the two basic levels, biotic and cultural (or societal) subject to different constraints, the one physical and external, the other moral and internal. A continuum was held to exist with the biotic (ecological) order at the base, followed by the economic and social, with the moral order at the apex.[26]

Park stressed the spatial manifestations of the forces at work, ecology being seen 'in some very real sense' as a geographical science though not, as Barrows had concurrently argued,[27] as identical with geography:

Human ecology ... seeks to emphasise ... space. In society we not only live together, but at the same time we live apart, and human relations can always be reckoned, with more or less accuracy, in terms of distance.[28]

Segregation of residence was symptomatic of the struggle for survival, or for the defence of status (in a sense of sublimated form of survival), among different religious, ethnic, social or occupational groups.

The physical or ecological organization of the community, in the long run, responds to and reflects the occupational and the cultural. Social selection and segregation, which create the natural groups, determine at the same time the natural areas of the city.[29]

These highly differentiated natural areas, with their disparate component groups, were to be found in close proximity, a situation likely to provoke social conflict, to the extent that the down-trodden 'sub-social' unit communicated upwards a 'pervasive sense of malaise': the feeling of being in the presence of 'something not quite understood and hence always a little to be feared.'[30] The final expression of these forces was a territorially-bound and socially relatively homogeneous community, delineated in Booth-like terms in Park's first important paper of 1916:

In the course of time every section and quarter of the city takes on something of the character and qualities of its inhabitants. Each separate part of the city is inevitably stained with the peculiar sentiments of its population. The effect of this is to convert what was first a mere geographical expression into a neighbourhood, that is to say, a locality with sentiments, traditions, and a history of its own.[31]

The half-century following the appearance of the Chicago paradigm has seen much criticism of it in its pure form. Exception has been taken to the stress on 'competition' as a key concept,[32] oversimplifying a social reality in which cooperation is simultaneously taking place; to a somewhat deterministic view which emphasises environmental controls over human action;[33] to a Social Darwinist emphasis wedded to a pathological view of urban society; and not least to an assumption of the capitalist order as the 'natural' and most highly evolved type of human organisation.[34]

It must be remembered, at the same time, that classical human ecology grew out of a long-standing perception of urban malaise. In the *laissez-faire* environment of the nineteenth- and early twentieth-century city, there *was* an elemental precarious quality[35] in urban existence which made the application of biological analogues, if not entirely congenial, at least not always inappropriate, as illustrated in sections of Chapter 9 of this book. Indeed, nineteenth-century metaphors of city life suggested comparison with infernal rather than biological levels of experience.[36]

The fact that, despite these criticisms, human ecological theory has survived is testimony to the underlying applicability of the Chicago work. Among the achievements were the demonstration that natural areas were often mismatched with administrative, an important piece of information for the urban (and the educational) planner. The concept of the natural area was itself a stimulus to later refinement of the notions of community and of the neighbourhood.[37] The American urbanist Louis Wirth concluded that while human ecology was not a substitute for it was a supplement to other methods of social investigation.[38] His own theory of urbanisation[39] emphasised the dehumanising and disorientating role of the city, as well as the complexity and interdependence of social life.[40] Other work which followed also accepted the necessity of incorporating cultural forces in ecological study, at the same time confining its attention to aggregate rather than individual data.[41]

The post-war period has seen the emergence of more sophisticated statistical techniques for aggregate studies of social areas,[42] and complex processing has been applied to census and other records to produce social area analyses of nineteenth-century towns and cities. Such work has constituted another example of the convergence of sociological and geographical thought, which chimed in well with the quantitative revolution experienced in geography in the 1960s. Meanwhile, sociologists continued to explore the spatial component in urban ecology, seeing the distribution and degree of residential segregation of various social groups within urban areas as representative of the strength of social division, and to accept 'locality' as a key variable in sociological enquiry.[43]

The late 60s, the 70s and the early 80s have seen a backlash against quantitative, aggregate analysis of the social world, viewed as reductionist in its neglect of the behavioural elements of reality. The ground-breaking work on the symbolic aspects of space was Firey's study of Boston, published in 1945, which argued that the cultural values and attitudes attached to particular locations could exercise a stronger influence than economic forces, such as changing land values.[44]

Increasing interest in the behavioural environment[45] has helped to shift the emphasis from aggregate population studies to the phenomenological investigation of individual or group actions,[46] which again has reinforced the convergence of sociological and geographical thinking. The essence of the phenomenological approach is that what phenomena *mean* rather than what they *are* defines their reality. It is more concerned with *intentions* towards phenomena than with the content of phenomena as such.[47]

APPLICATION TO EDUCATIONAL HISTORY

While the growth of ecological thinking is a process well known to urban geographers and sociologists, few historians of education have as yet attempted to get to grips with the concept. Sociologists, historians and geographers have, however, all drawn attention to the need to study school systems ecologically, though the conceptualisation of 'ecology' has tended to remain implicit. Murray, an historian, has espoused an ecological approach, but in broad and barely defined terms:

The study of the development and content of education cannot but be ecological. Systems do not flourish in the air. They affect and are affected by the social, political and religious structure as well as by the movements of their time. Of no period was this more true than of the last third of the nineteenth century.[48]

Eggleston, a sociologist, has stressed the locational variable, noting that people 'take on individual patterns of behaviour and accept different patterns of achievement' according to the geographical, economic, political or social situation they find themselves in. Ecological study is seen as having as much to do with the 'created' as the physical environment, and emphasis is placed on political responses to the disparate distribution of resources.[49] Among educational historians, Michael Katz has demanded an 'historical ecology of school systems', involving plotting the 'relationships of school structure and content to their environments'[50] and has successfully pioneered an aggregate ecological approach in the study of school attendance.[51] Two other historians, Kaestle and Vinovskis, have similarly stressed the need to study the development of schooling 'in relationship to the evolving social structure, economic system, and cultural relationships of community, region and nation.'[52] W. B. Stephens has argued for more careful investigation of regional variations in educational provision during the industrial revolution period,[53] in which is implicit an ecological view. Using a spatial-ecological approach, W. E. Marsden has provided studies of spatial inequalities in educational provision and take-up at national, regional, metropolitan, and local urban levels.[54] But aggregate ecological approaches to the relationships between education and society are not enough if the increasingly proselytised aim of producing 'grassroots' studies of education in the past, seeing its development more from the point of view of the recipients, and in other words trying to recreate the experience of schooling,[55] is to be achieved.[56] Such an aim demands a historical ecology of education which at the same time is not deterministic and embodies concepts of personal space.

Historians have also complained about the 'aerial views' which have emerged from the quantitative aggregate investigations of historical demographers and historical geographers, 'depicting a bleak land-scape, inhabited by statistical problems and sociological rocks ... the categories they deal in part company with the social reality they are intended to expose ...', as the radical social historian, Raphael Samuel, has commented. Samuel offers a preferred alternative:

> ... the historian can draw up fresh maps in which people are as prominent as places and the two are more closely intertwined. He or she can then explore the moral topography of a village or town with the same precision which predecessors have given to the Ordnance Survey ... Reconstructing a child's itinerary seventy years ago the historian will stumble on the invisible boundaries which separate the rough end of a street from the respectable, the front houses from the back, the boys' space from the girls' ...[57]

Similarly, Asa Briggs has insisted that valuable though studies based on quantitative data are, 'no urban history can afford to neglect the sense of place which must be the main theme of all studies of Victorian cities ...'[58] Even some of the quantifiers have come round to the view that their aggregate studies require complementing with the 'social flavours' of particular milieux that were an 'integral part of contemporary consciousness'.[59]

Kaestle and Vinovskis support this pluralist view and take the ecological approach as one suiting the complexity of educational history.[60] Their declared purpose is to work down from aggregate, state-wide data to more detailed comparative studies of the rural-urban continuum, and of different-sized towns. However, their study, immensely impressive at the aggregate level, is less convincing at the individual, relying on artificial, fictitious stereotypes of children (Sarah in Boxford and Benjamin in Lynn), based on generalisations from school and other local records, to communicate the experience of schooling.[61]

It must be stressed that relating socio-economic grouping to attendance rates,[62] while an important contribution to the study of links between education and society in the past, and an ecological one at that, is so at an aggregate level, and does not in itself serve to recreate the individual or group experience of schooling. A 'psycho-historical' approach to education demands equal sophistication in the experiential area. Such work has only recently begun, making use of oral evidence and of 'personal-history documents' such as letters, diaries and autobiographies.[63] Between the two is the even less explored level of the urban community, which requires micro-ecological and spatial study for its depiction.[64]

To cope with the complex methodological problems of such work the need for an *inter-disciplinary perspective* on the history of education is reinforced. Education in its social context has structural, temporal and spatial components, integral to the ecological concept, which offers essentially such an inter-disciplinary approach. 'Inter-disciplinary' needs careful definition, however. What is not advocated here is the search for the eldorado of some grand, all-embracing explanatory synthesis. What is suggested rather is the more limited notion of mutually beneficial partnership of Castells: '... the communication and inter-relating of results obtained *independently* by each discipline in relation to the same real object.'[65]

Harold Silver has outlined the tensions and balances between different scales and variables which need to be, and arguably can only be, resolved through such an approach:

Cultural history ... cannot be dominated by the composite ... It is not concerned solely with images, socio-economically defined groups, patterns of class relationships, the statistics of mobility. It is concerned with varieties as well as uniformities of experience, with teachers as well as the image of the teacher, the biographical re-construction of schooling as well as its relationship to the social order. This sense of variety and individuality is difficult to hold in view when history of education is pulled toward the grand scale – the cross-national explanation of capitalism, the role of the school, the mechanisms of control. A historical approach to cultures and subcultures is pulled in both directions, toward patterns and theories, and toward the individual biography in specific settings.[66]

Barbara Finkelstein has similarly pressed for a balance which goes

beyond the study of structure, beyond the analysis of macro-politics and economics, beyond the study of the work of élite-planners, to include the study of experience, of small face-to-face social contexts and processes, the consciousness of reformers, and the educational experience of ordinary people.[67]

For grassroots study in particular, the urban historian of education must therefore strive for a symbiosis of disciplines that gives due weight to cultural, experiential, ecological and territorial, as well as the more customary issues covered in the existing historiography of education.

In attempting to approach such a synthesis this book is divided into two main sections, the first dealing with national variations, and paying special attention to differentiation between urban areas. The first chapter in this section concentrates on the diffusion of a social innovation, mass educational provision, over England and Wales, in the period before the 1870 Act. The next one uses Lampard's structure in delineating those elements of urbanisation which strongly interpenetrated with educational provision. Chapters 4 and 5 of the book explore in turn the graduated system of urban schooling which surfaced in the second half of the century, and the niceties of the provision for the urban middle classes in this graduation. Chapter 6 is in a sense a transition chapter, stepping down the scale to the regional level, and investigating disparities in provision in Lancashire towns during the School Board period.

The second section focuses on variations within urban areas, again in the School Board period. Chapter 7 has both a regional component, in drawing attention on the basis of Booth's surveys to the educational disparities which existed at the metropolitan level, and a local grass-roots component, in using these surveys to highlight links between schools and slum and suburban communities in different parts of London. Chapter 8 is a case study of local decision-making, of relationships between central and local government, and the impact of these on educational provision in a Merseyside town. Chapters 9 and 10 are ecological micro-studies of schooling and communities in slum and suburban areas of Merseyside.

REFERENCES AND NOTES

1. 'Popular Education in England', *The British Quarterly Review*, vol. 8 (1846), p. 480.
2. See, for example, A. Wilson, 'Reticular Research', *The Times Higher Education Supplement*, 20 July 1984, p. 18.
3. D. Reeder, 'History, Education and the City: a Review of Trends in Britain', in R. K. Goodenow and W. E. Marsden (eds.), *Urban Educational History in Four Nations: the United States, the United Kingdom, Australia and Canada* (New York, forthcoming). See also D. Reeder, 'Predicaments of City Children: late Victorian and Edwardian Perspectives on Education and Urban Society', in D. Reeder (ed.), *Urban Education in the Nineteenth Century* (London, 1977), pp. 76–94.
4. Reeder, *op. cit.*, (forthcoming). See also G. Grace, 'Urban Education: Policy

Science or Critical Scholarship?, in G. Grace (ed.), *Education and the City: Theory, History and Contemporary Practice* (London, 1984), pp. 35–7.

5. E. E. Lampard, 'Historical Aspects of Urbanization', in P. M. Hauser and L. Schnore (eds.), *The Study of Urbanization* (New York, 1965), p. 519. See also E. E. Lampard, 'The Urbanizing World' in H. J. Dyos and M. Wolff (eds.), *The Victorian City: Images and Realities*, vol. 1 (London, 1973), pp. 3–57.

6. For a fuller discussion of a spatial approach to educational phenomena, see W. E. Marsden, 'Historical Geography and the History of Education', *History of Education*, vol. 6 (1977), pp. 21–42.

7. B. T. Robson, 'View on the Urban Scene', in M. Chisholm and H. B. Rodgers (eds.), *Studies in Human Geography* (London, 1973), p. 222.

8. See A. Buttimer, 'Social Space in Interdisciplinary Perspective', *Geographical Review*, vol. 59 (1969), pp. 418–20.

9. A. Buttimer, 'Social Space and the Planning of Residential Areas', *Environment and Behaviour*, vol. 4 (1972), p. 286.

10. See W. E. Marsden, 'Travelling to School: Aspects of Nineteenth-Century Catchment Areas', *Geography*, vol. 65 (1980), pp. 19–26. More extended discussion of the ideas in that paper can be found at various points in this text.

11. Rev. Canon Trevor, 'Elementary Schools in Small Town Populations', *Transactions of the National Association for the Promotion of Social Science* (York meeting, 1864), pp. 412ff.

12. *Reports of the Committee of Council on Education* (hereafter *R.C.C.E.*) (1871–2), Part 1, p. 72.

13. *R.C.C.E.* (1875), p. 408.

14. Grace, *op. cit.* (1984), p. 21.

15. Reeder, *op. cit.* (forthcoming). It is therefore being argued that both structuralist and ecological approaches are best seen as 'reticular research' in Wilson's terms (Reference 2), not incompatible, but addressing problems at different scales of study and with different intents. The pursuit of a grander synthesis, incorporating both, would seem to be the thrust of G. Grace, 'Theorising the Urban: Some Approaches for Students of Education', in G. Grace (ed.), *op. cit.* (1984), pp. 96–112, in which ideas drawn from Durkheim, Park and Burgess, Weber, Wirth, Pahl, Harvey and Castells are coalesced as a basis.

16. For a fuller discussion, see W. E. Marsden, 'Ecology and Nineteenth Century Urban Education', *History of Education Quarterly*, vol. 23 (1983), pp. 29–53.

17. See, for example, G. Pearson, *Hooligan: A History of Respectable Fears* (London, 1983).

18. T. S. Ashton, *Economic and Social Investigation in Manchester 1833–1933* (London, 1934), p. 13; and P. H. Butterfield, 'The Educational Researches of the Manchester Statistical Society, 1830–1840', *British Journal of Educational Studies*, vol. 22 (1974), pp. 340–5.

19. See M. J. Cullen, *The Statistical Movement in Early Victorian Britain: the Foundations of Empirical Social Research* (New York, 1975), p. 135.

20. The Booth Surveys are published in three main series: the 'Poverty' series of 1891 (following earlier surveys of poverty in East London); the 'Population Classified by Trades' series of 1892–7; and the 'Religious Influences' series of 1902–3. The whole can be found in C. Booth (ed.), *Life and Labour of the People in London* (London 1902–3), in 18 volumes.

21. For a complementary discussion of Booth's importance in the study of history of metropolitan education, see W. E. Marsden, 'Residential Segregation and the Hierarchy of Elementary Schooling from Charles Booth's London Surveys', in *The London Journal* (1986).

22. See E. P. Hennock, 'Poverty and Society Theory in England: the Experience of the

Eighteen-eighties', *Social History*, vol. 1 (1976), pp. 73–5.
23. R. E. Park, 'The City as a Social Laboratory', in T. W. Smith and L. White (eds.), *Chicago: an Experiment in Social Science Research* (Chicago, 1929), pp. 4–5. A more accessible source is the R. E. Park collection reprinted under the title *Human Communities: the City and Human Ecology* (Glencoe, Illinois, 1952).
24. R. E. Park, 'The City as a Natural Phenomenon', in *Human Communities, op. cit.* (1952), p. 118.
25. R. E. Park, 'Human Ecology' in *Human Communities, op. cit.* (1952), pp. 150–1.
26. *Ibid.*, pp. 151–7; also R. E. Park, 'Succession: an Ecological Concept', and 'Symbiosis and Socialization: a Frame of Reference for the Study of Society', both in *Human Communities, op. cit.* (1952), p. 228 and p. 258 respectively.
27. H. H. Barrows, 'Geography as Human Ecology', *Annals of the Association of American Geographers*, vol. 13 (1923), pp. 1–14.
28. R. E. Park, 'The Urban Community as a Spatial Pattern and a Moral Order', in *Human Communities, op. cit.* (1952), pp. 165–6.
29. *Ibid.*, p. 170.
30. R. E. Park, 'Symbiosis and Socialization', in *Human Communities, op. cit.*, p. 261.
31. R. E. Park, 'The City: Suggestions for the Investigation of Human Behaviour in the Urban Environment', in *Human Communities, op. cit.*, p. 17.
32. See M. Alihun, '"Community" and Ecological Studies', in G. A. Theodorson (ed.), *Studies in Human Ecology* (New York, 1961), pp. 93–7.
33. See W. E. Gettys, 'Human Ecology and Social Theory', in Theodorson (ed.), *op. cit.* (1961), pp. 98–103.
34. See A. B. Hollingshead, 'A Re-examination of Ecological Theory', in Theodorson (ed.), *op. cit.* (1961), pp. 108–114; and also D. Martindale, 'The Theory of the City', Preface to M. Weber, *The City* (New York, 1958), pp. 29–30.
35. See, for example, C. Booth (ed.), *Life and Labour of the People in London*, vol. 1 (London, 1891), p. 161.
36. See, for example, J. London, *The People of the Abyss* (London, 1903); G. Gissing, *The Nether World* (London, 1889); C. F. G. Masterman, 'The Social Abyss', *Contemporary Review*, vol. 71 (1902), pp. 23–25; 'A City Very Much Like Hell', *Pall Mall Gazette*, 31 July 1891 (reviewing Booth's 'Poverty' Series).
37. L. Wirth, 'Human Ecology', in Theodorson (ed.), *op. cit.* (1961), p. 73.
38. *Ibid.*, p. 76.
39. L. Wirth, 'Urbanism as a Way of Life', in P. K. Hatt and A. J. Reiss (eds.), *Cities and Society* (Glencoe, Illinois, 1957), pp. 46–63.
40. For a summary of Wirth's concept, see R. N. Morris, *Urban Sociology* (London, 1968), pp. 16–19.
41. See, for example, J. A. Quinn, 'The Nature of Human Ecology: Re-examination and Re-definition'; and A. H. Hawley, 'Ecology and Human Ecology', both in Theodorson (ed.) *op. cit.* (1961), pp. 135–41 and 144–51.
42. See, for example, E. A. Wrigley (ed.), *Nineteenth-century Society: Essays in the Use of Quantitative Methods for the Study of Social Data* (Cambridge, 1972); and R. Lawton (ed.), *The Census and the Social Structure: an Interpretative Guide to Nineteenth Century Censuses for England and Wales*, (London, 1978).
43. See, for example, C. Filkin and D. Weir, 'Locality' in E. Gittus (ed.), *Key Variables in Social Research*, vol. 1 (London, 1972), pp. 106–56; and M. Castells, 'Theory and Ideology in Urban Sociology' in C. G. Pickvance (ed.), *Urban Sociology: Critical Essays* (London, 1972), p. 70.
44. W. Firey, 'Sentiment and Symbolism as Ecological Variables', in Theodorson (ed.), *op. cit.* (1961), pp. 253–4.
45. See, for example, W. Kirk, 'Problems of Geography', *Geography*, vol. 48 (1963), pp. 357–71; and D. Lowenthal, 'Geography, Experience and Imagination: towards

a Geographical Epistemology', *Annals of the Association of American Geographers*, vol. 51 (1961), pp. 241–60.

46. See, for example, D. Mercer, 'Behavioural Geography and the Sociology of Social Action', *Area*, vol. 4 (1972), pp. 48–52; D. Harvey, 'Social Processes and Spatial Form: an Analysis of the Conceptual Problems of Urban Planning', in E. Jones (ed.), *Readings in Social Geography* (Oxford, 1975), pp. 288–306; E. Relph, 'An Enquiry into the Relation between Phenomenology and Geography', *The Canadian Geographer*, vol. 14 (1970, pp. 193–201); Yi-Fu Tuan, 'Structuralism, Existentialism and Environmental Perception', *Environment and Behaviour*, vol. 4 (1972), pp. 319–31; A. Buttimer, 'Grasping the Dynamism of Lifeworld', *Annals of the Association of American Geographers*, vol. 66 (1976), pp. 277–92.

47. See M. Billinge, 'In Search of Negativism: Phenomenology and Historical Geography', *Journal of Historical Geography*, vol. 3 (1977), p. 57 and pp. 60–1.

48. In F. H. Hinsley (ed.), *Material Progress and World-wide Problems 1870–1898* (New Cambridge Modern History, Vol. 11: Cambridge 1961), p. 177.

49. J. Eggleston, *The Ecology of the School* (London, 1977), pp. 15–16 and 111–12.

50. M. B. Katz, 'Comment' (on Urban Education), *History of Education Quarterly*, vol. 9 (1969), pp. 326–7; see also M. B. Katz, 'The Emergence of Bureaucracy in Urban Education: the Boston Case, 1850–1884', *History of Education Quarterly*, vol. 8 (1968), p. 157.

51. See, for example, M. B. Katz, 'Who went to School?', *History of Education Quarterly*, vol. 12 (1972), p. 433; and M. B. Katz and I. E. Davey, 'School Attendance and Early Industrialization in a Canadian City: a Multivariate Analysis', *History of Education Quarterly*, vol. 18 (1978), pp. 271–93.

52. C. F. Kaestle and M. A. Vinovskis, *Education and Social Change in Nineteenth-century Massachusetts* (Cambridge, 1980), p. 1.

53. W. B. Stephens, *Regional Variations in Education during the Industrial Revolution, 1780–1870: the Task of the Local Historian* (Educational Administration and History Monograph No. 1, Leeds, 1973).

54. For discussions of background methodology see references 6 and 16 above, and also W. E. Marsden, 'Census Enumerators' Returns, Schooling and Social Areas in the Late Victorian Town: a Case Study of Bootle', in R. Lowe (ed.), *New Approaches to the Study of Population Education, 1851–1902* (History of Education Society Occasional Publication No. 4 (Leicester, 1979), pp. 16–33.

55. See, for example, A. Briggs, 'The Study of the History of Education', *History of Education*, Vol. 1 (1972), p. 7; S. Cohen, 'The History of Urban Education in the United States: Historians of Education and their Discontents', in Reeder (ed.) *op. cit.* (1977), p. 123; and H. Silver, 'Aspects of Neglect: the Strange Case of Victorian Popular Education', *Oxford Review of Education*, vol. 3 (1977), p. 58.

56. Of the American texts on the history of urban education, those which to date most nearly approach a grassroots ecological study are perhaps S. K. Schultz, *The Culture Factory: Boston Public Schools, 1789–1860* (New York, 1973); C. F. Kaestle, *The Evolution of an Urban School System: New York City, 1750–1850* (Harvard, 1973), pp. 75–90; and sections of D. Ravitch and R. K. Goodenow (eds.), *Educating an Urban People: the New York City Experience* (New York, 1981); and R. K. Goodenow and D. Ravitch (eds.), *Schools in Cities: Consensus and Conflict in American Educational History* (New York, 1983).

57. R. Samuel, 'Local History and Oral History', *History Workshop Journal*, vol. 1 (1976), p. 195 and p. 199.

58. A. Briggs, 'The Human Aggregate', in Dyos and Wolff (eds.), vol. 1, *op. cit.* (1973), p. 100.

59. See A. Cowlard, 'The Identification of Social (Class) Areas and their Place in Nineteenth-century Urban Development', *Transactions of the Institute of British*

Geographers, vol. 4 (1979), pp. 254–5; also C. Booth, 'Life and Labour of the People in London: First Results of an Enquiry based on the 1891 Census', *Journal of the Royal Statistical Society*, vol. 56 (1893), p. 591.

60. Kaestle and Vinovskis, *op. cit.* (1980), pp. 1–2.
61. *Ibid.*, pp. 146–8 and pp. 178–9.
62. As in, for example, Katz and Davey, *op. cit.* (1978); and Kaestle and Vinovskis, *op. cit.* (1980), p. 90. A more 'atmospheric' work in this context is D. Rubinstein, *School Attendance in London, 1870–1904: a Social History* (Hull, 1969).
63. See G. J. Clifford, 'History as Experience: the Uses of Personal History Documents in History of Education', *History of Education*, vol. 7 (1978), pp. 183–96; and G. J. Clifford, 'The Life Story: Biographic Study', in J. H. Best (ed.), *Historical Inquiry in Education: a Research Agenda* (American Educational Research Association, Washington, 1983), pp. 56–74.
64. See, for example, C. Parsons, *Schools in an Urban Community: a Study of Carbrook, 1870–1965* (London, 1978).
65. Castells, *op. cit.* (1972), p. 83.
66. H. Silver, 'The Uses of Parochialism: Comparative and Cross Cultural Study', in J. H. Best (ed.), *op. cit.* (1983), p. 191. See also D. Angus, 'The Empirical Mode: Quantitative History', and J. Saunders, 'Education and the City: Urban Community Study', pp. 84–6 and pp. 223–4 in the same volume.
67. B. Finkelstein, 'Redoing Urban Educational History', in Goodenow and Marsden (eds.), *op. cit.* (forthcoming).

NATIONAL VARIATIONS
IN PROVISION

CHAPTER TWO

Diffusion and Regional Disparity in Educational Provision in England and Wales 1800–1870

> The migration of ideas, like the migration of people,
> helped to shape Victorian society and schooling.[1] (Tyack,
> 1978)

The purpose of this chapter is to describe and explain the diffusion of an important nineteenth-century social innovation, the monitorial system of schooling, and related regional variations in provision as they shifted in the period before the great Education Act of 1870. The term 'diffusion' is used here in its social rather than scientific sense, and means the spread and application of ideas or innovations. Diffusion takes place in three dimensions: temporal, in that innovations take time to spread; geographical, in that they are dispersed over space; and social, in that they are disseminated through society.

In so far as a complex process can be classified, it may be useful to employ Baker's distinction of two types of diffusion: contagious and hierarchical.[2] Contagious diffusion reflects the ability of an 'infected' body to affect neighbouring bodies. Here a friction of distance effect operates, with contact and therefore ability to infect becoming more tenuous with increasing distance.[3] The process was apparently well understood in an argument put to the House of Commons in 1876 over the compulsory school attendance issue:

The contagious influence upon neighbouring areas of the system at work, in what might be called the compulsory areas, had prepared the minds of those still outside for the more distant enactment of a universal compulsory law.[4]

Sending children to school in a situation where attendance was not compelled was in fact a form of conspicuous consumption, which could spread contagiously from household to household in a neighbourhood.

At the institutional level, innovations are less likely to spread in this way, but rather by a hierarchical process. Geographically, this will result in spatial leap-frogging, with the direction of movement from the centre to the peripheral regions, generally down the settlement hierarchy. Socially, the process normally descends the class structure.[5] In practice, as Robson has indicated, contagious and hierarchical diffusion may happen concurrently, radiating from the centre contagiously to small neighbouring settlements, at the same time leap-frogging to larger provincial centres in hierarchical fashion.[6]

Necessarily there are time-lags in the uptake of innovations. These are likely to be less where there is strength in the initial impetus, whether in terms of the quality of the idea, the zeal with which it is espoused, the power of the resource base, or the capacity of the channels of communication established. The rate of spread varies with the degree of technological advance. The early stages of diffusion are usually associated with slow but gradual acceleration, followed by rapid adoption, then deceleration.[7] In the early stages there is therefore likely to be considerable regional variation in uptake, giving rise to 'leading' and 'lagging' regions.[8] Later, more rapid uptake leads to a filling in of gaps, reducing the range of variation.

Another vital factor in the diffusion process is the presence of change agents or agencies. Armytage has considered these in the context of the late eighteenth century, an age 'running mad after innovation', and a time when a number of the ideas which preoccupied educational promoters in the nineteenth century were generated. Scientific and educational ideas were 'incubated in' and disseminated from the learned societies, laboratories, lecture halls and, not least, the London coffee-houses, where 'men from the provinces could hear about what was afoot'.[9] The social context was conducive to change. It was a time when gentlemen and wealthy men did not disdain to meet rugged men of business.[10] Ideas thrashed out at institutions such as the Royal Society and Royal Society of Arts were translated into innovations and widely disseminated.

The seed-beds of change were in the first place the two great cultural capitals of Britain: London and Edinburgh. Edinburgh men, such as Henry Brougham, and journals, such as the *Edinburgh*

Review, had an important influence on the early development of mass education in England.[11] Later the provincial capitals gained in stature, with Liverpool, Leeds, Manchester and Birmingham exercising considerable pressure for change at the national level at different points in time in the nineteenth century.[12]

A question here is whether impulses to *educational* change in the early nineteenth century were contagiously or hierarchically diffused, or indeed in both ways. Another is how these processes related to regional variations. Three issues will be discussed. The first is the geographical spread of an early nineteenth-century educational innovation, the 'new plan' or the monitorial system. This embodied a technical change which made mass provision of elementary education an economic proposition. The development of this provision through the British and National Societies will be outlined as far as 1870. The second reflects the contemporary interest in the non-uniform distribution of crime and its relationship with educational provision. The third concerns the extreme regional variations which existed as a result of uneven diffusion in the cases of two borderland areas, the northern counties adjoining Scotland, and Monmouthshire adjoining Wales, respectively a 'leading' and a 'lagging' region, particularly in the early stages of development.

They serve to illustrate the caution which must be exercised in studying the pattern of diffusion and regional variation. Comparison of Figs. 2.1/2.2 makes clear that the northern counties, a leading region in terms of school enrolments, had hardly been touched by the spread of 'new plan' schools. It was already well supplied by the standards of the time. On the other hand, there was a stronger diffusion of 'new plan' schools into Wales and the Welsh borderland, a lagging region in 1818, in which an initiative was sorely needed.

THE DIFFUSION OF SCHOOLS ON THE 'NEW PLAN'

Fig. 2.2 indicates that by 1818 the schools on the 'new plan', even where most firmly established, were in a considerable minority. They were relatively strong in Hampshire and other south-eastern counties, Welsh and Welsh borderland counties and weak, as we have seen, in the northern counties, related to an earlier pattern of provision. The mining and manufacturing counties were also as yet hardly touched but, unlike the northern counties, were greatly in need of provision (Fig. 2.1).[13] The 'new plan' schools were of more influence than their

Fig. 2.1. Percentage in Day Schools to Child Population (taken as ⅙ total population), 1818

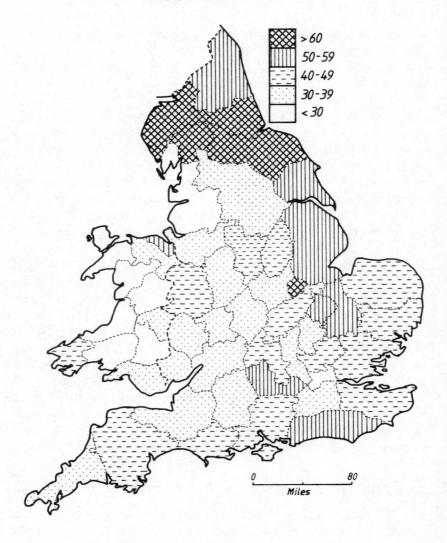

numbers at this stage would suggest, however, for they were the advanced elementary schools of their time, embodying the highest level of provision that could be afforded for the masses. They were supported by the resources of two societies of nationwide repute, the British and the National, and they were expanding in numbers.

Fig. 2.2. Elementary Unendowed Day Schools on 'New Plan',
1818 (National and British)

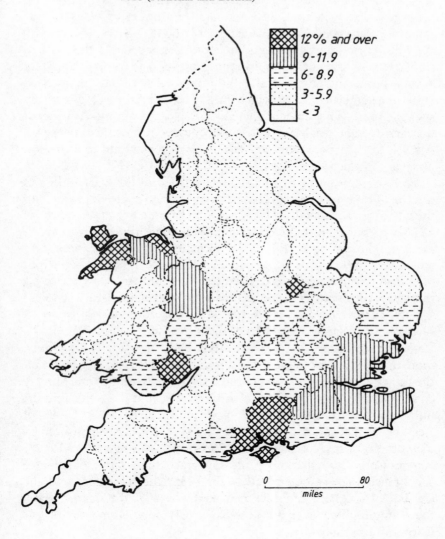

THE BRITISH SOCIETY

Lancaster's original school (1798), located in Borough Road, South-wark, became the centre for the dispersal of his version of the monitorial system. There were two main ways in which Lancasterian ideas were disseminated. One was through provincial tours by

Lancaster and his disciples. The other was through using Borough Road as a teacher-training institution, relying on its products to propagate the system. Lancaster made a number of visits to, for example, Liverpool and Manchester, in the 1800–10 period.[14] William Allen, the Quaker and a staunch supporter of the system, similarly was 'indefatigable' in spreading knowledge of the system both at home and abroad.[15] Indeed, it may be said that the overseas effort consumed energies which might have been more effectively spent at home. The same happened with teacher training. As many of the early women teachers trained at Borough Road worked in Buenos Aires as in Liverpool, and twice as many men went out to St Petersburg as to Lancashire.[16]

The distribution of British schools was, from the start, thin and uneven. This might be expected in an early stage of development, but the situation continued. According to the British Society's Report of 1812, which it admitted to be incomplete, there appears evidence of metropolitan strength (Fig. 2.3).[17] But leaving aside London and adjacent counties, little progress had been made, apart from the hint of spread to the large industrial cities of the midlands and north. By this stage, the majority of counties had few or even no British schools.

Some of the schools which developed in the industrial centres were, however, very large in size. In Manchester, for example, the Royal Lancasterian School in Marshall Street had, by 1825, 1,000 pupils, more than the city's National day schools put together.[18] In Liverpool, the Lancasterian system was operated at Circus Street day and Sunday charity school, and at the Welsh charity school.[19] At the former, numbers rose from 98 in 1804 to 593 in 1813. By 1824, 53.4% of weekday elementary scholars in the city were in schools sponsored by dissenting groups, as against 31.7% Church of England and 6.2% Roman Catholic. After this promising start, the relative position of the British Society deteriorated. By 1836, the dissenters and the Church of England each claimed about 36% of the day scholars, the Catholics just over 10%, while nearly 15% attended the two Corporation schools.[20]

By 1846, on the evidence of Joseph Fletcher's survey, there had been some overall progress, with a thickening of the distribution from the 1812 position.[21] At the same time, apart again from the metropolis, the dots for each school can still be placed with some ease on a small-scale map of England and Wales (Fig. 2.4). By 1846, a more distinctive pattern of development in the provinces can be discerned,

Fig. 2.3. Distribution of British Schools, 1812

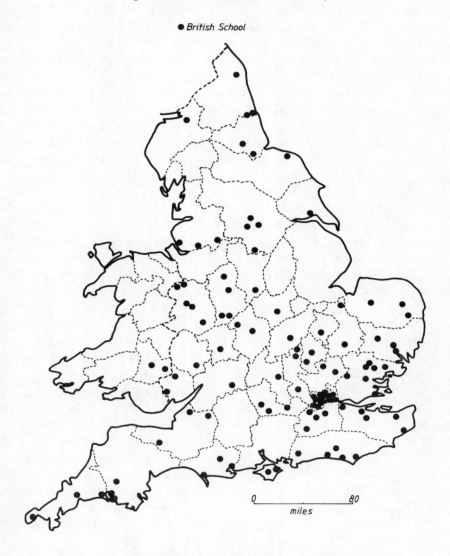

● *British School*

miles

0   80

concentrated on the conurbations. Little progress had been made in the rural counties. It must be noted, however, that Fletcher's figures referred to inspected schools, and may well have underestimated the spread which a straight comparison of all British schools in 1812 and 1846 would have indicated.

Fig. 2.4. Distribution of Inspected British Schools, 1846

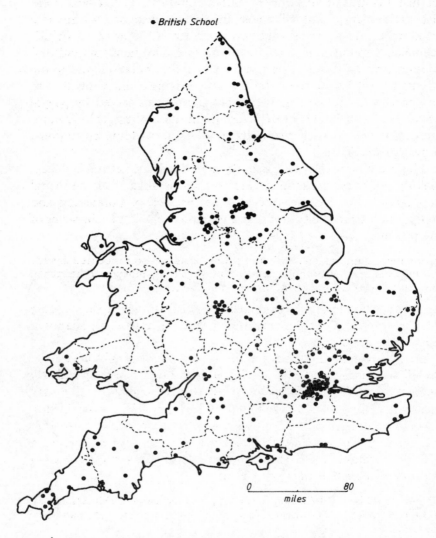

While his function as school inspector was to survey the British schools, Joseph Fletcher (see also page 65) additionally undertook a private survey of the moral and educational state of England and Wales. He provides interesting insight into the barriers to the spread of British schools. He divided the country for his purposes into broad regions: 'agricultural counties'; 'agricultural and maritime

counties'; 'agricultural and mining counties'; 'mining and manufacturing counties'; and 'metropolitan counties'. The regions were
also divided into least and most instructed portions. Within this
framework Fletcher assessed prospects for the spread of British
schools. He found poor soil in the southern and Midlands agricultural
counties, owing to the scale and dispersal of population, and to the
strength of the Established Church. The thriving country towns were
exceptions, for in these active school committees served by people
with a 'superior amount of education and leisure' might be found.
Unfortunately, in such towns the need for expanding educational
provision was least.[22]

The situation was also bleak in the combined agricultural and lace-
making counties, containing 'the most miserable of all our rural
population', but here less because of the lack of population and
competition from the Church, and more because of the character of
the parents.

Every item connected with Bedfordshire seems to be influenced by the
combination of remote ignorance with a profligate dependence of the man in
part, upon the earnings of the women and children.

By contrast the lack of impact of the British system in the extreme
northern counties could be attributed to the quantity and quality of
existing provision (pp. 46–50).[23]

In the great mining and manufacturing counties of Lancashire,
the West Riding and the Midlands, conditions were 'peculiarly
unfavourable' to the establishment of British schools, 'in the very
spots where they are most needed'.[24] Thus while, as Fig. 2.4 indicates,
schooling had been planted to a greater extent here than in most other
places, 'yet the growth of evils against which its progress is matched is
yet more onwards'. The stony ground was the gross indifference of
parents of the labouring population:

whatever may be the deficiency in the supply of the means of education ... it
is, on the whole, greater than the demand in the perception of the parents of
the children.[25]

The extent to which Fletcher's strictures applied to the efforts of the
British Society as such, as distinct from educational provision in
general is, however, not always clear. Certainly his reasoning can be
supported in respect of rural areas. Here the structure of Nonconformity was often looser than that of the Established Church. As
Everitt has indicated, Nonconformity was strong in parishes with

many small independent freeholders, and in areas of dispersed settlement, but weak in estate parishes where there was a nucleated settlement pattern, and the power of the local squire or parson was great.[26]

In the towns, the situation was different. Even here the infrastructure of the dissenting groups was weaker than that of the Church,
though the Anglicans also were to find the traditional parish structure
inappropriate to urban requirements.[27] The British Society was fully
aware of the escalating demands which followed early nineteenth-
century industrialisation. But the scale of its provision tended to be at
the level of *ad hoc* local enthusiasms, without an adequate central
support. Contacts between the London office of the British Society
and the provinces were, according to Sanderson,[28] minimal. While its
efforts sufficed to plant a certain number of schools in large provincial
towns, the network never took wing.

The British Society was inevitably unable to compete financially
with the National Society, supported as it was by the resources of the
Established Church.[29] The flow of funds from Lancashire to head-
quarters in London was 'almost derisory' in its smallness, and in turn
Lancashire British schools were handicapped by lack of assistance
from the centre.[30] Indeed, in many cases, the centre was not even clear
as to what were and what were not associated schools. When Treasury
grants became available, 70% went to the National Society during
1833–9, giving it a cumulative advantage. British Society revenues,
relatively speaking, became even more thinly spread.

By and large, it seems that Nonconformity in any case gave less
priority to educational than to other provision, notwithstanding the
fact that its Lancasterian system pioneered the move into universal
elementary education. As M. E. Jones's study of the Charity School
movement was shown, the Methodists of the eighteenth century were
signally backward in providing schools for the poor, believing it
necessary to concentrate their efforts on missionary activity among
adults. They were disposed also to think in terms of *ad hoc* phil-
anthropy rather than structured effort.[31] Similarly, early nineteenth-
century Lancashire opinion suspected that education was not high on
the list of Nonconformist priorities when it involved distributing
money. A Blackburn newspaper pointed out in 1827 that while the
Methodists alone had raised £45,000 for foreign missions, the Nonconformists as a whole had found £9,000 for the British Society.[32]

Increasingly plagued by lack of resources, therefore, yet supported
by much sophisticated and influential, but financially less than

powerful, opinion, made up of secular educationalists, radical philanthropists and the like, Nonconformity showed less and less interest
in shoring up the efforts of the British Society as a major pro-
vider of schools, and became increasingly sympathetic to the ideas
of a national educational system. Successful diffusion was inhibited
therefore both by a lack of priority being given to this particular
innovation, and the limited provision of formal channels of communication, essential in a hierarchical diffusion process.

Relying on raw totals of 'British' schools can, however, occasion
under-estimation of the influence of the system. Most Dissenting
schools used the British system or variants of it, but many did not
belong to the British Society. In 1851 there were 514 British schools
with nearly 83,000 pupils. In his introduction to the 1851 Education
Census, Mann calculated that in all there were probably over 850
schools with nearly 125,000 children linked with particular bodies
who were using the system. And if schools receiving teachers from the
British normal schools were added, the number of 'British' scholars
would be well in excess of 200,000. Problems of definition arose
particularly from the fact that the British Society did not affiliate
local institutions. However, the number of British schools grew
significantly between 1841 and 1851. In this decade 449 were established, as compared with 357 in the period before 1841.[33]

By the time of the Newcastle Commission, British schools were
strong in Wales and round the head of the Severn estuary, were
perhaps relatively weaker in the Home Counties and in London, and
had made a slight advance in Devon and Cornwall. But over most of
the country there was a relatively even but thin spread. Overall the
British school provision stood far behind the National Society's with
less than 10% as against over 75% of the total. And while the British
Society raised as much for education in 1859 as the National Society,
its annual income in 1858–9 from non-government sources was less
than a tenth as much.[34]

THE NATIONAL SOCIETY

Bell's Madras System ran concurrently and competitively with the
Lancasterian System in the early decades of the nineteenth century.
In practice, these 'new plan' systems were so similar as to cause
surprise that so much could have been made of the minor differences
that existed. But the controversy was important as a symbol and

harbinger of the century-long educational rupture between the Church and Nonconformity.[35]

As with the Lancasterian, the Madras System was disseminated from a central school, Baldwin's Gardens, established in 1812 in Gray's Inn Lane, its prime function the training of teachers. As the 1820 National Society report stressed:

The first object which claims their [the Committee's] attention is the state of the Central School . . . a practical model of the [Madras] System in its greatest perfection.[36]

The educational funds available to the National Society were, as a policy, distributed differentially. The intent was to give preference to the most populous places, in the first instance in the metropolis and its vicinity.[37] But the emphasis then shifted: 'the manufacturing county of LANCASTER has obtained their particular attention', observed the 1832 report.[38] Similarly, the 1843 Report noted that the special fund for the establishment of schools in manufacturing and mining districts had been preferentially used for Lancashire, followed by the West Riding, Cheshire and Staffordshire. The Battersea Training Institute had been designed to train masters for the manufacturing and mining districts.[39]

In a study of the roots of Anglican supremacy in education at this time, Sanderson expertly traces the process whereby in Lancashire channels of communication were established for the transmission of ideas and resources, and a local infrastructure organised, in the attempt to ensure that the initial introduction of the Madras System was followed by its diffusion and implementation. In this area, the Church had allowed the control over day schooling, which it had exercised in the eighteenth century through the Society for the Promotion of Christian Knowledge, to lapse.[40] But Lancashire was brought to the notice of the National Society movement from the very beginning. The Bishop of Chester, in whose diocese the county lay, was present at the Society's initial meeting. Chester was one of the first diocesan societies to be formed, in 1811. Owing to its large sphere of influence, district societies or committees were also required, and these were established first in Blackburn and Manchester, and from 1832 in 12 other centres.[41] In the 1830s a Diocesan Board of Education was established to help the dispensation of Privy Council funds for education. By 1839, a tightly organised regional structure had been developed, in stark contrast to the limited presence of the British

Society in the region.[42] An early project was the establishment of a Training College at Chester.

The Established Church was also helped by the able quality of its leadership at Chester. The occupants of this See in the 1820s and 1830s were in turn Blomfield and Sumner, on their way to becoming respectively Bishop of London and Archbishop of Canterbury. Both regularly attended meetings of the National Society in London, and Sumner in particular ensured that the needs of the region were kept in the forefront of the thinking of the Society. In addition, the spread of National Schools was helped by the presence of interested and efficient local clergy in such important centres as Blackburn, Warrington, Liverpool and Manchester.[43] Grants made by the National Society to places in Lancashire rose from £100 in 1817 to £1,000 in 1825 and £8,700 in 1833. Of Treasury grants to the Society in the first five years of operation, over 20% were sent to Lancashire.[44] From two day schools in Union in 1814, the number grew to 49 in 1820, 110 in 1830, and 239 in 1838.[45]

Like Lancaster, Bell acted as publicist for his system, and the National Society from an early stage used agents to spread his ideas. One of Bell's disciples, Bamford, was appointed superintendent of the Bluecoat School in Liverpool,[46] which in later years became a showplace for the Madras System, and a cell for the training of teachers in its methods, though in fact Liverpool was not one of the major beneficiaries of early National Society funding in the north-west region.[47]

Even these major initiatives were insufficient to keep pace with the demand of the manufacturing counties, which explains why in absolute terms Lancashire ranked low in actual provision. At the time of the Society's Report of 1831,[48] Lancashire, with the West Riding, Middlesex, Nottinghamshire and Shropshire, and some Welsh counties, lay in the lowest quintile of provision, with figures of 13% and below of National scholars to total scholars.[49] The greatest strength of provision in this respect remained in the traditional Anglican strongholds of the southern and south-eastern agricultural counties. While in absolute terms the Society was pouring more funds into the manufacturing districts than in rural, it was still only providing for the minority of scholars.

Fig. 2.5, showing grants from the National Society in proportion to the population, confirms its continuing support for the manufacturing counties.[50] For Lancashire, Yorkshire, Cheshire, Stafford-

Fig. 2.5. Grants from the National Society, 1846–47

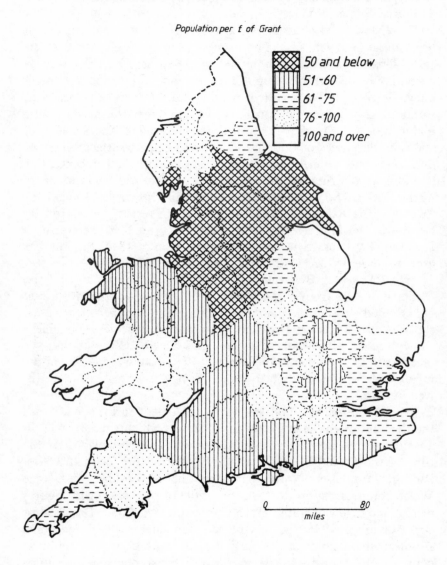

Population per £ of Grant

50 and below
51 -60
61 -75
76 -100
100 and over

shire and Derbyshire, there were fewer than 50 people for every £ of grant dispensed. At the other extreme, receiving less grant per capita, were the South Wales counties, Monmouthshire and Herefordshire, and the eastern counties. Significantly, the pattern of giving was almost converse (Fig. 2.6). Thus in response to the Queen's Letter of

Fig. 2.6. Collections for National Society under the Queen's
Letter 1843

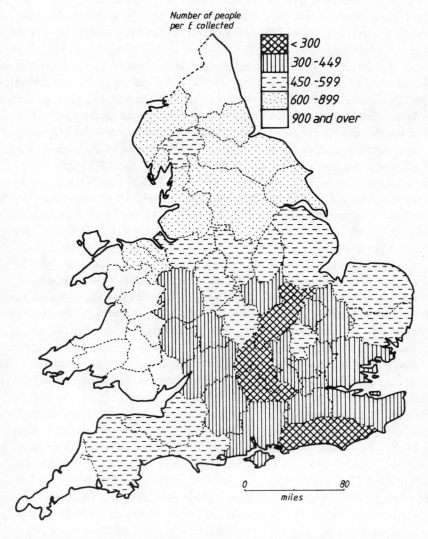

Number of people
per £ collected

< 300
300 -449
450 -599
600 -899
900 and over

0   80
miles

1843, exhorting her people to donate generously to the educational
work of the National Society, the biggest returns were from London,
the Home Counties and the south-east coast counties, and the smallest
from the north and from the Celtic extremities.[51] Here over 600 people
were required to collect each £, as against fewer than 450 in most

of the counties in the south-eastern quadrant of England and in
the West country. Taking the rank orders for the two sets of figures,
out of 42 counties, Staffordshire, Cheshire, Yorkshire, Derbyshire
and Lancashire were the first five for receipt of grants, and were
respectively 33rd, 31st, 34th, 30th, and 36th in their responses to the
Queen's letter.

Notwithstanding its compensatory efforts, however, the National
Society was not reaching the majority of the children of the industrial
proletariat, nor indeed providing the majority of school places in the
large urban centres, a lack of impact to be confirmed in the 1851
census. The Society's impact was strong in its agricultural heartland
of the south and south-east (excepting the metropolis). But important
initiatives had also continued in the coastal counties of North Wales.
Following the 1847 Report on education in Wales, the thrust towards
Anglicanization through schooling intensified. In Welsh-speaking
counties, however, the national schools were 'isolated in a sea of
dissent', and their influence nullified by the pre-eminence of the
Welsh language in the Nonconformist Sunday schools.[52]

Taking Church of England schools as a whole, and not merely
National schools, the Newcastle Commission[53] makes clear the overall
dominance of the Established Church. There was a clear pattern of
strength in agricultural counties and relative weakness in the metropolitan (Middlesex and Surrey), mining and manufacturing counties.
The failure in Lancashire was in a sense a crucial symbol of defeat.
Although even here Established Church schools were in the majority
(1,125 departments out of 1,553, in ordinary day schools) this represented nationally a relatively weak position, in the lowest quintile,
hardly adequate return for the effort that had been expended. A
rapidly growing population, a strong Catholic presence, and the complications of the half-time system, all presented barriers. The early
voluntary initiatives in the area, however, resulted in Lancashire
and Cheshire having proportionally fewer school boards than other
counties after 1870. Paradoxically, the *near absolute* failure of the
Nonconformists to establish an adequate spread of schools gained
them their objective of a rate-supported system. The *relative* failure of
the Anglicans, which had embodied an enormous effort, was not
sufficient to preempt, from their point of view, this feared outcome.
One of their critical omissions was in diffusion through the social
ranks. The gaps they had left were in the great towns and cities and
often in the poorer parts of them.

REGIONAL VARIATIONS IN CRIME AND EDUCATION

The idea that social unrest could be muted by educational provision was a decisive factor in the case for state intervention in education in the mid-nineteenth century. If it could be established that man for man the criminal element in the population was less well educated than the rest, then a vital piece of evidence would be to hand to justify the expense.

Early scientific studies of crime made considerable use of cartographic techniques, and 'geographical schools' of criminology flourished in France and England in the 1830–80 period.[54] Ecological studies probed the non-uniform territorial distribution of crime,[55] attempting to relate its spatial variation to other social variables, such as poverty and lack of educational opportunity. The statistical experts were not disinterested scientific observers. They were bent on influencing social policy. Their territorial investigations of relationships between crime and social conditions, including educational provision, became increasingly popular following the appearance of Guerry's work, *Essai sur la Statistique Morale de la France*, published in Paris in 1833.[56] Some of the impetus came from the need to disprove Guerry's inconvenient finding that education was *not* effectual in reducing crime. A similar discovery by a non-establishment statistician, Joseph Bentley, on the basis of a survey, with six agents, of crime and education in Worcestershire, excited scornful disapproval from the mainstream group at the British Association meeting of 1840.[57] Porter,[58] Rawson[59] and Fletcher,[60] among other prominent statisticians bent on the social application of their findings, attacked those of Guerry.

In 1840, for example, Rawson, Honorary Secretary of the Statistical Society, published the results of an investigation into the educational condition of criminal offenders in England and Wales. He carefully separated 'education' from 'instruction', contending that the latter, divorced from moral training, was unlikely in itself 'to repress criminal passions'.[61] Notwithstanding this distinction, Rawson proceeded to categorise criminals as 'instructed' and 'un-instructed' (which was all he could do on the basis of the data available to him), and juxtaposed the figures, on a county by county basis, with percentages of persons signing the marriage register with a mark. He found that only 10% of the criminal offenders committed for trial in

England and Wales were able to read and write well. But in spatial terms there were considerable variations, from 39% in Rutland, 23% in Leicestershire, and 20% in Sussex, to 2% in Bedford and Durham.[62] The discrepancies were described rather than accounted for. Though Rawson was unable to demonstrate at this date that the provision of education reduced crime, he was able to stress that lack of instruction, and still more of education, prevailed among the large majority of the criminal classes, and that considerable variations existed between areas.

Joseph Fletcher, barrister, inspector of British schools, secretary of the Statistical Society of London, and editor of its *Journal*,[63] was obsessively concerned with the relationship between crime and education. He sought, on the basis of empirical evidence, to denounce the view that education was a social irrelevance. He translated his spatial data into a series of shaded maps, an approach suggested to him by Prince Albert.[64] The potential of the shading technique used for reinforcing the moral point was not lost. 'In the following Shaded Maps it will be observed that it is always the *favourable* end of the scale, morally considered, that receives the lightest tone.'[65]

Fletcher used the proportion of signatures of the marriage register by mark for each county, above and below the average for England and Wales as a whole, as a telling comparative index of ignorance. As Fig. 2.7 indicates, considerable spatial variation existed, with the northern counties, east Yorkshire, the metropolitan area and Surrey emerging as areas of relatively high levels of literacy. Ignorance was correlated with other social variables, including crimes against persons, crimes against property, improvident marriages, bastardy, and disperson of population. Taken at face value, the figures revealed an inconvenient association between, for example, high levels of literacy and high crime rates in the metropolis. In a lengthy and tortuously argued account, Fletcher rightly showed the issues to be more complex than this, emerging with the conclusion that on balance education supplied a 'detergent [sic] influence',[66] and emphasising not only the spatial differentiation present in all his social indices, but also the powerful influence on social well-being of the forces of industrialisation and urbanisation, as well as education of the people.

Henry Mayhew similarly investigated national variations in density of population, intensity of criminality, intensity of ignorance, numbers of illegitimate children, and other variables, as part of his mammoth study of the pathology of London society.[67] Using less complex

Fig. 2.7. Ignorance in England and Wales 1844
(as indicated by the men's signatures by marks in the
marriage registers)

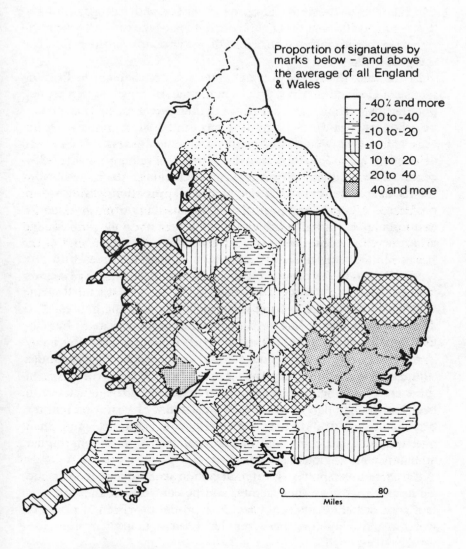

Proportion of signatures by
marks below – and above
the average of all England
& Wales

	-40% and more
	-20 to -40
	-10 to -20
	±10
	10 to 20
	20 to 40
	40 and more

0   80
Miles

REDRAWN FROM JOSEPH FLETCHER'S MAP
(QUARTERLY JOURNAL OF THE STATISTICAL SOCIETY 1849 VOL. 12, p.176)

techniques than Fletcher, he found the two most densely populated counties, Middlesex and Lancashire, to be the most criminal. Unlike Fletcher, he was sceptical of the power of education to improve the lot and attitudes of the poor and criminal classes, and was critical of the 'overweening disposition to play the part of pedagogue . . . to the poor [which] proceeds rather from a love of power than a sincere regard for the people'.[68]

In the mid-1850s, the Reverend John Clay, chaplain of Preston House of Correction, drew attention to relationships between crime, popular instruction, attendance at religious worship, and number of beer-houses, again on a county by county basis.[69] Statistics from criminal returns were linked with occupational returns and details of educational attendance and religious observance from the 1851 census. The counties were grouped and percentages above and below the mean for the four variables correlated. Attention was drawn to problems of interpretation posed by variations within the regional entities, and the lack of administrative uniformity in the punishment of offences between places.[70]

Fig. 2.8, based on Clay's statistics, suggests that areas with low crime figures, the northern counties, Yorkshire, the north Midlands and the south-western counties had all, apart from the north Midlands, well below the average number of beer and ale houses. The anomaly in the north Midlands was seen to be compensated by relatively good church and school attendance. In contrast, the deficiency in religious worship and school attendance for the northern counties (though Fletcher's and Mayhew's maps indicate high literacy levels in these areas) was held to be more than matched by the deficiency in beer-houses. Similarly, on an individual county basis, Monmouth's bad record for drinking, as compared with Cornwall, more than over-weighted its equivalent educational provision and its higher attendance at religious worship.

Clay's figures showed greater deviation in numbers of beer and ale houses than his other factors, and he concluded that while certain good social effects could accrue from the provision of places of worship and schooling, these were less positive than their promoters would have hoped.

It is a mere truism to say that the progress of popular education, and the formation of religious habits, are fatally opposed by the temptation to animal pleasures, which abound wherever BEER-HOUSES and ALE-HOUSES abound . . . our present system of popular education is of little or no efficiency

Fig. 2.8. Relation between Crime, Popular Instruction, Attendance
at Religious Worship and Beer Houses, 1850s (based on
Rev. J. Clay)

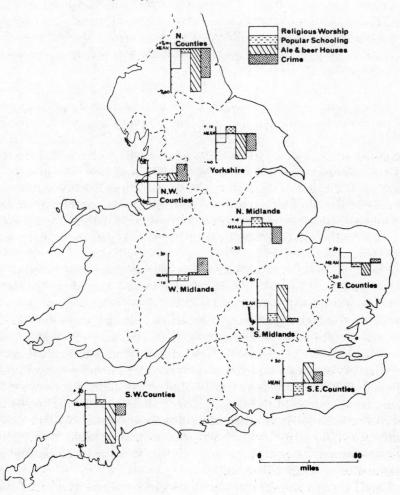

in saving the industrial classes from the moral dangers created by those
drinking houses.[71]

Although in some ways the results of these investigations were
inconclusive, and there might even be the suspicion that interpretations of the figures were manipulated, albeit without deliberate
intent, to achieve the desired conclusion, they represent vitally important early attempts to get to grips with the diseases of the body

politic,[72] and highlight the regional and local variations contained within the national picture, tantalisingly difficult though these variations were to explain. They also provide early evidence of the difficulties faced by educational providers in diffusing their wares down the social ladder, a problem later confirmed in the large towns and cities where, as we have seen, the voluntary agencies by 1870 had failed to fill in the gaps.

'LEADING' AND 'LAGGING' REGIONS: THE NORTHERN COUNTIES AND MONMOUTHSHIRE

Fig. 2.1 makes clear the striking regional disparities which existed in the early stages of the growth of mass elementary education,[73] with a range of from over 60% in day schools in the northern counties to less than 30% in Middlesex and Lancashire, the two most densely populated counties, and over much of Wales. Henry Brougham made full use of the strengths and deficiencies revealed in the national surveys he promoted in the 1816–18 period. A product of Edinburgh High School and an advocate of the Scottish parochial system of education, he drew attention to the achievements of the northern counties, setting an example for the rest of the country. 'Were he not afraid of fatiguing the house', he said, 'he could show, as in a map, how education was spread over the country'.[74] He quoted the contrast between Middlesex and Lancashire, respectively three times and twice as badly educated as the rest of the country, and Cumberland and Westmorland, twice as well educated. The proportion of the poor in the Lakeland counties was only half of that elsewhere. Brougham was also surprised by the fact that most parents here paid for their children's education. Only 48 out of 2,700 were educated free in Westmorland. This he took as a sign of the value that people attached to education. At the other extreme, over half of those in the lace-making counties were provided with free education; 16,000 out of 27,000 in Wiltshire and Somerset; and 30,000 out of 54,000 in the three eastern counties (Norfolk, Suffolk and Essex). The situation of Westmorland was a replica of Scotland, and showed 'the zeal and earnestness of parents in procuring instruction for their children'.[75]

Other commentators had applauded and were to applaud this strength of provision in the northern counties. Thus of Westmorland, Bernard wrote in 1809:

How much superior in morals, in intellect, and in happiness, the peasantry of those parts of England are which have opportunities of Instruction, to the same class in other situations ... the peasantry of Westmorland and ... adjacent counties, if their physical and moral qualities be taken together, appear to possess a considerable degree of superiority over the peasantry of any part of the island.[76]

Parson and White in 1829 were similarly impressed by the 'temperate, social, humane, industrious and enlightened people' of Cumberland and Westmorland, a state of affairs brought about by the provision for the 'humbler classes' of 'numerous and well conducted *endowed* and *subscription* schools'.[77]

Hill's survey of the 'State of Education in England' in 1836 also found the northern counties in good shape, with the labouring people of Northumberland, for example, seen to be more polite, in language and address 'decidedly superior', and more free from crime than the same class in southern England. One of Hill's correspondents was clear as to why this was so: 'A principal cause of this, I have no doubt, arises from the education they receive from the schools scattered through the country', in which the bible was the 'grand school-book', symptomatic of the value the people placed on religious observance.[78]

One reason given by Hill for this extensive diffusion in the north was, at least by implication, the 'contagious' influence of Scotland, with its envied parochial system of schools:

on the south Tweed ... though there is no established system as in Scotland ... the education of the lower orders is very general, and sought after with great avidity ... Where a taste for knowledge is once spread among a people, and education has become so common as to convey a reproach to those who are destitute of it, I find that it goes on very well without extraneous patronage or support.[79]

A more recent commentator, Professor Stone, quotes Sir Francis Doyle in 1843 as commenting on the high educational level in Northumberland as compared with the south, noting that some social stigma was attached to parents who did not secure for their children an elementary education – 'every nerve is strained to procure it', both at individual and community level, with a 'school attached to almost every village'.[80] Stone lends support to the 'contagious diffusion' argument, viewing Scotland as enjoying a superior elementary system to England, and setting an example for those south of the border to emulate. Education in this region, he argues, was favoured by the large endowment of elementary schools in the seventeenth and eighteenth centuries, testifying to a long-standing regard for education; the lack of opportunities for child labour before industrialisation took place; and the long, hard winter giving time to attend to educational improvement. As a result, boys might stay at school until 13 or 14, three or four years longer than in the south.[81]

It was, however, particularly towards the Lakeland counties that the plaudits were directed. The Schools Inquiry Commission (1868) referred back to late eighteenth-century accounts of the greater commitment of ordinary people to education than was the case in the south, noting that 'in London, the compting houses are much supplied with country lads from Cumberland and Westmorland', attributing the advanced educational state in some degree to the 'keen and pure air' of these counties.[82] J. D. Marshall too, in his 1971 study of *Old Lakeland*, identifies the rigorous environment as a reason for training youthful talents for 'emigration' to town employment outside the region.[83]

The Schools Inquiry Commission also contained a memorandum from Richmond on the reasons for 'the unusual diffusion of classical learning' in Westmorland. He ascribed the situation to a social system characterised by the presence of 'statesmen' or small landowners, and a democratic outlook unusual in eighteenth- or nineteenth-century society. The 'statesmen' were not rich enough to use the high-class boarding schools, but at the same time

had very different notions about education from those which are often to be discerned among farmers and tradespeople in more southern counties. They did not regard the gentility of a boarding school; they had no thought of their sons learning manners among those who might pass with the world for their betters. A spirit of strong independence and self-sufficiency, a certain contempt for mere externals, a pride of class which admitted no desire to struggle out of that class, led the Westmorland 'statesmen' to look at home for their education. There was no unwillingness to consort with the children of the poor. If the village schoolmaster could teach Latin and Greek the 'statesman' would look no further for the schooling of his boys.[84]

If the local schoolmaster were not a scholar, the boy would walk every day to the nearest village at which the Classics were taught. It was very much the norm that a younger son from these families should become a clergyman, and was often ordained from the village school. It was understood that his later sphere of operations would be the local township where he would function as schoolmaster as well as curate, and carry on the tradition of learning.[85] For these reasons a multiplicity of schools over the years were endowed.

In his pioneering exploration of education and social movements, Dobbs later interpreted this healthy state of affairs as a response to fundamental social and cultural dispositions, helped by the region's close proximity to the educational influence of Scotland.

The study of education cannot be divorced from that of the social system in which it arises. One of the reasons which have been assigned for the growth in Scotland of a democratic scheme of education, is that a strong educational tradition had been established there before society was divided by the influx of wealth.[86]

He argued that differentiation of social life and attitudes between areas related back to early racial influences, as between, for example, Anglo-Saxon and Celtic regions.[87] Another factor was stage in a process of social diffusion. Thus Lancashire and Yorkshire on the eve of the Industrial Revolution were in some respects passing through a phase which had been achieved two centuries previously in more advanced agricultural districts. Similarly, the northern grammar schools had been established later than those of 'traditional England', founded by a prosperous yeomanry in the fifteenth century.[88]

Thus Dobbs noted the English lakes area as a region of powerful Viking, and even earlier Celtic, stock, its isolation quarantining it for centuries from outside commerce. It therefore developed a 'store-house of racial energies' and an individuality of character and social habits. These survived in the Cumberland 'statesmen' of the eighteenth century. The 'social order harmonised with ... rude, wholesome surroundings'.[89] Here a more democratic society than known elsewhere prevailed, with the priest and the schoolmaster forming the 'upper class', but neither wealth nor destitution were obvious.

Thus arose a consensus interpretation of a highly favoured educational environment. It seems likely, however, that under the influence of the Lakeland poets and the discovery of the scenic glories of the district, this became translated into a romanticised cultural stereotype, of an ideal harmony between man and nature, education, society and physical surroundings.

Among the hills of Athol he was born;
Where, on a small hereditary farm
An unproductive slip of rugged ground,
His parents, with their numerous offspring dwelt;

A virtuous household, though exceeding poor!
Pure livers were they all, austere and grave,
And fearing God; the very children taught
Stern self-respect, a reverence for God's word,
An habitual piety, maintained
With strictness scarcely known on English ground.

From his sixth year, the Boy of whom I speak,
In summer tended cattle on the hills;
But, through the inclement and the perilous days
Of long-continuing winter, he repaired,
Equipped with satchel, to a school, that stood
Sole building on a mountain's dreary edge,
Remote from view of city spire, or sound
Of minster clock! From that bleak tenement
He, many an evening to his distant home
In solitude returning saw the hills
Grow larger in the darkness; all alone
Beheld the stars come out above his head,
And travelled through the wood, with no one near
To whom he might confess the things he saw.

So the foundations of his mind were laid ...[90]

Other regions, overtaken by mining and manufacturing activity, presented a grim contrast to this northern Utopia. One of the counties
worst-hit by industrialisation and rapid population increase was
Monmouthshire, lying at the eastern end of the South Wales coalfield
and iron district. To this area, recently affected by Chartist riots,
Seymour Tremenheere was despatched by the Committee of Council
in December 1839 to report on the state of elementary education. He
concentrated on the industrialised townships of the eastern valleys of
Glamorgan and Monmouthshire.

The valleys have there attained a high elevation, are susceptible of but scanty
culture, and are separated from each other by tracts of cheerless moorland.
The people are for the most part collected together in masses of from four to
ten thousand. Their houses are arranged round the works in rows, sometimes
two to five deep, sometimes three stories high ... The surface of the soil
around is frequently blackened with coal, or covered with high mounds of
refuse from the mines and the furnaces. The road between the rows is so
imperfectly made as to be often, in wet weather, ankle-deep in mud ... The
house of the master or resident director stands conspicuous amidst a small
group of stunted and blackened trees. About a dozen other houses of decent
exterior may be seen, inhabited by the surgeon, the agents, and other officers
belonging to the works. These ten or twenty superior members of the

establishment, a few small shopkeepers, and many thousand people depending on daily labour, constitute for the most part the respective divisions of society among these colonies in the desert.[91]

Unlike Westmorland, there was no tradition, outside a few larger settlements, of providing endowments for education. The Welsh Circulating Charity School Movement, a peripatetic means of combating mass illiteracy, which reached Monmouthshire in 1738 and collapsed in the 1770s, was no adequate substitute though Davies suggests that it began a tradition of education in many parishes.[92]

Tremenheere was convinced that the slow rate of educational advance in the area was caused by parental indifference. It was apparent that children could gain a living at an early age without the aid of schooling.[93]

The steady demand for labour, and the rates of wages in the last seven years, have been such that the earnings of children of a very early age can rarely have been absolutely necessary to the father of a family.[94]

Effecting improvement was not just a matter of providing resources, though this was important, but of changing attitudes. As Tremenheere concluded:

in order to give an improved system of education on any scale a fair chance, it appears indispensable that many circumstances of the first importance as affecting the moral and social condition of this people, should be earnestly considered in the proper quarters. The state of the population, as regards spiritual superintendence, will naturally be a prominent object of solicitude.[95]

In explaining the backwardness of education in Monmouthshire in the first half of the century, Davies points out that the country was divided into large unwieldy parishes, appropriate to an earlier economic stage, but anachronistic in the changing circumstances of the industrial revolution. The Established Church was as a result badly placed to provide schools for the burgeoning valley communities. The small Nonconformist chapels were better able to meet the new demands as they sprang into being in association with the influx of population.[96] But resources were small and the quality of provision poor.

The Chartist riots of the late 1830s promoted not only Tremenheere's despatch to the area, but also an extension of elementary education through the medium of works' schools mostly associated with ironworks.[97] These, plus the formation of the Llandaff Diocesan

Board of Education and the prospect of more government help at about this time, constituted belated steps in 'filling in the gaps' in Monmouthshire.

Monmouthshire remained in 1851 an educationally backward area. The proportion of children at school on census day was less than 50% in all areas except the district of the county town, Monmouth, and that was less than 60%. In his 1847 report on the state of education in the county, Symons had written:

Evil in every shape is rampant in this district; demoralization is everywhere dominant, and all the good influences are comparatively powerless. They drink to the most brutal excess ... are savage in their manner, and mimic the repulsive rudeness of those in authority over them. The whole district and population partake of the iron character of its produce; everything centres in and ministers to the idolatry of profit; physical strength is the object of esteem, and gain their chief God.[98]

This points the contrast between the authoritarian economic and social relationships of the mining districts and the democratic ones of Lakeland. It also repeats the environmental determinism evident in Tremenheere's pioneering report of 1839, despite a sensitivity to the fact that the workers' materialist ways could have been inculcated by their economic masters. It presented a contrasting cultural stereotype to that of the Lakeland counties.

Change was to come, however. In his 1856 report on the mining districts of Glamorgan and Monmouthshire Tremenheere detected an improvement on his 1839 visit. He felt the Chartist riots had at least led the employers, through factory schools and improved houses, to take 'some steps towards providing for their people better means of moral and religious and general instruction'. Neglect and indifference to education he saw now as reduced to exceptions.[99] Similarly HMI Hernaman noted that between 1853 and 1860 the number of annual grant schools had risen from seven to 18; of certificated teachers from six to 25; and pupil teachers from 24 to 42.[100] The Newcastle Commission's figures indicated that, in proportion of children at day schools, Monmouthshire had risen to 24th ranking among English counties, not a lofty position, but a sign that it was probably a late start as much as the local dissipation of the population that had held back progress, and that the earlier tendency to indulge in deterministic explanations was questionable.[101]

On the other hand, all was not well with the schools of the Lakeland counties, on the evidence given to the Newcastle Commission. Thus the Lord Bishop of Carlisle declared that the small endowed schools which abounded in Cumberland and Westmorland were by then in a poor condition.

I believe I state a fact, which admits of no controversy, that as a whole those schools are worse than any others, and that either their endowments should be consolidated so as to make from the funds of many, one good middle class school, or confiscated as hindrances to the real work which ought to be secured.[102]

Assistant Commissioner Foster confirmed that the leading educational feature of the area was the large number of endowed elementary schools transmitted down from past generations. But he found the people less educated than he had expected. 'Literature among them appears as the remains of an old civilization fast wearing out'. The statesman class was rapidly diminishing, with the consolidation of small holdings into large estates owned by more wealthy people. The people were in a transition state between their former 'rude independence' and the condition of a normal agricultural community. Nevertheless

That these institutions were once valuable means of education is evinced by the fact that there lingers among the most illiterate of the people a traditional feeling of belonging to an educated race, and they treasure in their houses books which their ancestors understood, if they do not.[103]

Foster related the decline to the lower quality of the teachers now found. Some of the so-called 'grammar schools' had sunk to the position of mixed elementary schools. The 'moral infirmities' of some of the teachers, with drunkenness a 'prevailing vice', seemed less deplored than their intellectual deficiencies. Foster thought such teachers could not be removed unless parliamentary enactment vested the endowment for the benefit of the school rather than the master. He quoted the Bishop of Carlisle's observation that the endowed schools were the 'curse of his diocese'.[104]

  D.C. Richmond who, in his Memorandum on Westmorland schools to the Taunton Commission, had stressed the high early quality of education provision in the area (page 48), noted that there had been much social change over the last 50 years which had had deleterious effects. The break-up of the independent statesman class had resulted in a loss of demand for the dual system, which had provided in the same school both an elementary and classical education. The offices of the curate and schoolmaster had been separated, to the spiritual benefit of the community, but the curates had been replaced by lower ability masters and the standard of teaching had suffered.[105] Similarly, J. H. Tremenheere, in his report to the Agricultural Commissioners in 1868–9, quotes a witness as testifying to the decline in the custom of 'statesmen' training their second and younger sons for the Church, as a result of it being too costly for their present economic situations.[106]

Notwithstanding this evidence of decline, there remained, in Parliament at least, the impression that educational provision in the northern counties continued to be sound. In the debate over the Second Reading of the Agricultural Children's Bill in 1867, it was argued strongly that the view that the education of rural children was in a disgraceful state did not apply in the north of England, where such education was 'highly creditable' in quality. Northumberland, Cumberland, Westmorland, and the North Riding of Yorkshire were again singled out as the best educated counties in England.[107]

It could well have been that Northumberland remained isolated from the kind of social pressures which seem to have plagued the Lake Counties. At all events, the accumulated evidence suggests an increasingly complex picture as industrialisation on the coastal coal and ironfields, and the spread of railways into the valleys of Cumbria, brought change to a formerly self-sufficient and apparently highly educated populace. At the same time, there was a reluctance to abandon the rhetoric that had fostered the favourable 'mental maps' of the region.

CONCLUSION

No unequivocal conclusion can be offered as to the nature of the diffusion process in the case of the northern counties. The patterns of the map (Figs. 2.1 and 2.2) suggest contagious diffusion. In the case of the spread of 'new plan' schools it would seem at first sight that the friction of distance factor had operated with weak uptake at the extremities, leaving an impression of educational lag. Fig. 2.1, however, makes it clear that in the case of the northern counties, elementary provision was already present. This was presumably the result of an earlier cycle of diffusion. But from where?

At the institutional level, Dobbs is clear that the diffusion of small country grammar schools, offering both an elementary and a classical education, arrived late in this region, and from the south.[108] The likelihood is that a hierarchical diffusion was involved. The schools took firm root in a social and economic system which promoted favourable attitudes towards schooling. It is tempting to conjecture that at the level of individual or community attitudes, there was some contagious influence from Scotland. But it may also be that the physical and cultural settings of both sides of the border, being similar, encouraged concurrently favourable attitudes. Obviously at the formal level, the systems were quite separate, and there was no question of hierarchical diffusion southwards.

The Lakeland counties also illustrate the point that those early in the field did not of necessity maintain their lead. By the late nineteenth century the utopian picture promoted by their idyllic physical setting and progressive attitudes towards education, and drawn to the attention of a wider public by the romantic poets and the railways, was being clouded by the social changes which improved access engendered. Elsewhere too, as in the case of voluntary provision in certain towns of Lancashire, achieving a lead at an early stage in the 1830s, '40s and '50s could be followed by complaints about the obsolescence of the accommodation provided in the 1880s and 1890s, as the diffusion of modern urban board schools responded to higher levels of expectation of elementary provision.[109]

There was no uncertainty about the direction of diffusion in the Welsh border region. Monmouthshire, essentially a part of Wales, was at the opposite extreme from the Lakeland counties, suffering a dual unfavourable cultural stereotype, of being a mining and manufacturing county, and Welsh-tainted. Scotland meant Edinburgh and high European culture, and educational pioneers such as Brougham, Pillans, Stow and Owen. Wales was equated with a low indigenous culture, its development hampered by what was regarded in England as a primitive and dying language. The diffusion into Wales was aggressively hierarchical: a form of cultural colonisation.

Hierarchical diffusion of social innovations is, however, a notably frail and uncertain process where it meets resistance among the consumers. It requires local lubrication as much as the power of the initial impetus to produce the desired wave effects. Thus influential individuals or groups on local managing bodies and school boards could do much to hasten or slacken the pace of change. Anglicisation of all but peripheral areas of Wales did not succeed.

The process of educational diffusion by the voluntary societies down the social ladder also failed, reaching too late the most deprived social groups. The impetus for the diffusion of mass education had come from the great towns and cities. Paradoxically, while voluntary provision spread far and wide, by 1870 it had not dug deep enough into urban society. A new cycle of diffusion was about to start in the attempt to fill the gaps.

REFERENCES AND NOTES

1. D. B. Tyack, 'The Spread of Public Schooling in Victorian America: in Search of a Reinterpretation', *History of Education*, vol. 7 (1978), p. 178.
2. A. R. H. Baker, *Historical Geography and Geographical Change* (London, 1975), pp. 26–9.
3. See T. Hagerstrand, 'Quantitative Techniques for Analysis of the Spread of Information and Technology', in C. A. Anderson and M. J. Bowman (eds.), *Education and Economic Development* (London, 1971), pp. 253–4 and p. 256, for reference to the contagious influence of early compulsory education in Denmark on the Swedish province of Scania.
4. *Hansard*, CCXXIX (1876), col. 1906.
5. C. A. Anderson, 'Patterns and Variability in the Distribution and Diffusion of Schooling', in Anderson and Bowman (eds.), *op. cit.* (1971), p. 315.
6. See B. T. Robson, *Urban Growth: an Approach* (London, 1973), p. 137.
7. Baker, *op. cit.* (1975), p. 23.
8. *Ibid.*, p. 24.
9. W. H. G. Armytage, 'Education and Innovative Ferment in England 1588–1805', in Anderson and Bowman (eds.), *op. cit.*, pp. 377–92.
10. See H. Perkin, *The Origins of Modern English Society* (London, 1969), pp. 67–9.
11. See E. Kerr-Waller, 'Scottish Influence on English Education between 1800 and 1840' (Unpublished University of London (King's College) M.A. Thesis, 1952).
12. See, for example, D. Fraser, 'Education and Urban politics c. 1832–1885', in D. Reeder (ed.), *Urban Education in the Nineteenth Century* (London, 1977), pp. 11–26.
13. It must be accepted that the data collected in the early educational surveys should be looked at with caution. There is clearly more margin for error than is desirable. On the other hand, in relative terms, there is no reason to believe that at the general level, as between the traditional counties, one would be more accurately enumerated than another. Where errors were much more likely to occur lay in the rapidly growing towns. Some encouragement can be gained from the fact that broadly the patterns shown are reflected in contemporary qualitative pronouncements on the nature of regional differentiation. In addition, the information contained in the surveys was used as a basis on which to promulgate policy and particularly by Henry Brougham.
14. M. Sanderson, 'The National and British School Societies in Lancashire 1803–1839: the Roots of Anglican Supremacy in English Education', in T. G. Cook (ed.), *Local Studies and the History of Education* (London, 1972), p. 8.
15. F. Smith, *A History of English Elementary Education* (London, 1931), pp. 81–2.
16. Sanderson, *op. cit.* (1972), p. 24.
17. Note that it was impossible in the event to trace eight schools that were listed in the British Society's 1812 report.

18. E. Baines, *History, Directory and Gazetteer of the County Palatine of Lancashire* (Liverpool, 1825), vol. II, p. 142.

19. J. Murphy, 'The Rise of Public Elementary Education in Liverpool: Part One, 1784–1818', *Transactions of the Historic Society of Lancashire and Cheshire*, vol. 116 (1964), p. 184.

20. J. Murphy, 'The Rise of Public Elementary Education in Liverpool: Part Two, 1819–35', *Transactions of the Historic Society of Lancashire and Cheshire*, vol. 118 (1966), p. 117.

21. See *Minutes of the Committee of the Privy Council on Education* (hereafter *M.C.C.E.*) (1846), Part 2, pp. 25–8.

22. *Ibid.*, p. 25.

23. *Ibid.*, pp. 26–7.

24. *Ibid.*, p. 27.

25. *Ibid.*, pp. 80–1.

26. A. Everitt, 'Nonconformity in the Victorian Countryside', in Cook (ed.), *op. cit.* (1972), pp. 45–55.

27. See, for example, Rev. Canon Trevor, 'Elementary Schools in Small Town Populations', *Transactions of the National Society for the Promotion of Social Science*, York meeting, 1864 (London, 1865), pp. 412–20.

28. Sanderson, *op. cit.* (1972), p. 8.

29. *Ibid.*, p. 1.

30. *Ibid.*, pp. 13–14.

31. M. E. Jones, *The Charity School Movement: a Study of Eighteenth-century Puritanism in Action* (Cambridge, 1938; repr. Cass, 1964), pp. 138–42.

32. Sanderson, *op. cit.* (1972), pp. 14–15.

33. *British Parliamentary Papers* (hereafter B.P.P.) 1692 (1852–3), pp. lxii–lxiv.

34. *Report of the Royal Commission on the State of Popular Education in England and Wales (The Newcastle Report)*, vol. 1. (1861), p. 18 and p. 583.

35. Smith, *op. cit.* (1931), p. 77.

36. National Society, *Ninth Report* (London, 1820), pp. 9–10.

37. National Society, *First Report* (London, 1812), p. 16.

38. National Society, *Twenty-first Report* (London, 1832), p. 12.

39. National Society *Thirty-second Report* (London, 1843), pp. 36–7.

40. Sanderson, *op. cit.* (1972), p. 3.

41. *Ibid.*, p. 6.

42. *Ibid.*, p. 7.

43. *Ibid.*, p. 11.

44. *Ibid.*, pp. 12–13.

45. *Ibid.*, p. 18.

46. Murphy, *op. cit.* (1964), p. 186.

47. Murphy, *op. cit.* (1966), p. 112–13.

48. National Society, *Twentieth Report* (London, 1831), pp. 39–41. The tables were 'according to returns obtained', i.e. not fully complete.

49. It must be emphasised that the percentage figures in this case can serve only for comparative purposes, as they measure scholars actually on the rolls of National Society schools against a theoretical judgment for the proportion of the population that 'ought' to have been in school, not one that was actually in attendance.

50. National Society, *Church School Inquiry, 1846–7* (London, 1849), p. 3.

51. National Society, *Thirty-fourth Report* (London, 1845), p. 54.

52. D. A. Pretty, *Two Centuries of Anglesey Schools 1700–1902* (Anglesey Antiquarian Society, 1977), p. 59.

53. See *Newcastle Report*, vol. I. (1861), tables 596–616.

54. P. D. Phillips, 'A Prologue to the Geography of Crime', *Proceedings of the Associa-*

tion of American Geographers, vol. 4 (1972), pp. 86–8.

55. Y. Levin and A. Lindesmith, 'English Ecology and Criminology of the Past Century', in G. Theodorsen (ed.), *Studies in Human Ecology* (New York, 1961), pp. 14–21.
56. See T. Morris, *The Criminal Area* (London, 1957), pp. 44–51.
57. M. J. Cullen, *The Statistical Movement in Early Victorian Britain: the Foundations of Empirical Social Research* (New York, 1975), pp. 139–40.
58. G. R. Porter, 'The Influence of Education, shown by Facts Recorded in the Criminal Tables for 1845 and 1846', *Journal of the Statistical Society*, vol. 70 (1847), pp. 316–44.
59. R. W. Rawson, 'An Enquiry into the Condition of Criminal Offenders in England and Wales, with Respect to Education', *Journal of the Statistical Society*, vol. 3 (1840), p. 331 and pp. 348–9.
60. J. Fletcher, 'Moral and Educational Statistics of England and Wales', *Journal of the Statistical Society*, vol. 10 (1847), pp. 193–233; vol. 11 (1848), pp. 344–66; vol. 12 (1849), pp. 151–76 and pp. 189–335; also J. Fletcher, *Education, National, Voluntary and Free* (London, 1851), p. 91.
61. Rawson, *op. cit.* (1840), p. 331.
62. *Ibid.*, pp. 348–9.
63. See N. Ball, *Her Majesty's Inspectorate, 1839–1849* (Edinburgh, 1963), p. 89.
64. Fletcher, *op. cit.* (1851), p. 85.
65. *Ibid.*, p. 91.
66. Fletcher, *op. cit.* (1849), p. 234.
67. H. Mayhew, *London Labour and the London Poor* (London, 1861; repr. Cass 1967).
68. Quoted in E. Thompson, 'The Education of Henry Mayhew', in *The Victorian Poor* (4th Conference Report of the Victorian Society, 1966), p. 14.
69. J. Clay, 'On the Relation between Crime, Popular Instruction, Attendance at Religious Worship, and Beer-Houses', *Journal of the Statistical Society*, vol. 20 (1857), pp. 22–32.
70. *Ibid.*, pp. 22–3.
71. *Ibid.*, p. 27 and p. 32.
72. See Fletcher, *op. cit.* (1847), pp. 193–4.
73. Anderson, *op. cit.* (1971), p. 314, sees access to schools as quite unequal until late in the process of educational development.
74. *Hansard*, 2nd Series, vol. II (1820), col. 63.
75. *Ibid.*, cols. 64–5.
76. T. Bernard, *Of the Education of the Poor* (London, 1809; repr. Woburn Press, 1970), p. 47.
77. W. Parson and W. White, *History, Directory and Gazetteer of the Counties of Cumberland and Westmorland* (Leeds, 1829), p. 25.
78. F. Hill, *National Education: its Present State and Future Prospects* (London, 1836), vol. 1, pp. 243–5.
79. *Ibid.*, pp. 240–1.
80. L. Stone, 'Literacy and Education in England, 1640–1900', *Past and Present*, vol. 42 (1969), p. 123.
81. *Ibid.*, pp. 123–4.
82. *Schools Inquiry (Taunton) Commission*, vol. 9 (1868), p. 903.
83. J. D. Marshall, *Old Lakeland* (Newton Abbot, 1971), p. 59.
84. *Schools Inquiry (Taunton) Commission*, vol. 9 (1868), pp. 902–3.
85. *Ibid.*, p. 903. See also W. B. Marker, 'The History of Elementary and Secondary Education in Westmorland 1870–1914' (Unpublished University of Durham M.Ed. thesis, 1967), pp. 17–25.

86. A. E. Dobbs, *Education and Social Movements, 1700–1850* (London, 1919), p. 34.
87. *Ibid.*, pp. 48–51.
88. *Ibid.*, pp. 52–3.
89. *Ibid.*, pp. 61–2.
90. W. Wordsworth, *The Excursion*, Book First (Oxford 1951 edition), p. 592, lines 108–32.
91. Tremenheere's report was in effect the prototype of later HMI reports. See *M.C.C.E.* (1839–40), Appendix 2, pp. 76–7.
92. T. Davies, *Monmouthshire Schools and Education to 1870* (Newport, 1957), p. 54 and pp. 61–3.
93. Tremenheere in *M.C.C.E.*, pp. 182–3.
94. *Ibid.*, pp. 183–4.
95. *Ibid.*, p. 192.
96. Davies, *op. cit.* (1957), p. 83.
97. *Ibid.*, pp. 93–4.
98. *B.P.P.* 871 Part II (1847), p. 290.
99. *B.P.P.* 2125 (1856), p. 24.
100. *R.C.C.E.* (1860–1), Appendix B, p. 33.
101. *Newcastle Report*, vol. I. (1861), pp. 594–5.
102. *Ibid.*, vol. V, p. 122.
103. *Ibid.*, vol. II, p. 335.
104. *Ibid.*, p. 336.
105. *Report of the Royal Commission on Schools not comprised within Her Majesty's two recent Commissions on Popular Education and the Public Schools (The Taunton Report)*, pp. 904–5.
106. *B.P.P.* 4202–I (1868–9), pp. 553–4.
107. *Hansard*, 3rd series, CLXXXIX (1867), cols. 500–2.
108. See reference 88.
109. See W. E. Marsden, 'Variations in Educational Provision in Lancashire during the School Board Period', *Journal of Educational Administration and History*, vol. 10 (1978), pp. 15–20.

CHAPTER THREE

Urban Change, Urban Experience and Educational Responses

The race between Education and Population is, no doubt, far from being a neck-and-neck one.[1] (Ludlow and Jones, 1867)

Nineteenth-century Britain experienced the most brutal onslaught of urbanisation that the world has yet witnessed, an encroachment on the physical environment and an irritant to bodies politic. While towns and cities became the loci of new occupational and cultural opportunities, they also generated a climate of anxiety, related to runaway population increase, crime and social unrest in general. In response to these problems, education was prescribed as a powerful emollient.[2] So on the one hand, schools were mandated to deliver society from the baneful effects of urbanisation while, on the other, hyperactive population change created acute difficulties for the various providing agencies.

DEMOGRAPHY

The concentration of population in towns and cities was in fact an irresistible force confronting educational planners. They had to take account of all the variables of demographic structure and change: size of population; natural increase or decrease; varying age structure and sex ratios; the timing and pacing of population spurts; and the migrations at various scales of territorially fluid populations.

Over England and Wales as a whole, the population grew from 8.9 millions in 1801 to 32.7 millions in 1901, with the highest percentage growths in the early decades of the century, and the largest incremental gains in the later ones.[3] Population increases alone engendered problems enough for the educational providers. But these inevitably were exacerbated in a historical context first of increasing parental demand for schooling, and later of compulsory attendance. The overall growth of population conceals, however, wide variations between town and country, and between different types of town.

The most dramatic aspect of population growth was its concentration in urban areas and, even more, in large towns and cities.[4] Nowhere, as Weber's comparative figures indicated, was the urbanisation process more pronounced than in England and Wales, where the number of towns of over 5,000 inhabitants grew from 106 in 1801, to 263 in 1851 and 622 in 1891.[5] Urban areas contained about one-third of the population in 1801, one-half in 1851, and three-quarters in 1901.[6]

From the educational point of view, the structure of the population in the urban areas was as important as the numbers involved. By modern standards, the population was predominantly youthful. Families were large. The balance of birth and death rates occasioned a relative dearth of elderly and a surplus of young people. In 1871, for example, 36% of the population was made up of children under fifteen, as compared with 23% in 1961. The 'dependent' population was therefore concentrated at the bottom end of the population pyramid, with obvious connotations for school provision, particularly in towns and cities experiencing rapid growth.

Within towns and cities, pulses of population growth and decline were of great importance. A sudden influx, or gradual gain followed by loss, or loss by gain, all complicated the arithmetic, and in some cases made a mockery of what was or was not being provided educationally. Exceptionally rapid growth led to demands which could not be matched by even the most active school boards. Barrow in the 1870s and 1880s was a case in point.[7] Suburbanisation,[8] a process shifting both funds and respectable children to the periphery, posed major and differential problems for the educational providers.

Some areas benefited from their salubrious residential nature. Among these were the seaside resorts, which also functioned as dormitory and retirement centres.[9] The presence of both an elderly and a socially-high-status population reduced the pressure on public provision of schooling. Sex ratios were unbalanced in such areas, in part because women were longer-lived, and in part because unmarried females were imported for domestic service. As a contemporary researcher summarised, there was a surplus of men in mining counties and towns, barrack towns and steel towns, and of women in textile towns (employment opportunities), seaports (men at sea) and especially at watering places.[10] The contrasts are illustrated on the population pyramid comparing Southport and Birkdale (a seaside resort and dormitory centre), with Bootle (a Merseyside dock town), Lancashire, in 1901 (Fig. 3.1). Notice the abnormal proportion of females in the population from about the age of fifteen upwards in Southport and Birkdale. Many were domestic servants. Notice too the much greater proportion of young people in Bootle. This and the poorer nature of its population made educational provision a greater economic strain than in Southport and Birkdale.

In towns such as Bootle, the social norms, family life-cycles and large numbers of married women in the child-bearing age groups ensured high birth rates. Thus in 1860, the national average age of women at the birth of their last child was over forty, as against under thirty in 1950. The mean ultimate family size of women marrying aged 20 to 24 was seven in 1860, eight in 1880, but only 2.3 in 1950.[11]

Declining death rates helped to boost natural increase, although the drop between 1850 and 1900 was less dramatic than is sometimes imagined. Expectation of life at birth was 40 years for males and 42 for females in 1841, and 49 and 52 respectively by the end of the century. Infantile mortality rates remained high throughout the period, but varied between good and bad years, rather than exhibiting consistent decline. In a condition of high infantile mortality there remain high birth rates. And even short life expectations maintain large numbers of children for schools to accommodate.

Apart from natural change, the other great variable in demographic development is migration.[12] The territorial mobility of nineteenth-century people was remarkable, though it was mostly restricted in range. High fertility rates and family sizes increased the 'push' to move, while the presence of employment, social opportunities and a flexible housing market in the towns and cities provided the 'pull'. Much of the migration was short in step, in some cases moving up the settlement hierarchy from rural areas, and ending in provincial capitals or in London itself. The larger the place, the greater the pull it exerted.[13] Rural districts in consequence lost young people and, with an aging population, the impetus to provide schooling.

For the most part, England and Wales escaped the complications

Fig. 3.1. Population Pyramids for Southport/Birkdale and Bootle, 1901

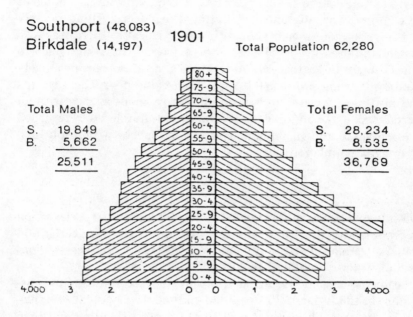

Southport (48,083)
Birkdale (14,197)   1901   Total Population 62,280

Total Males   Total Females

S.   19,849   S.   28,234
B.   5,662   B.   8,535

     25,511   36,769

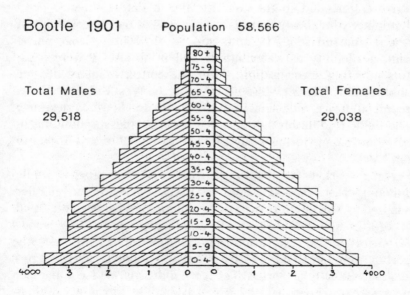

Bootle 1901   Population 58,566

Total Males   Total Females

29,518   29,038

posed by large-scale immigration. The significant exception was the influx of poor Irish, which gathered momentum during the time of the potato famines of the 1840s, but which was present through much of the century. The migrants concentrated on the cities and notably on Liverpool, the major point of entry.[14] Locally, there was also massive variation in the concentration of poor Irish, who tended to congregate, or be segregated, in dockland ghettos, increasing already daunting housing problems.[15] Apart from being poor, the migrants were also mostly Catholic, providing that religious agency with an onerous task in the building of the schools and churches they regarded as essential to the moral and spiritual rescue of a multiply disadvantaged population.

URBAN STRUCTURE

This is here taken to subsume such important aspects as specialisation of economic function, occupational make-up, social stratification and related questions of status and mobility, and residential segregation, to all of which schooling had to react.

Steam power and the division of labour were fundamental discoveries of the Industrial Revolution and the development of industrial capitalism. The uses of coal first for metal-smelting and then to drive engines led to the concentration of late eighteenth- and early nineteenth-century manufacturing centres on the coalfields of northern England, the Midlands and South Wales. Geographical terrain, availability of water supply and prior history were other factors affecting specialisation. Thus the cotton industry became localised mainly in Lancashire, woollens in the West Riding of Yorkshire, metallurgical industries in the Midlands and South Wales, steel in Sheffield, Middlesbrough and in Cumbria, and shipbuilding in Barrow, and along the major estuaries of the Clyde, Mersey, Tyne and Wear.[16]

Existing market centres in general grew less rapidly, while maintaining their long-standing functions. Ports formed another specialised group, with growing differentiation, as between the naval bases of Portsmouth and Plymouth, the fishing ports of Fleetwood, Hull, Grimsby, Lowestoft and Great Yarmouth, and the already important commercial ports such as Glasgow, London, Liverpool and Bristol. The coastal resorts, like many industrial and commercial centres, were offshoots of railway expansion. The way in which their demographic structure affected educational provision has already been noted. They also made good use of their environmental advantages to attract private schools (Chapter 10).

The consequences of this differentiation of function for education were appreciated at the time, though too readily used in deterministic explanations of regional differences in educational provision and achievement. In the second decade of the century, for example, Henry Brougham found the greatest deficiencies in schooling in large cities and densely populated counties, where crime was rife and the population viewed as ignorant and vicious.[17]

There were attempts to link educational development, or lack of it, with regional specialisation of occupation. Thus Joseph Fletcher[18] found conditions for the establishment of British and Foreign Society schools 'peculiarly unfavourable' in such areas as the lace-making, mining, manufacturing and metropolitan counties. While moneys had been spent on building schools, the evils of child labour and the perceived indifference of parents precluded success.[19]

Arguably the most striking example of the adjustment of schooling to the demands of industry lay with the half-time system, especially popular in the textile districts of Lancashire and Yorkshire. Its basis was to combine schooling and wage-earning. For a time it was thought to be providing the best of both worlds, acting as an incentive to children to attend school regularly and pass through the standards quickly to gain total exemption from schooling,[20] and additionally to bolster inadequate family income and in so doing enhance the self-esteem of children as contributors to the domestic welfare.[21] The system was used in certain places, as for example Burnley,[22] to hide accommodation deficiencies, however. The attempt of vested interests to legitimate half-timing on educational grounds was officially denounced as a preposterous fallacy.[23] As Fig. 3.2 suggests, elementary attendance in the cotton and colliery districts of Lancashire in 1851 was markedly below the rest of the country, a consequence of the continued demand in these occupationally specialised areas for youthful labour. The relative success of the industrial interest is clear from Fig. 3.3, which shows that in a national situation of improved average attendance in the large towns and cities, the most obvious 'lagging region' was still in 1896 made up of the textile districts of the West Riding and in particular of Lancashire.

Fig. 3.2. Children at School

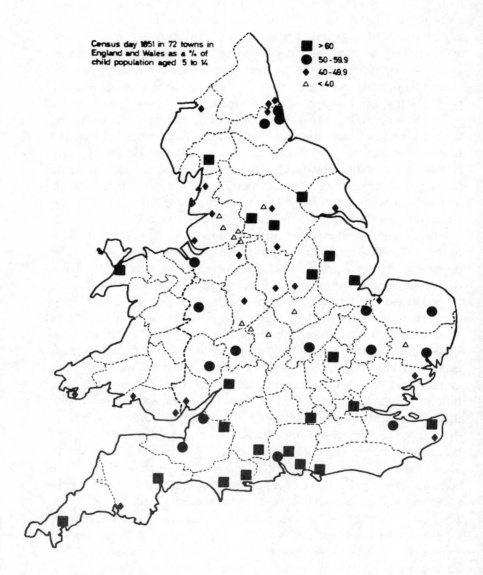

Census day 1851 in 72 towns in
England and Wales as a % of
child population aged 5 to 14

■   > 60
●   50 - 59.9
◆   40 - 49.9
△   < 40

Fig. 3.3. Elementary Schools

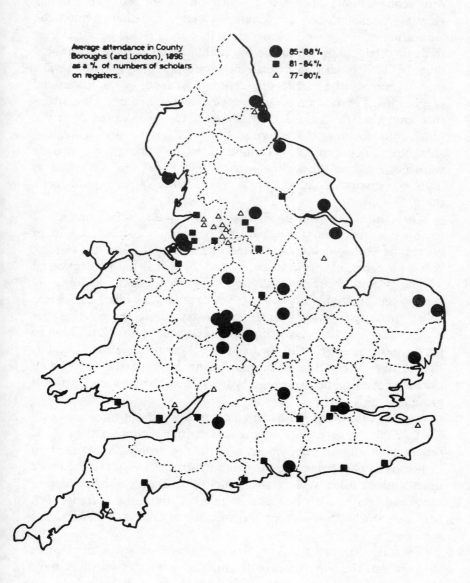

Average attendance in County Boroughs (and London), 1896 as a % of numbers of scholars on registers.

● 85-88%
■ 81-84%
△ 77-80%

SOCIAL STRATIFICATION

Most conventional histories of education reflect the 'two nations' view of nineteenth-century English society: one that divided the 'education of the poor', taking place in public elementary schools, from 'the education of the rich', taking place in private 'public' schools. This is no doubt relatively appropriate to a conflict view that represents the nineteenth century as a period of 'industrial revolution'. There is well-documented evidence of a new class structure emerging from the industrialisation taking place early in the nineteenth century, characterised by 'class feeling' and increasing antagonism between socio-economic groups.[24] The groups at odds were polarised as 'proletariat' and 'bourgeoisie' and presented as 'radically dissimilar ... as unlike as difference of race could make them'.[25]

What this view neglects is one of the great social changes of the nineteenth century, the 'tertiary' revolution, associated with an enormous enlargement and differentiation of the middle classes, based on urban service industries, and an increasing perception of 'solidarity' with the respectable working classes, notwithstanding the serious tensions which developed between 'white-collar' and 'blue-collar' groups. Shrewd observers of the day, while appreciating vast differences of wealth as existing at the extremes, found it difficult to perceive distinct breaks in the class structure at the centre.[26] And as Parkin has observed, the 'no-man's-land between the entrenched classes proved to be extremely hospitable to the new occupational groups'.[27]

Preoccupation with status was a diagnostic trait of these groups.[28] Status can be regarded as a more differentiated concept than class, related to it but not synonymous with it. It refers to social estimation or prestige. This being the case, any interpretation of the nature of nineteenth-century society involving the placing of education in the social fabric, must be made in a more differentiated framework than that of the 'two nations' distinction, to take account of status aspirations.

When Archdeacon Sandford wrote in 1864 that it was 'impossible to exaggerate the importance of' the middle classes, he was thinking of their dual role, both as a moral guide to the working classes below, and as invigorators of the upper class above.[29] The middle classes were the creators of wealth through hard work, thrift, careful investment and deployment of resources. Subscription to these values could both make possible and legitimate upward mobility. Elite status had to be earned both economically and morally. The middle classes were intent on lifting the moral tone of society and rising socially. If social mobility could not be attained by the current generation, education could provide a ladder for the next.

The upper middle classes looked to the public schools to effect the change. Their colonisation successful, by the end of the century they were the staunchest supporters of this exclusive system. By far the wealthier segment of the upper middle class was centred on London and not, as has sometimes been supposed, in the manufacturing belts of the north.[30] London's was more tied to the 'old society' and had either retained or constructed links with the metropolitan upper classes, through a reformed and extended public school system, predominantly Anglican in tone. The system became increasingly concentrated in the south-eastern segment of the country, and particularly around London.[31]

Apart from the rising influence of the upper middle classes, important shifts were taking place in the ranks just below. The occupational transition from secondary to tertiary activities produced an increasing differentiation. A well-marked divide, distinguishable by the extent to which servants were kept,[32] opened between the upper and lower middle class. The lower middle class, in essence an urban phenomenon, consisted of the classic *petit bourgeoisie* of shopkeepers, joined in the second half of the century by the new white-collar groups of clerks, commercial travellers, elementary school-teachers, and the like. There were 144,000 white-collar employees in 1851, 262,000 in 1871, 535,000 in 1891 and 918,000 in 1911. The most rapidly growing occupation was that of clerk, and clerks of different types increased in numbers from about 92,000 in 1861, to 370,000 in 1891 and over 560,000 in 1911.[33]

The financial affairs of the lower middle class were congenitally insecure. As much as they were enticed by the prospect of social advance, so they were obsessed by the fear of social descent, which could follow inexorably from dismissal from a post, or failure of a family business.[34] Even though both his parents were at work, his mother as a board school teacher, Richard Church ascribed the humility, furtiveness and timidity of the lower middle class to fears of submergence by 'the ever-rising waters of the indifferent masses'.[35] It was difficult to sustain aspirations toward genuine middle-class status on what was often little more than a working-class income, probably in the £100 to £150 per annum range. Many artisans, without the need to spend money on, for example, respectable clothes for work, were essentially better off. The low wages of clerks were cited in explanation if not in justification of cases of embezzlement.[36]

Elementary school-teachers embodied lower-middle-class neuroses about status, and were embittered by the low esteem in which they were held by the upper ranks of society. One commentator of the 1840s ranked the 'office of educator' as 'of low caste, even beneath the common rank of successful tradesmen and shopkeepers'.[37] And while *The Times*, following the 1870 Act, saw a 'boundless prospect opening up before the teaching profession', it drew attention to the ambiguous position and narrowness of outlook of its practitioners.

They have too much education to be quite at home with smaller farmers and shopkeepers, while they have not the knowledge or the manners which are acquired in good society. They can scarcely avoid being pedants or mere pedagogues ... When teachers have no congenial society to which to betake themselves when the day's work is over, and when they have nothing to do but to give lessons to pupil-teachers, or improve their own minds, they must find themselves year by year in a more contracted circle of ideas and sentiments.[38]

The parents of the more respectable children they taught were equally obsessive over socio-economic status, and looked to the schools to promote social mobility, or at least to maintain the hard-earned position they had already won.[39]

The lower middle class shaded indeterminately into the upper reaches of the working class. Many families included members in both. Though a good deal of the literature of social, economic and educational history hands down a concept of a homogeneous working class, many Victorian commentators were aware of the existence of 'the very various classes which subdivide the great proletarian order'.[40] It was in the interests of politicians and social reformers to draw attention to the worth of the respectable working class, to point up the contrast with the disreputable orders which threatened society from below. In a contribution to the 1884 meeting of the National Association for the Promotion of Social Science, Professor Levi enumerated 70% of the population as making up the working class. 'But they comprise many scarcely distinguishable from the middle classes', including those 'as far removed from common labourers and miners as clerks and curates are from those who have reached the highest places in the liberal professions'. While a large number remained 'low and degraded, ignorant and miserable', their condition should 'not be allowed to be diagnostic of the state of the class as a whole'.[41]

It was equally in the interests of respectable working men to concur with such judgements. Thus Thomas Wright, 'journeyman engineer', indicated that there was 'no typical working man', and that in no other section of society were there 'so many and widely differing castes as among the working classes'.[42]

It is difficult to make clear-cut distinctions between the lower middle and upper working classes. Respectability was a plaudit attached to both groups. The fact that respectability characterised the bourgeoisie has led to the charge of *embourgeoisement* of the upper working class, implying an uncritical adoption of middle-class culture and values. Tholfsen has opposed too ready an acceptance of this interpretation, pointing to the distinctive middle-class definitions of respectability, from which emerged the 'deferential worker' stereo-type, and the ideology of the working class itself, which saw it more in terms of self-respect and independence.[43] The labour aristocratic group, while generating its own rigid occupational distinctions at the work-place, is seen as being solid in its resentment of patronising lower-middle-class attitudes to blue-collar work.[44] It may be that individual workers were able to switch on the deferential and self-respecting independence roles when it suited them.

At the group level, therefore, the late-nineteenth century witnessed a reinforcement of working-class unity, as a result of structural changes in employment and the growth of socialist political activity.[45] At the level of family decision-making, however, there seems no similar evidence of a shift of upper-working-class opinion away from the desire for upward social mobility, or a rejection of the opportunities offered by an increasingly ambitious elementary pro-vision of schooling. Labour aristocrat children continued to rub shoulders with those of the lower middle class in the upper standards and in the higher grade schools of the late-Victorian period.[46] Such schools effectively assisted in the enlargement of the middling groups of society, rather than helping the ascent of the lower middle classes. Not all middle-class observers liked the fraternisation. Indeed, as one, admittedly extreme, commentator suggested, 'they stood like Frankenstein aghast at the monster they have created'.[47]

The writer may well have been guilty of falsely homogenising the working classes in his polemic, but reflected a growing middle-class anxiety about the magnitude and corrupting power of the residuum. Many were still unaware of the gradations which existed within the working classes. The degree of ignorance increased with nineteenth-century residential segregation, to be considered shortly, with wealthy and more 'moral' groups moving out leaving the poor in their ghettos to become 'poorer, more ignorant and more degraded'.[48]

It was again difficult at the margins to distinguish between respectability and disreputability. An important factor determining whether a family lived in comfort or poverty was income, not only its amount, but also its regularity. Equally significant, and especially so at the margins, was the way in which family income was used. An increasingly accepted view was that the budgeting skills of the housewife were crucial,[49] reinforcing the demand for domestic economy classes in the elementary schools.

RESIDENTIAL SEGREGATION

The on-the-ground manifestation of class and status differentiation was the segregation of residential areas. Dwellings of markedly different character and density of development constituted an almost uncontrollable extension of the built environment, and reflected the speculative judgements of their builders about the residential preferences of incoming populations, as the process of suburbanisation gained momentum:

the middle-class suburb was an ecological marvel. It gave access to the cheapest land in the city to those having most the security of employment and leisure to afford the time and money spent in travelling up and down; it offered an arena for the manipulation of social distinctions to those most conscious of their possibilities and most adept at turning them into shapes on the ground; it kept the threat of rapid social change beyond the horizon of those least able to accept its negative as well as its positive advantages.[50]

The suburbanisation process was well under way by the middle of the century. Garwood, writing in the early 1850s, was alert to some of its consequences:

I am disposed to consider very important ... the gradual separation of classes which takes place in towns by a custom which has grown up, that every person who can afford it lives out of town ... Now this was not so formerly: it is a habit which has, practically speaking, grown up in the last half-century. The result of the old habit was, that rich and poor lived in proximity, and the superior classes exercised that species of silent but very efficient control over their neighbours ... They are now gone, and the consequence is that large masses of population are gathered together without those wholesome influences which operated upon them when their congregation was more mixed; when they were divided, so to speak, by having persons of a different class of life, better educated, among them.[51]

But the classic ecological forces of invasion and succession, outlined in the first chapter, were inexorably promoting a middle-class flight to the suburbs. The Rev. Gover, Principal of the Worcester, Lichfield and Hereford Training College, wrote to the Mayor of Birmingham, George Dixon, to draw his attention to the impact of this process on the social life and educational provision in inner areas of his city in comparison with the developing parts of the conurbation:

At some parts of the Borough, schools lie so thickly together that one can thrive only at the expense of some of its neighbours ... In central districts, where dwell the most necessitous, and where the residents above the manual labour class are becoming fewer, from want of extraneous help a small School feebly lingers on in buildings designed for larger numbers; or, because the fees must be low in these quarters, reduction of expense is purchased by reduction in the staff and efficiency of the teachers. In outlying districts a class better off by their readiness to pay higher fees outbids the poorer for the limited space, so that the latter are left untaught ...

... all those who possess a moderate competency, or even secure a tolerable income, fly from the town itself to dwell in the purer air of suburbs or of villages of villas by railway sides. The separation of classes, however unavoidable, ... becomes a deadlier evil daily. The opulent fashion their own communities outside, the labouring or the necessitous classes are left to form societies solely by themselves within the town. It is almost in vain that ministers of religion seek to enlist ... the sympathies of the richer, who live apart from, for plans of social good within, their densely-crowded courts: vainer far for them to ask the means of providing instruction for every child from the population which throngs around them, living from hand to mouth.[52]

As Chapter 4 indicates in general, and later chapters the particular cases of London and Merseyside, through the medium of the adjustable school fee, the education system of the second half of the century was matched to a nicety with the subtle gradations and shifts of tertiary urban society.

URBAN-TYPE ATTITUDES AND BEHAVIOUR

But though true worth and virtue in the mild
And genial soil of cultivated life
Thrive most, and may perhaps thrive only there
Yet not in cities oft, – in proud and gay
And gain-devoted cities; thither flow,
As to a common and most noisome sewer,
The dregs and faeculence of every land.
In cities foul example on most minds
Begets its likeness. Rank abundance breeds
In gross and pamper'd cities sloth and lust.
And wantonness and gluttonous excess.
In cities, vice is hidden with most ease,
Or seen with least reproach . . .

I do confess them nurseries of the arts,
In which they flourish most; where in the beams
Of warm encouragement, and in the eye
Of public note they reach their perfect size.
Such London is, by taste and wealth proclaim'd
The fairest capital of all the world,
By riot and incontinence the worst.[53]

(W. Cowper, 'The Task')

Cowper's was an early salvo in the compulsive debate which followed the savage yet invigorating onslaught of the urban revolution. It was feared that it heralded a new and dangerous 'urban type' of behaviour. Public opinion was polarised and ambivalent and no wonder, for the city was a Jekyll and Hyde creation. In the 1840s, Robert Vaughan was taking the more positive line that was one part of Cowper's argument, looking upon cities as centres of intellectual opportunity.

Cities . . . are the natural centres of association . . . Men live there in the nearest neighbourhood. Their faculties, in place of becoming dull from inaction, are constantly sharpened by collision. They have their prejudices, but all are likely to be assailed.[54]

Edward Baines similarly urged people to look beneath the 'unpleasing exterior' of manufacturing centres, to see them as promoting opportunity through education, for the concentration of population made schooling an economic enterprise. Competition improved the arts of teaching. 'Every man has space in which to make trial of his favourite method. The observers are many, and the stimulus is proportionate'.[55] In an address to a British Association meeting at Bradford in 1873, the 'greater manifestation of intellectual vigour' in towns and cities was ascribed to this factor,[56] while writers such as Fletcher (1849)[57] and Conan Doyle (1888)[58] drew attention to the special advantages of London in this respect.

But favourable interpretations could readily be countered by the strengthening perception that unhindered urban growth was producing a dangerously deprived mass of people. Urban revolution at home combined with political revolution abroad generated a dread of the poorer classes, as 'a Leviathan that was fast learning his strength'.[59] The poorer districts, as in the East End of London, acquired the public image of the nether regions.[60] William Booth pointed the comparison, not the contrast, with the barbarian denizens of the primaeval equatorial forest:

... while brooding over the awful presentation of life as it exists in the vast African forest, it seemed to me only too vivid a picture of many parts of our own land. As there is a darkest Africa is there not also a darkest England? Civilisation, which can breed its own barbarians, does it not also breed its own pygmies?[61]

In such a climate of opinion there grew a stereotype of the city as a slum-bearing monster.[62] Though highly differentiated milieux to their inhabitants,[63] to outsiders slums were homogeneous, alien and degenerate. An outcast London seemed to threaten 'the very idea of an urban civilisation',[64] and the slum became in effect 'a mental landscape within which the middle class could recognize and articulate their own anxieties about urban existence'.[65]

Anxieties had been reinforced by the application to the social domain of Darwin's ecological concepts of natural selection and survival of the fittest. As early as 1865 Morgan, physician to the Salford hospital, asked the 'momentous question':

May not nations, like individuals, curtail their day of power in the world's history, by over-taxing the physical and mental energies at their disposal, thus prematurely consuming that national life-blood on which permanent greatness mainly depends?[66]

Out of the anxieties had thus grown what has been categorised as 'urban geopolitical thinking', encompassing not only the tangible aspects of urban pathology, but also a moralistic and deterministic perception of the deviance of the slum as an outcome of the 'behavioural, physiological and even genetic effects of overcrowded living conditions'.[67] As a corrupting environment was to blame, it was the environment that required treatment to cure the infection. The most potent long-term immunisation agency was thought, despite decades of experience which pointed somewhat to the contrary, to be education, a panacea for the ills of drunkenness, crime, over-population[68] and disease. City life directly, and indirectly in its dispiriting influence on poorer families, was seen as subverting the social and moral development of the young. The cry went up to 'Save the Children'.[69]

In taking urchin children off the streets, educational reformers generated fearful problems. Indeed, some contemporaries regarded the effort as wasted, schools teaching young thieves just enough 'to pilfer the articles marked at the highest figures'. And while philanthropists took exception to Mayhew's critique of the ragged schools,[70] they were unable to disguise the difficulties experienced in dealing with indescribably unkempt and foul-smelling 'street arabs'.[71] Apart from the cosmetic problems, there was the distressing fact of endemic disease, some of it lethal. The main juvenile killers were measles, whooping cough, diphtheria, scarlet fever and infantile diarrhoea. By the 1890s cholera and smallpox had disappeared. School Boards such as London, with doubtful legality,[72] established both school medical and meal services in the 1890s which, though laudable in principle, brought further pressures on the poorest families in introducing an additional layer of confrontation with authority. From its early years the London County Council conducted campaigns against verminous children and the hair inspection became enshrined in the folklore of elementary school experience (Plate 5).

The association between schooling and disease was a two-way process. Early death removed children from or, very frequently, prevented them from reaching, the school registers. Illness took a terrible toll of attendance. Regularly acquainted with disease, disability and death, parents and teachers were obsessively concerned over what were seen as environmental hazards: 'odours and emanations (miasmas)', cold and damp, and the perils of urban living, regarded as fundamental causes of disease at a time when the role of micro-organisms had yet to be understood.[73]

In the period following the 1870 Act, the schools were identified as promoters of disease, both mental and physical. The 'over-pressure' movement[74] disseminated the view that the stresses of mass education were damaging to the health of children, and culminated in the

Crichton-Browne Report of 1884. The controversy was fanned by various pressure groups, not least the medical establishment. The system of cramming children to get them through the standards, and the burden of 'home lessons', were said to increase the incidence of nervous diseases, sometimes causing death, in the 5–15 age group.

The Education Department was criticised for not reacting to the view that schooling was 'exerting some serious and deadly influences among a large number of sound and wholesome ones'.[75] Schools were also responsible for the spread of infectious diseases, which were disseminated like wild-fire through the congested and ill-ventilated elementary classrooms, and were often not reported until epidemic proportions were reached, for fear of schools being closed and attendance grants lost. Medical opinion again found the Education Department proving 'singularly stubborn' in not compelling absence in the case of infection, but allowing such to count towards the attendance grant.[76] In 1893, in fact, a grant to allay financial loss caused by epidemic illness was introduced.[77]

Among the recommendations of the Crichton-Browne Report were the provision of regular medical inspection and free school milk and meals. The late nineteenth-century slum school increasingly became a social welfare institution. An important means of improving attendance was to entice half-starved children into schools by offering free breakfasts and dinners. Pioneered by Miss Burgwin, the Head-mistress of Orange Street School (Plate 1), in Southwark in the 1870s and 1880s,[78] they were seen in Birmingham in the mid-1880s as having had a 'wonderful effect' on attendance, in improving afternoon work, in compensating for deficient growth, and in some cases in revo-lutionising the 'moral nature' of the beneficiaries.[79]

Poverty was implicated with truancy in other ways also. In the large cities there was little chance of preventing children from taking on casual employment. As the surveys of Gorst[80] and Edith Hogg[81] showed, a good deal of this work was undertaken either on the street or just off it, in neighbourhood shops or in domestic work such as child-minding. Street-trading children mixed promiscuously with truants, playing in slum streets and commercial thoroughfares from morning till night.

When such children were swept into school, a new set of problems faced the teacher. Some were seen as 'shifty' and some as 'bright enough' little fellows. But a ubiquitous and aggravating trait was their inability to concentrate. Few teachers could 'keep the wild youngster's eye from wandering', his mind being always 'on the alert for something new to see, or something new to steal'.[82] Implicit in such statements was a psychological theory: that the city was creating nervous strain and subversive over-stimulus in its youth.[83] Domestic privation was compensated by 'the excitement of the crowd ... the familiar noises and flaunting brilliance of the streets'.[84] Thus Reginald Bray, a settlement worker and member of the London Education Authority, characterised the impact of urban surroundings on the child. If the deprived districts of cities were calculated to rear an unhealthy race in physical terms, the moral and mental effects were even worse:

A mass of impressions are hurled at the observer, a thousand scenes sweep by him; but there is nothing to hold them together, nothing to produce a sense of order, nothing to give a perception of similarity ... This continuous panorama of shifting scenes produces no conception of a world of connected phenomena, and merely serves to fill the mind with a whole lumber room of useless, though perhaps entertaining, rubbish.[85]

The temptations of the street (Plate 6) were not compensated by stability in the home, where over-crowding and lack of privacy allowed no peace and order. The 'ceaseless babel of noise' in the home added to the strain on the nerves of urban children, seen as notably more highly strung than rural.[86]

To the socialising agencies of the family and the school were added the urban peer group and its preferred milieu, the street, enlivened by the 'rhythmic chant, unceasing, discordant, cheerful and not unpleasing' of child life.[87] The street's glamour brought some compensation to the lives of children otherwise blighted by squalor and often brutalised relationships in the home, and the monotony and oppressive discipline of the school.

... the daily path to school yields a succession of stolen joys which make it compare very favourably with the formal promenade of the little West-ender in fashionable clothes and clean hands ... I have seen a letter from a girl of this age describing the delights of the street dance and the meeting of friends, which, though perfectly simple in expression, was almost passionate in its intensity of feeling, and made me realise ... the impossibility of getting these young girls out of London or into a quiet domestic life.[88]

But the general feeling of social commentators was despairing, for below the outward problems of city life they detected an 'invisible spirit, which makes for neuroticism, decadence, moral drift, instability and national decay'.[89]

The physical, social and moral hazards presented by urbanisation demanded a broader curriculum than that initially allowed for. The physical demands of certain types of urban employment, and still more those of military service, necessitated a reconsideration of the curriculum base. Weber pointed out that while the power to read and write was more advanced in the town than in the country, it was generally misapplied, whether in the interests of industrial competition, in feeding 'that sensational interest in sport and crime which absorbs the attention of the masses in their non-working hours', or in contributing to the townsman's 'glib tongue' and 'showy intellectual shop-front'.[90]

As the Inter-departmental Committee on Physical Deterioration later reported, physical degeneracy in the population was largely confined to the poorer areas of large towns, while there was no evidence of retrogressive deterioration of the population as a result of the urban state, as had been argued by the eugenicists.[91] But the fears had been sufficient to compel the introduction of health-promoting activities into the curriculum, as well as the provision of milk, meals and medical inspection. One activity was drill, first applied on hard military lines but later, under the aegis of the London School Board, ameliorated in a less rigid form of physical education.[92] On the social side, just as the factory system had broken up the natural but irregular tempo of country life, and set a tightly prescribed schedule for work, so the school timetable would help to replace the jagged rhythms of town life, stressing the virtues of order, punctuality and regularity.

Celebration of empire served to distract attention from the privations of urban life.[93] The school could play its part. Like other subjects, geography and history had been set back by the Revised Code of 1862, but were soon reintroduced as grant-earning 'specific' or 'class' subjects. One inspector extolled geography as the subject *par excellence* suited 'to children of a race like ours', one 'born to create empires'.[94] In history and geography books, the customs, modes of life and values of foreigners were caricatured and adversely stereotyped. Thus in a geography text for pupil teachers, the English character was counterpointed as 'liberty-loving, independent, enterprising, wealth-respecting, law-abiding, steadfast, illogical and rather solemn', and the chief national vices identified as 'drunkenness and gambling'.[95] Desirable Anglo-Saxon traits were normally projected as decaying in distance away from the Straits of Dover. Turks, Negroes and Papists excited special disapproval.[96]

Another palliative was to introduce the urban child to country ways of life. Here too geography could assist in awakening a consciousness of a lost rural content, 'to counteract the misfortune of living in a large town'.[97] The idea that the urban child might benefit from the study of his personal milieu was slow to come, as the professional journals stressed the need for the rural field excursion.[98] Penstone, in her pioneering text on *Town Study*, presented a somewhat ambivalent viewpoint:

We do not forget what has often been pointed out – that the sights and sounds of city life may have very little educative value in themselves. This is especially true with regard not only to the slum, but even more to the mean and monotonous suburbs which form such large areas in London and other great cities.

Even mean streets required study for the indirect benefit of making apparent to the children the possibility of improvement and, prophetically, incitement of a 'divine discontent'.[99]

Despite the broadening of the late nineteenth-century elementary school curriculum, Bray remained dissatisfied by the lack of moral impact it was having on urban youth.

It must ... be confessed that the schools have not realised the sanguine expectations formed when the Education Bill of 1870 came into operation. The effect of the discipline of the children and their ability to read and write have undoubtedly led to important results. But the influence on their character is not strongly marked; the majority leave school without any desire to continue their education, and the traces of their training, instead of being permanent, gradually disappear.[100]

He identified the problem as stemming from the narrow instructional view of education held by its promoters. The board schools were condemned for their isolation from the local community, with the teachers descending daily as aliens from more salubrious parts of the city.[101] The voluntary schools in particular were pervasively overcrowded, and dispensed 'an air of gloom and rusty antiquity', replicating the disturbance and nervous excitability characteristic of the urban community.[102] Education should strive for more coherent learning, bringing order to the facts purveyed, and emphasise the expressive and moral areas of the curriculum. The school should give priority to functioning as a community centre in which welfare agencies might operate and evening classes be given.[103]

Others, and perhaps too much the educational reformers themselves, judged the growth of nineteenth-century urban school pro-

1. The 3rd Class at Orange Street, Southwark, a '1d Board' School and one of London School Board's 'Schools of Special Difficulty'.

2. Children of Oxford Gardens School, North Kensington, the parents of which petitioned the London School Board to fix a high fee to keep it select. Starting with fees of 6d, it was by 1891 one of the two board schools in London to have the maximum fee of 9d.

3. An impressive London Board School, Mansfield Place (later Holmes Road) in Kentish Town, of which the architect, E. R. Robson suggested its fault might lie 'in being somewhat beyond the mark of an Elementary and suggesting in appearance rather the uses of a Secondary or Grammar School'.

4. Leipsic Road, Camberwell in the early years of this century with the Board School at back left.

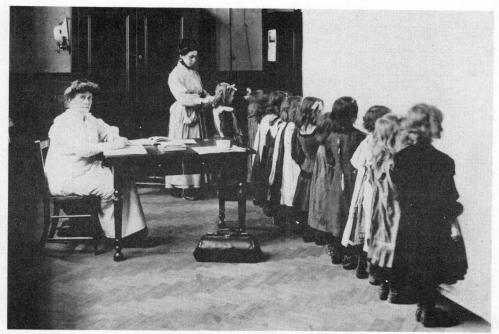

5. A hair inspection in a London school in the early years of this century.

6. 'Children of Bootle': an undated photograph of play in a Bootle side street.

7. Bootle's south-western slum: the backs of houses of Mann and Emley Streets prior to clearance in the 1930s.

8. The docks near Bootle's northern boundary: the main catchment area of Salisbury Road Board School.

vision to have been beneficial. There was a satisfied feeling in the later decades that the schools were effecting some social reconstruction. As families produced second and third generation scholars they were seen as becoming more acclimatised and sympathetic towards compulsory public education. Thus in 1875, HMI Kennedy, reporting on the Manchester district: 'I get abundant testimony that the formerly rude and violent "residuum" is unquestionably and greatly softened and enlightened'.[104]

Kennedy qualified his optimism by saying that such was only the case where parental cooperation was present. Hence the school boards continued to battle for large numbers of truants, and nowhere more so than in the metropolis.[105] But there too there was widespread agreement that by the 1890s the battle for universal urban provision was largely won, and that the attitudes and behaviour of urban parents and children were gradually improving.

As an East End schoolmaster replied to Booth's query about the changes wrought by education: 'Where are the rebels and young villains of a dozen years ago?'[106] An alternative view was that a permissive educational system had moved them up the age cohort. The 'sentimental brigade' on the school board had made possible 'the reign of the rough'.[107] A new cycle of anxiety about the delinquent adolescent emerged.[108]

Whatever be the disease which is investigated, those who diagnose it put the finger on these all-important years of adolescence as the chief breeding ground of the evil ...[109]

In the streets appeared 'gangs of ruffians known as Hooligans',[110] the product, as one reverend gentleman asserted, of 'the modern public-house, the modern tenement dwelling, and the modern education system'.[111] The school, the 'ultimate opponent' of street anarchy,[112] could cage children for only so long and was for some having a disappointing long-term influence.

Juveniles, like urban people in general, were by the 1880s and 1890s enjoying more private time than previously available. But to be gainful leisure, like work time, needed supervising.[113] A fitting means of control was the voluntary but formal youth organisation, providing both moral and physical training, taking over from the school 'after hours' and also beyond the span of school life, thus functioning as an informal agency of education.[114]

CONCLUSION

The mass rediscovery of the almost lost world of leisure enhanced the prospects of achieving a life, even an urban one, worth living, beyond preoccupation with the crude necessities of existence. But leisure time, in diffusing down the social gradient, was seized upon by those in positions of power and influence as of dangerous precedent. Their response, the glorification of not only Christian, but also rural and pioneering values, was at once a diversion from the continuing glaring inequalities of town life, which the nation's urban educational system both mirrored and reinforced, and a means of reasserting middle class values and interests through extending a particular custodial form to less reputable groups. But the intervention failed to achieve its most fundamental objective. The preaching was to the converted. Thus while the youth movements provided for very many young people purposeful and enjoyable activity, like the best elementary schools, they had largely been colonised by lower-middle- and upper-working-class groups. Like the schools, the youth movements were too ulterior an assuagement to transfigure the deprivation and disenchantment of the Brixtons and the Toxteths of long ago. Anxieties about the threat of the residuum were no doubt exaggerated, but nineteenth-century urbanisation cumulatively opened up social sores too deep for eighty succeeding years to heal. On the other hand, the Victorian city established the fortunes of millions of families. As the novelist John Fowles has suggested, *Dr. Jekyll and Mr. Hyde* is possibly 'the best guidebook to the age'.[115]

The educational system was presented with the dual and onerous tasks of acting as a palliative for the wide-ranging ills of urban society and at the same time of providing opportunities for upward mobility for the relatively comfortable urban masses. The second half of the nineteenth century witnessed the evolution of more subtle and successful responses to these responsibilities than the period has been given credit for, as subsequent chapters will suggest.

REFERENCES AND NOTES

1. J. M. Ludlow and L. Jones, *Progress of the Working Class, 1832–1867* (London, 1867), p. 148.

2. See section on 'Regional Variations in Crime and Education' in Chapter 2, pp. 41–6.
3. See *Census of Great Britain, 1851* (London, 1854), p. 90; and *A Digest of the Results of the Census of England and Wales, 1901* (London, 1903), p. 1.
4. See, for example, R. Lawton, 'Census Data for Urban Areas', in R. Lawton (ed.), *The Census and Social Structure: an Interpretative Guide to Nineteenth-Century Censuses for England and Wales* (Frank Cass, London, 1978), pp. 82–3; R. Lawton, 'Population and Society, 1730–1900', in R. A. Dodgshon and R. A. Butlin (eds.), *An Historical Geography of England and Wales* (London, 1978), p. 342; and J. A. Banks, 'The Contagion of Numbers', in H. J. Dyos and M. Wolff (eds.), *The Victorian City: Images and Realities*, Vol. 1 (London, 1973), p. 105.
5. A. F. Weber, *The Growth of Cities in the Nineteenth Century* (Ithaca, New York, 1899; reprinted 1963), p. 43, p. 46 and p. 151.
6. See B. T. Robson, *Urban Growth: an Approach* (London, 1973), pp. 53–4.
7. See Chapter 7; also T. R. Phillips, 'The Elementary Schools and the Migratory Habits of the People 1870–1890', *British Journal of Educational Studies*, vol. 26 (1978), pp. 177–88.
8. See, for example, R. Lawton, 'An Age of Great Cities', *Town Planning Review*, vol. 43 (1972), pp. 213–17; D. A. Reeder, 'A Theatre of Suburbs: some Patterns of Development in West London, 1801–1911', in H. J. Dyos (ed.), *The Study of Urban History* (London, 1968), pp. 253–71; D. A. Reeder, *Suburbanity and the Victorian City* (Leicester, 1980); and T. W. M. Crosland, *The Suburbans* (London, 1905).
9. See C. M. Law and A. M. Warnes, 'The Changing Geography of the Elderly in England and Wales', *Transactions of the Institute of British Geographers*, New Series, vol. 1 (1976), p. 461, for the continuing impact of such change.
10. Rev. A. W. Worthington, 'On the Unequal Proportion between the Male and Female Population of some Manufacturing and Other Towns', *Journal of the Statistical Society of London*, vol. 30 (1867), pp. 68–70.
11. W. V. Hole and M. J. Pountney, *Trends in Population, Housing and Occupancy Rates 1861–1961* (London, 1971), pp. 15–16.
12. For a general account of the situation in late nineteenth-century England and Wales, see T. A. Welton, *England's Recent Progress: an Investigation of the Statistics of Migration, Mortality, etc. in the Twenty Years from 1881–1901, as Indicating Tendencies towards the Growth and Decay of Particular Communities* (London, 1911), p. 9; see also R. Lawton, 'Population Changes in the later Nineteenth Century: an Analysis of Trends by Registration Districts', *Transactions of the Institute of British Geographers*, vol. 44 (1968), pp. 55–74.
13. For a famous contemporary discussion of migration patterns see E. G. R. Ravenstein, 'The Laws of Migration', *Journal of the Statistical Society of London*, vol. 48 (1885), pp. 198–9; see also R. Lawton, 'Mobility in Nineteenth-century British Cities', *Geographical Journal*, vol. 145 (1979), p. 223.
14. See, for example, J. A. Jackson, *The Irish in Britain* (London, 1963); R. Lawton, 'Irish Migration to England and Wales in the Mid-nineteenth Century', *Irish Geography*, vol. 4 (1959), pp. 35–54; L. H. Lees, *Exiles of Erin: Irish Migrants in Victorian London* (Manchester, 1979); S. Garratt, *The Irish in London* (London, 1852).
15. See C. G. Pooley, 'The Residential Segregation of Immigrant Communities in Mid-Victorian Liverpool', *Transactions of the Institute of British Geographers*, New Series, vol. 2 (1977), pp. 364–82; and R. Lawton, 'The Population of Liverpool in the Mid-Nineteenth Century', *Transactions of the Historic Society of Lancashire and Cheshire*, vol. 107 (1956), pp. 104–5 and p. 119.
16. The interaction of industrialisation and education has to date received fuller

attention than the interaction of urbanisation and education. See, for example, E. G. West, *Education and the Industrial Revolution* (London, 1975); E. G. West, 'Literacy and the Industrial Revolution', *Economic History Review*, 2nd Series, vol. 31 (1978), pp. 369–83; M. Sanderson, 'Literacy and Social Mobility in the Industrial Revolution in England', *Past and Present*, vol. 56 (1972), pp. 75–104; and, for a more detailed study of interaction between home, school and work in a Birmingham industrial quarter, see C. Heward, ' "Father Gets such Low Wages": the Problems of the Introduction of Compulsory School Attendance in the Birmingham Jewellery Quarter', in R. K. Goodenow and W. E. Marsden (eds.), *Urban Educational History in Four Nations: the United States, the United Kingdom, Australia and Canada* (New York, forthcoming).

17. *Hansard*, 2nd Series, vol. 2 (1820), col. 63.
18. Joseph Fletcher was the school inspector for grant-aided British Society schools in the 1840s.
19. See *M.C.C.E.*, vol. 2 (1846), pp. 25–31.
20. See, for example, HMI Freeland on the Bury District of Lancashire in *Reports of the Committee of Council on Education* (1881–2), p. 294.
21. See T. P. Sykes, 'The Factory Half-timer', *Fortnightly Review*, vol. 52 (1889), p. 82.
22. See Chapter 6.
23. See H. Silver, 'Ideology and the Factory Child: Attitudes to Half-time Education', in P. McCann (ed.), *Popular Education and Socialization in the Nineteenth Century* (London, 1977), p. 157; also in H. Silver, *Education as History: Interpreting Nineteenth- and Twentieth-Century Education* (London, 1983), p. 51.
24. See H. Perkin, *The Origins of Modern English Society, 1780–1880* (London, 1969), p. 176.
25. F. Engels, *The Condition of the Working Class in England in 1844* (London, 1892; Panther Books reprint, 1969), p. 124.
26. W. H. Mallock, *Social Equality: a Short Study in a Missing Science* (London, 1882), p. 7.
27. F. Parkin, 'Social Stratification', in T. Bottomore and R. Nisbet (eds.), *A History of Sociological Analysis* (London, 1979), pp. 605–6.
28. See W. G. Runciman, 'The Three Dimensions of Social Inequality', in A. Beteille (ed.), *Social Inequality: Selected Readings* (Harmondsworth, 1969), p. 49.
29. Rev. J. Sandford, *Middle Class Education, or our Endowed and Commercial Schools* (London, 1864), pp. 9–10.
30. See W. D. Rubinstein, 'The Victorian Middle Classes: Wealth, Occupation and Geography', *Economic History Review*, 2nd Series, vol. 30 (1977), pp. 609–10.
31. *Ibid.*, p. 621.
32. See, for example, G. Best, *Mid-Victorian Britain 1851–1875* (London, 1971), p. 90.
33. See G. Crossick, 'The Emergence of the Lower Middle Class in Britain: a Discussion'; and G. L. Anderson, 'The Social Economy of late-Victorian Clerks', both in G. Crossick (ed.), *The Lower Middle Class in Britain* (London, 1978), p. 19 and p. 113 respectively.
34. See, for example, H. Corke, *In our Infancy: an Autobiography, Part 1, 1882–1912* (Cambridge, 1975), p. 44 and p. 78.
35. R. Church, *Over the Bridge* (London, 1955), p. 51.
36. G. L. Anderson, *Victorian Clerks* (Manchester, 1976), p. 41.
37. 'The Social Position of Educators', *The Scholastic Journal*, June 1840, p. 321.
38. Quoted in *The Schoolmaster*, 22 June 1872, p. 269.
39. See H. McLeod, 'White Collar Values and the Role of Religion', in Crossick (ed.), *op. cit.* (1978), p. 72.

40. G. Gissing, *Thyrza* (London, 1927 edition), p. 37.
41. L. Levi, 'What is the Social Condition of the Working Classes in 1884 as Compared with 1857 ...?', *Transactions of the National Association for the Promotion of Social Science*, Birmingham meeting, 1884 (London, 1885), pp. 589–90.
42. T. Wright, *The Great Unwashed* (London, 1868; Cass reprint, 1970), p. 5, pp. 7–8, p. 14 and p. 21.
43. T. Tholfsen, *Working Class Radicalism in Mid-Victorian England* (London, 1976), p. 18.
44. G. Crossick, *An Artisan Elite in Victorian Society: Kentish London 1840–1880* (London, 1978), p. 137.
45. R. Q. Gray, *The Labour Aristocracy in Victorian Edinburgh* (Oxford, 1976), p. 169 and p. 183.
46. See Chapters 4 and 5.
47. E. F. Hinder, *The Schoolmaster in the Gutter: or a Plea for the Middle Class* (London, 1883), p. 21.
48. Ludlow and Jones, *op. cit.* (1867), p. 298.
49. See Wright, *op. cit.* (1868), p. 31.
50. H. J. Dyos and D. A. Reeder, 'Slums and Suburbs', in Dyos and Wolff (eds.), *op. cit.*, vol. 1 (1973), p. 369.
51. J. Garwood, *The Million-people City: or One-half of the People of London made known to the Other Half* (London, 1853), pp. 9–10.
52. Rev. W. Gover, *Day School Education in the Borough of Birmingham: our Progress, Position and Needs* (London, 1867), pp. 13–15.
53. W. Cowper, 'The Task', Book 1, Lines 678–99, in *The Works of William Cowper*, vol. 6 (London, 1854), p. 23.
54. R. Vaughan, *The Age of Great Cities: or, Modern Society viewed in Relation to Intelligence, Morals and Religion* (London, 1843; repr. Woburn Press, 1970), p. 146 and p. 152.
55. E. Baines, *The Social, Educational and Religious State of the Manufacturing Districts* (London, 1845; repr. Woburn Press, 1969), p. 54.
56. H. Clarke, 'On the Influence of Large Centres of Population on Intellectual Manifestation', *Transactions of the British Association for the Advancement of Science*, Bradford meeting, 1873 (London, 1874), p. 186.
57. J. Fletcher, 'The Moral and Educational Statistics of England and Wales', *Quarterly Journal of the Statistical Society of London*, vol. 12 (1849), p. 176.
58. A. Conan Doyle, 'On the Geographical Distribution of British Intellect', *The Nineteenth Century*, vol. 24 (1888), p. 185.
59. J. L. and B. Hammond, *The Town Labourer, 1760–1832* (London, 1918), p. 94.
60. See, for example, the *Pall Mall Gazette*, 31 July 1891, which heads its review of an early Charles Booth survey volume, 'A City very much like Hell'; also J. London, *The People of the Abyss* (London, 1903); C. F. G. Masterman, 'The Social Abyss', *Contemporary Review*, vol. 71 (1902), pp. 23–35; and G. Gissing, *The Nether World* (London, 1889).
61. W. Booth, *In Darkest England, and the Way Out* (London, 1890), p. 11.
62. The word 'slum' is derived, according to Wohl, from 'slumber', and came to mean 'a sleepy, unknown back alley'. See A. S. Wohl, *The Eternal Slum: Housing and Social Policy in Victorian London* (London, 1977), p. 5.
63. See C. Parsons, *Schools in an Urban Community: a Study of Carbrook, 1870–1965* (London, 1978), p. 140. See also R. Roberts, *The Classic Slum: Salford Life in the First Quarter of the Century* (Manchester, 1971), p. 11, in which the author from personal experience testifies to the presence of 'awesomely respectable' families in the slum, striving to gain their children a more reputable status.
64. D. A. Reeder, 'Predicaments of City Children: Late Victorian and Edwardian

Perspectives on Education and Urban Society', in D.A. Reeder (ed.), *Urban Education in the Nineteenth Century* (London, 1977), p. 77.

65. G.S. Jones, *Outcast London: a Study in the Relationship between Classes in Victorian Society* (Oxford, 1971), p. 151.

66. J.E. Morgan, 'The Danger of Deterioration of Race from the too Rapid Increase of Great Cities', *Transactions of the National Association for the Promotion of Social Science*, Sheffield meeting, 1865 (London, 1866), p. 427.

67. D. Ward, 'The Victorian Slum: an Enduring Myth', *Annals of the Association of American Geographers*, vol. 66 (1976), p. 322.

68. In the case of over-population, dating back of course to T. Malthus, *An Essay on the Principle of Population*, vol. 3 (London, 5th edition, 1817), p. 199.

69. See Reeder, in Reeder (ed.), *op. cit.*, p. 85.

70. See E. Thompson, 'The Education of Henry Mayhew', in *The Victorian Poor*, 4th Conference Report (Victorian Society, 1966), pp. 13–14.

71. See C.J. Montague, *Sixty Years in Waifdom, or the Ragged School Movement in English History* (London, 1904; repr. Woburn Press, 1969), p. 115.

72. See J.S. Hurt, *Elementary Schooling and the Working Classes 1860–1918* (London, 1979), pp. 128–33.

73. G.M. Howe, *Man, Environment and Disease in Britain: a Medical Geography through the Ages* (Harmondsworth, 1976), p. 195.

74. For a fuller account, see A.B. Robertson, 'Children, Teachers and Society: the Over-pressure Controversy, 1880–1886', *British Journal of Educational Studies*, vol. 20 (1972), pp. 315–23.

75. See 'Death in the Primer', and 'Over-pressure in Elementary Schools', both in *British Medical Journal*, 9 Feb. 1884, p. 279; and 21 June 1884, pp. 1212–13, respectively.

76. See 'Schools and Infectious Diseases', *British Medical Journal*, 24 Sept. 1881.

77. See D. Rubinstein, *School Attendance in London, 1870–1914* (University of Hull Occasional Papers in Economic and Social History, No. 1, 1969), p. 77.

78. See Hurt, *op. cit.*, p. 106 and Part 2 in general; also W.J. Reese, 'After Bread, Education: Nutrition and Urban School Children, 1890–1920', *Teachers College Record*, vol. 81 (1980), pp. 496–525; and, for a negative contemporary reaction, Mrs. B. Bosanquet, *Rich and Poor* (London, 2nd edition, 1908), p. 182.

79. *School Board Chronicle*, 3 Sept. 1887, p. 233.

80. J.E. Gorst, 'School children as Wage-earners', *The Nineteenth Century*, vol. 46 (1899), pp. 11–13.

81. E.A. Hogg, 'School children as Wage-earners', *The Nineteenth Century*, vol. 42 (1897), pp. 241–2.

82. *School Guardian*, 21 Oct. 1882, p. 678.

83. Reeder, in Reeder (ed.), *op. cit.*, p. 87.

84. R.A. Bray, *The Town Child* (London, 1907), p. 17.

85. R.A. Bray, 'The Children of the Town', in *The Heart of Empire: Discussion of Problems of Modern City Life in England* (London, 1901), p. 115.

86. *Ibid.*, pp. 119–22; see also J.J. Findlay, *The Children of England: a Contribution to Social History and to Education* (London, 1923), p. 161.

87. R.A. Bray, 'The Boy and the Family', in E.J. Urwick (ed.), *Studies of Boy Life in our Cities* (London, 1904), p. 3.

88. H. Dendy, 'The Children of Working London', in B. Bosanquet (ed.), *Aspects of the Social Problem* (London, 1895), pp. 246–7.

89. J.L. Paton, 'The Secondary Education of the Working Classes', in C. Norwood and A.H. Hope (eds.), *The Higher Education of Boys in England* (London, 1909), p. 546.

90. Weber, *op. cit.*, p. 399.

91. *Report of the Inter-departmental Committee on Physical Deterioration*, vol. 1 (London, 1904), pp. 13–14.
92. See J. S. Hurt, 'Drill, Discipline and the Elementary School Ethos', in McCann (ed.), p. 170 and p. 187.
93. See J. Springhall, *Youth, Empire and Society: British Youth Movements, 1883–1940* (London, 1977), p. 16.
94. *Reports of the Committee of Council on Education* (1878–9), p. 643.
95. J. M. Yoxall, *The Pupil Teacher's Geography* (London, 2nd edition, 1891), pp. 17–32. For similar activity in history textbooks see F. A. Glendenning, 'School History Textbooks and Racial Attitudes 1804–1969', *Journal of Educational Administration and History*, vol. 5 (1973), p. 33.
96. See W. E. Marsden, 'The Royal Geographical Society and Geography in Secondary Education', in M. Price (ed.), *The Development of the Secondary Curriculum* (London, 1986), p. 193.
97. S. S. Laurie, *Occasional Addresses on Educational Subjects* (Cambridge, 1888), note on pp. 96–7.
98. See J. B. Reynolds, 'Class Excursions in England and Wales', *The Geographical Teacher*, vol. 1 (1901), p. 33; though see also E. J. Orford, 'Home Geography in London', *The Geographical Teacher*, vol. 3 (1906), pp. 264–6.
99. M. M. Penstone, *Town Study: Suggestions for a Course of Lessons Preliminary to the Study of Civics* (London, 1910), p. 2.
100. Bray, *op. cit.* (1901), p. 139.
101. *Ibid.*, p. 143.
102. *Ibid.*, p. 153.
103. *Ibid.*, pp. 161–2.
104. *Reports of the Committee of Council on Education* (1875–6), p. 314.
105. See, for example, D. Rubinstein, *op. cit.* (1969); also T. A. Spalding and T. S. A. Canney, *The Work of the London School Board* (London, 1900), pp. 120–36.
106. In *Miscellaneous Interviews*, Group B, vol. 225 (Booth Collection, London School of Economics Library), insert at p. 67.
107. *The Board Teacher*, 1 Oct. 1884, p. 21.
108. J. R. Gillis, 'The Evolution of Juvenile Delinquency in England, 1890–1914', *Past and Present*, vol. 67 (1975), p. 96. For an earlier 'cycle of anxiety', see M. May, 'Innocence and Experience: the Evolution of the Concept of Juvenile Delinquency in the Mid-nineteenth Century', *Victorian Studies*, vol. 17 (1973), pp. 7–29.
109. Paton, *op. cit.*, p. 547.
110. *School Guardian*, 3 Nov. 1900, p. 869; see also G. Pearson, *Hooligan: a History of Respectable Fears* (London, 1983), pp. 51–118.
111. *School Guardian*, 16 Feb. 1901, p. 120.
112. M. Lazerson, *Origins of the Urban School: Public Education in Massachusetts, 1870–1915* (Cambridge, Mass., 1971), p. 243.
113. See J. Addams, *The Spirit of Youth and the City Streets* (New York, 1912), p. 6.
114. See Springhall, *op. cit.*, for the overall story; also M. Barratt, 'The Early Years of the Boys' Brigade: its Aims and Activities', in K. S. Dent (ed.), *Informal Agencies of Education* (Leicester, History of Education Society of Great Britain, 1979), pp. 71–6.
115. J. Fowles, *The French Lieutenant's Woman* (London, 1969; St. Albans, paperback edition, 1977), p. 319.

CHAPTER FOUR

A Graduated System of Urban Schooling

There ought to be made a considerable Difference
between the Children of inferior People, and those of
Rank, with regard to their Tuition.[1] (Nelson, 1756)

The graduation principle in English education has an extended
lineage. Reaching its apogee in the late nineteenth century, it subtly
reflected shifts in the social structure, whether defined in terms of
pre-ordained orders or estates, as in the seventeenth century, or in the
socio-economic, class conflict terms of industrial society, or in the less
tangible spectrum of status-consciousness that became increasingly
characteristic in the late nineteenth century.

So far as the mid-seventeenth century was concerned, Nelson, in
his *Essay on the Government of Children*, offered advice about the
appropriate type of education for each of the five social groups he
identified. For the nobility and gentry, a learned education was
essential. This, suitably modified, was also applicable to the genteel
trades, for the commercial aspirations of the nation demanded contact between men of trade and the gentry. While applauding the
social ambitions of the respectable trading classes, Nelson was less
sympathetic towards the 'ostentatious education' sought by some
common tradesmen, for whom a learned education was 'needless and
improper' and 'even hurtful'. Their curriculum should include the
three R's, drawing and knowledge of maps, but exclude the classics
and foreign languages. The lower orders in turn were seen as having
'but a small Share either of Time or Abilities for Instruction'. Nelson
distinguished, however, the agricultural peasantry, who were particularly in this situation, from their peers in London, who possessed
the same ignorance but not the same degree of innocence. For these he

advocated some basic education to qualify for useful employment, at the same time holding out little hope that it would reform character.[2]

Nelson's concept was thus a harbinger of more refined nineteenth-century responses to a social situation in which it was both seen as necessary to maintain the stability of the existing order, while at the same time enabling a modicum of mobility for the deserving:

The principal Aim of Parents should be, to know what Sphere of Life their Children will act in; what Education is really suitable for them; what will be the Consequence of neglecting that; and what Chance a superior Education will give them for their advancement to posts of Dignity. Education is often wasted on us either by being improper for our Station, or by engaging us in things we are unfit for.[3]

The classification of Mrs Sarah Trimmer (1801), on the other hand, related specifically to education for the lower orders. She regarded it as proper to offer an educational opportunity to all the poor, 'to rescue the lower kinds of people from that deplorable state of ignorance, in which the greatest part of them are suffered to remain', but it could not be right

to train them *all* in a way which will most probably raise their ideas above the very lowest occupations in life, and disqualify them for those servile offices, which must be filled by some members of the community, and in which they may be equally happy with the highest, if they will do their duty.[4]

It was right, she felt, that schooling should reflect the finer gradations of society, and such gradations existed even among the poorer ranks:

and if it be improper to educate the children of the higher classes pro-miscuously, it surely must be equally so to place all the children of the poor upon the same footing, without any regard to the different circumstances of their parents, or their own genius or capacity ...[5]

In the charity schools, however, the different grades of the poor were mixed together. Mrs Trimmer's strategy was to integrate the charity schools, schools of industry and Sunday schools into a graded system of popular provision. *The Charity Schools* would offer a more comprehensive tuition for the *first degree* of the lower orders, who might be trained as charity school teachers, as traders' apprentices, or as higher grade domestic servants. The day *Schools of Industry*, by mixing labour and learning, would be 'particularly eligible' for children who would later be employed in manufacturing industry or 'other inferior offices of life, as well as for training those who are usually called *common servants'*. The *Sunday Schools* would provide religious instruction for poor children whose labour could not be spared during the week, and would also 'serve as probationary schools to try the capacities of children previous to their admission into *Charity Schools'*. The Charity Schools would thus provide the most 'liberal instruction' that could be envisaged, for a relatively limited number of scholars from the 'superior stations of humble life',[6] in which they would be protected from contact with 'the offspring of thieves and vagabonds'.[7]

These were far from reactionary views for their time, for the principle of mass provision of popular education had still to be established. By the 1820s, the battle was largely won, and attention could be concentrated on the social objectives. In a period of shift from the closed divides of the 'old society' to the new class society of the industrial revolution, priority had to be given to social control. Even the more advanced thinkers on education were not disposed to regard popular schooling as an agency of social change. Wyse, for example, was committed to educational provision for the masses as a social emollient, noting that the discontent which had caused riots and insurrections in the late eighteenth century was now terminating in meetings and subscriptions. 'Disorder has diminished with ignorance, bigotry with communication'.[8] But the level of 'communication' required was seen as different for different groups, for grading in the social system was the necessary determinant of the nature of instruction, 'applicability' being the keynote.[9]

A similarly close linkage between the grades of society and education was envisaged in Wade's *History of the Middle and Working Classes* (1833), which argued that the differences in the wants of society led to diversities of occupation and in social condition.

They all co-operate for the common good, and that jealousy between the several classes of the community, which some persons have very inconsiderately endeavoured to excite, would be quite as senseless as jealousy between the several members of the body, or faculties of the mind ...[10]

Yet while arguing against classification and making of distinctions, a contradictory 'primary maxim' controlled his thinking on social education. This should be adapted to the future occupations of life.

As education ought to have reference to the atmosphere in which we are destined to live and move – a different course of instruction is prescribed for the different orders of society ... a merchant, manufacturer, or even an artisan, requires knowledge that would be comparatively valueless to a ploughman.[11]

Wade did not, however, 'interdict to any class of society' the pursuit of knowledge of any kind, 'useful or ornamental'.[12] But the general regulation was clear, and the viewpoint in essence little advance on that of Trimmer, or indeed of Nelson.

Such thinking persisted in influential statements of the 1850s and 1860s. Thus in a sermon at Salisbury (1868), James Fraser, a major contributor to the Newcastle Commission on popular education, insisted that the American 'common school' system, open to all classes, was only possible in a young society where wealth had not yet set up class barriers, whereas

in England, the grades of society, so marked and manifest, will always probably demand, and in fact necessitate, a corresponding graduation of schools ... as far as I care to look forward ... the inevitable basis of our educational organization ...[13]

Similarly Matthew Arnold promulgated the idea of class-related school provision (1863–4):

The education of each class in society has, or ought to have, its ideal determined by the wants of that class, and by its destination ... We have to regard the condition of classes, in dealing with education; but it is right to take into account not their immediate condition only but their wants, their destination – above all, their evident pressing wants, their evident proximate destination.[14]

The complexity of class and status differentiation by the 1860s was heightened by the increasing concentration of population in large towns and cities, and the consequential residential segregation. The variety of social and economic circumstance that characterised urban society offered the opportunity for a sophisticated gradation of schools, as an article in the *Educational Reporter* of 1869 indicated:

This completeness of classification is one of the greatest makeweights afforded to a town school. The larger the town, the more complete should be the graduation of its school children for purposes of instruction, and in the largest towns the *schools themselves* should be grouped into classes. Not, however, that they may become 'class chools'. We have already had too much of that sort of thing. 'Distinctions' there should be, but not 'social' ones. Let the scholars distinguish *themselves* – not their 'order'. There will be plenty of time for the cultivation and development of caste after school life is over. We want 'schools classed' – not 'class schools'.[15]

Opinion in the 1860s was thus veering towards a meritocratic view: that the aspirations of different social groups and the needs of state justified an educational system that at all levels could develop relevant skills and promote a degree of occupational mobility.

Mass urban provision threatened, as Sarah Trimmer had antici- pated, the promiscuous mixing of the lower orders of society. The Newcastle Commissioners accepted that the most intractable problem was that posed by pauper and vagrant-criminal children, to be dis- tinguished from the 'independent poor'. These disreputable children were characteristically accommodated in the lowest class of school provided, the 'ragged school', the epithet 'ragged' having been pre- fixed, according to Watson (1872), to ward off self-respecting parents.[16]

Mary Carpenter, a pioneer in the provision of day and boarding schools for neglected and delinquent children, had been even more uncompromising in her designation of 'ragged schools', as designed

expressly for the class of children who, by their poverty and vice, are virtually excluded from the numerous educational establishments which abound in all our great cities, and who, if admissible, would be wholly unwilling and unfit to remain there; – schools for those who are called the 'canaille', the 'scum of the populace' ...

At the same time, she rated these 'vermin' as people with 'mental and bodily powers often of the first order', and also as possessing 'mortal souls' in need of rescue by the school.[17]

In taking such children off the streets, the philanthropists faced fearful problems, not least cosmetic ones. Montague recounts the tribulations of the early voluntary women teachers in ragged girls' classes, the habits of whose occupants must have been 'abhorrent to delicately nurtured ladies' and whose physical appearance and smell was also offensive, in a period of 'bad and incomplete water supply' and 'a tax on soap'.[18]

Another major social reformer, William Booth, painted a lugu- brious portrait of the consequences of introducing destitute children into the public elementary system:

The rakings of the human cesspool are brought into the school-room and mixed up with your children. Your little ones, who never heard a foul word and who are not only innocent, but ignorant, of the horrors of vice and sin, sit for hours side by side with little ones whose parents are habitually drunk, and play with others whose ideas of merriment are gained from the familiar spectable of the nightly debauch by which their mothers earn the daily bread

... It is good, no doubt, to learn the A.B.C., but it is not so good if in acquiring these indispensable rudiments, your children should also acquire the vocabulary of the harlot and the corner boy ...[19]

Compulsion meant sweeping more and more unkempt children into the schools, in which circumstances respectable parents were held to have the right to demand 'separate development'. *The Edinburgh Review* (1874) pointed to the need for a 'conscience clause against the contagion of infectious disease or the worse contagion of bad example'.[20] The *School Board Chronicle* (1872) contended that the schools were not the arena in which to indoctrinate 'the rising generation of the working and labouring classes with the dogma of equality'. If 'unqualified mixture of grades' caused the more well-to-do 'repugnance, indignation and rebellion', then 'some special arrangement must be made for the uncivilised'.[21] T. W. Sharpe, HMI, was equally explicit in an 1873 Report:

Without sympathising with the innumerable class distinctions which abound in every grade of English life, great allowance should be made for the mother's dislike of the society of children whose home circumstances interpose difficulties of modesty or even decency ... Besides children who are proper inmates for reformatories or industrial schools, there are many degrees of dirty habits and filthy language, whose mere presence would deter the mothers of many of the nicest children.[22]

Educational justifications for the grading of schools were also advanced, one of which, in another guise, was language. The *School Guardian* (1880) noted that home language and school language were very different, domestic colloquialisms and slang constituting 'almost a separate tongue'. Similarly, the narrowness of parental interest served to 'furnish them with a vocabulary not much more extended than that of the inhabitants of the South Sea Islands'. Thus a lowest rung of graded schools was needed in which the curriculum was confined to the most basic rudiments of learning.[23]

While official opinion was slow to acquire an appreciation of the subtleties of the class structure, those working at the grassroots had for some time been aware of distinctive and differentiated responses among working class consumers towards education, many of them not at all negative.

Thus J. P. Norris, HMI, in his 1851 Report on Cheshire, Staffordshire and Shropshire, attacked the stereotyping of working-class attitudes to education, and urged a more sensitive reaction:

If education really be instruction in a certain curricule of book learning, it is plainly absurd to expect an illiterate set of parents to appreciate it. But is this *their* definition of education? I do not say that their's is more likely to be right than our's; the presumption is quite the other way; yet it is very possible, nay highly probable, that there may be some portion of truth in their notion, and some admixture of error in our own; enough at least to make it well worthwhile to consider attentively what their definition is.[24]

The Newcastle Commissioners were to find this type of appeal to working-class opinion useful in that, like the lower-middle-class opinion previously cited, it tended to support an instrumental view of education consistent with the terms of reference of the Commission itself, which were to see what measures, if any, were required for the provision of 'sound and cheap elementary instruction to all classes of the people'.[25]

By the 1850s, the well-to-do working, joined by the lower middle classes, were seeking educational provision at modest cost which provided useful knowledge and avoided mixture with children of the low poor. This could be achieved through private adventure schools, which some parents chose. But their uninspected nature and variability in quality discouraged their widespread use. A gap existed which was quickly plugged by voluntary school managers, particularly in the Wesleyan and 'British' school sectors, who from the 1850s sought to provide a more exclusive elementary tuition. Thus in his report to the Newcastle Commission, Ralph Lingen noted that the children attending these schools consisted

to a very great extent, of that class which is either the top of the working class or the bottom of the shop-keeping class; and, with regard to these persons, the contribution which they make to the schools is very much represented by a graduated set of fees.[26]

Matthew Arnold had in fact already drawn attention to this phenomenon:

The Wesleyan schools have established, generally speaking, a rate of payment on the part of their scholars higher than that which is made in other elementary schools that I have seen. This rate of payment varies from 2d to 8d per week for each scholar; in some schools a majority of the scholars pay 3d, others 4d; but in none less than 2d. It is obvious that these rates of payment must generally exclude the children of the very poor ... on the whole, the Wesleyan schools which I have seen must be considered as existing for the sake of the children of tradesmen, of farmers and of mechanics of the higher class ...[27]

Arnold attached no blame to the Wesleyans for such opportunism (having been given an assurance from the Wesleyan Training Institution that there was no deliberate policy in this respect), arguing that they were responding to a legitimate demand. He also felt it only to be expected that a management committee able to fill a school with children paying 4d or 6d a week would not refuse to admit them in order to find room for those able to pay only half that, thus encouraging the trend for less profitable, irregularly attending children to be 'gradually eliminated to make room for a more desirable body of scholars'.[28]

The fact that separate inspectors had been recruited to oversee British, Wesleyan and other non-Anglican and Catholic denominational schools, brought this important development into the open. In his report on the eastern counties for 1858, Alderson noted that in the larger towns the Nonconformist schools he visited contained most children from the small tradesman, artisan, and public service groups (policemen, railway clerks, porters, etc.). From the Wesleyan school at Lincoln, for example, he obtained the information that 135 children came from families in the small shopkeeper class and above, and only 48 from labouring and other poor groups. Similarly, in the majority of rural schools of this group, there were in the first classes (top classes) mostly children of parents in thriving circumstances, though they had started school together with labouring children.

In this – the infusion into the ranks of a school intended for the labouring classes of children belonging to a higher grade of society – there seems to me to be unquestionable advantage and some danger.

The advantages related to finance, social prestige, and civilizing influences. The dangers lay in the possibility of teachers devoting more time to the more 'inviting' upper part of the school, where the children were more regular, more intelligent and better behaved.[29]

J. D. Morell, HMI, covering Nonconformist schools in the Lakeland counties and Lancashire, noted in his evidence to the Newcastle Commission the practice of raising the fees to improve the school, attracting middle-class children and driving out the poor. Another policy was to graduate the fees within the school, allowing a wider social mix lower down, but not in the higher standards. Morell was well aware that graduation of fees was promoting social differentiation. If a school charged below 3d per week, the better class of children was withdrawn, as parents of lower-middle-class and upper-working-class children were prepared to pay up to 6d per week. When asked whether the effect of this process was to 'pauperise' relatively affluent parents, he agreed that there was ambiguity in the situation. The justification was that such parents were taking up places because of the quality of education being provided, and not to evade paying for schooling.[30]

Morell returned to these 'ambiguities' in his Report for 1861. He did not accept the popular opinion that government funds were being widely used for the education of middle-class children. He interpreted the problem as deriving from the varied circumstances of parents termed 'working-class'. The working people of the manufacturing district were often as affluent as members of the lower middle classes.

To exclude the children of well paid working men on the ground of their parents being laborious, provident, and successful, would be inflicting . . . a very unjust and impolitic penalty upon merit and industry . . . Unless indeed these families who float between the lower and middle classes were to gain some benefit from the public school grants, they would be manifestly placed in a less favourable position than any other part of the community.

The only alternative was the cheap boarding or private adventure day school, giving an inferior education, for the better schools of this type were enormously expensive.[31]

One of the Newcastle Commission witnesses, H. S. Skeats, an ecclesiastical historian who had presumably come to the attention of the Commission through an article he wrote for the *Christian Spectator* entitled 'Results of Government Education 1857', was dismayed by the thought of the middle classes taking advantage of the 'superior system of the state-aided schools', forsaking private academies. If they had the right to do this, then 'let us all assert our moral and equitable claim to be supplied, at the public expense, with broughams and horses, fine houses and furniture, the best "Havannahs", and nothing inferior to hock at lunch and champagne at dinner'.[32]

The Rev. John Scott, Principal of the Wesleyan Training College, refuted the charge that Wesleyan parents were generally more well-to-do than those of Anglican elementary scholars, though he believed that in general they had better habits and were more industrious, and therefore better off than much of the working class. The fact that they paid fees meant that the pauperisation principle did not apply. In any case, many managers asked richer parents to pay a subscription in addition to the fees, kept the same for children of all groups.[33] The Rev. William Unwin, Principal of the Congregational Training College, Homerton, argued that the idea of bringing together the children of the more affluent workers and tradesmen with poorer children was a sound one, a healthier education being produced by the blending of children of different classes. The fact that the Congregational schools had to be self-supporting meant that they needed to charge fees of at least 3d and 4d. There were, however, few instances of fees over 6d.[34]

Figures collected by the Newcastle Commission indicated the higher dependence of British and other dissenting schools on fees: 5s 10½d in the case of Church of England Schools as against 8s 1d in British schools. Twenty per cent of dissenting/British school children were paying fees of 4d and more, as against just under 6% in Church of England schools and 3.5% in Catholic. Only 17.5% paid fees of less than 2d compared with 37% of Church of England and no less than 66% of Catholic children.[35]

The figures must be kept in proportion, of course. In his evidence to the Commission, Lingen quoted official records to show that only 14% of the elementary population was paying fees of 4d and more, as against 34% 2d and less than 3d, and 39% less than 2d. But it was clear that a new order of school had been established for the upper-working-class/lower-middle-class fringe population, that was very much 'in the nature of a proprietary school for the lower classes', largely self-supporting, and regulated in its clientele by a general scale of fees that was beyond the means of the poor.[36]

The debate heated up in the 1860s. Graduated fees were a new mechanism of selection. Far from driving children from schools, they increased attendance for the reason which George Melly advanced in the debate in the House over education in the towns and cities, to the effect that the working classes had

as many social castes, as many political and religious prejudices, among them as there are among those above them; and the well-to-do-Conservative artizan, and the small Radical shopkeeper, will continue to send their children to their Church and Dissenting schools.[37]

This referred of course to the more respectable, higher-feed schools run by those groups.

A situation in which relatively well-to-do parents were being subsidised out of government grant, still perceived as primarily intended for the education of the poor, continued to excite disapproval. D. R. Fearon, in his contribution on Liverpool and Manchester to the official 1869 'Return on schools for the poorer classes in four great provincial cities', maintained that the intentions of the 1861

Code were being flouted in so far as children from the lower middle classes were being allowed into elementary schools designed for those of the poor. Nine of 95 uninspected schools in Manchester, with 310 children on the rolls, were largely filled with middle-class scholars. Managers, not surprisingly, found it difficult to draw the line between the social groups. The more advantaged children earned grant more easily. The inspectors appealed to managers to do their duty, but were preoccupied with supervising annual examinations, and rarely went beyond exhortation.[38]

Horace Mann, architect of the 1851 Education Census was, like Skeats, appalled at a situation which could be regarded as pauperising those above the pauper class:

Gradually the circle which defined the assisted and assumed-to-be-needy classes has expanded, until now, as we have seen, it includes well-nigh three quarters of the population, and there is no longer any pretence for believing that the aided schools are schools for the poor alone.

The logical conclusion was that the state should 'go the whole hog', and apply subsidised education to all classes of the community.[39]

By the time of the 1870 Act, therefore, the social pressure for a 'higher level' elementary provision was inexorable. Through the Nonconformists in particular an important principle in the extension of popular education had been implanted, one that had led to, and was increasingly to foster, a hierarchy of schools within the elementary sector.

Mass elementary education had been diffused relatively successfully over the country by 1870. But the impact had not been comprehensive in the towns and cities. As we have seen, the voluntary societies, and especially the Nonconformists, were moving up-market, and failing to cater for the more deprived social groups. The intention of the 1870 Act was to fill these gaps. Among the many burning questions which followed were those regularly posed by voluntaryist interests, faithfully reflected in their journal, the *School Guardian*, in articles entitled: 'What is the Proper Use for Board Schools?',[40] or 'For What Class of Children are our Board Schools Intended?'[41]

The voluntaryists took the view that as subscriptions formed a major part of their income, it was appropriate that they should attract children whose parents could afford to pay reasonable fees. If elementary schools were to be subsidised by the rates, it should be the function of rate-supported board schools to concentrate on provision for the more needy who, as the *School Guardian* in 1876 delicately observed, 'do not feel comfortable among the more orderly and well-dressed children who are found in most of our Primary Schools'.[42]

The board school sector was not generally content to assume this lower status role. Certainly board schools in general acquired a stigma. For many respectable parents, the voluntary school maintained a higher esteem, as for one of the novelist George Gissing's characters:

Clara went to a Church school, and the expense was greater than the new system (i.e. of board schools) rendered necessary. Her father's principles naturally favoured education on an independent basis, but a prejudice then (and still) common among workpeople of decent habits made him hesitate about sending his girl to sit side by side with children of the street.[43]

T. W. Sharpe, HMI, in his 1873 report drew attention to the view that the prime function of board schools would be to replace ragged schools: 'It seems to be tacitly assumed by managers of voluntary schools that an increase in fees would elevate their schools above the lowest stratum, which might be left to the board schools'.[44]

The situation did not evolve so straightforwardly, however. Well-to-do parents soon became aware of the qualitative advantages possessed by schools resourced by the rates. School boards such as London's were by the late 1870s erecting the most ambitious elementary schools yet envisaged.[45] The *School Board Chronicle*, organ of the school boards, foresaw in 1876 that while in the early stages the voluntary sector would be able to attract the more select children, the superior resources of the board schools would later reverse this trend, already operative by the mid-1870s, as J. D. Morell, HMI, noted in his report on Greenwich and the City of London (1875):

The idea which at first prevailed when the new board schools were started was that they would be filled by scholars of a lower class, driven in by the operation of the compulsory clauses, and that the voluntary school would approach somewhat to the middle-class type adapted to the requirements of those who object to the indiscriminate mixture of their own children with those of rougher description. This idea, I find, has not by any means been realised. So far from that the tendency is rather the contrary, the board school, where circumstances favour it, showing a much more decided tendency to assume a middle-class form than the others.[46]

One of the factors underlying change was the territorial flight of people to the outer suburbs. These had hitherto been heavy subscribers to the voluntary system in inner areas, but were now withdrawing their resources with their children. In his report for 1878–9 on the schools of Lambeth, J. G. Fitch, HMI, pointed out that already more children were attending board schools than voluntary schools in his area, with the ratio increasing still further in favour of the board schools. The reason was clear:

In the densely-peopled districts of Walworth, Kennington and North Camberwell there are few or no rich residents, the inhabitants are chiefly shopkeepers and others who form the class most keenly sensible of the pressure of the rates, and most likely to regard the existence of the education rate as a reason for withholding all subscriptions from Church or other voluntary schools.[47]

At the same time, the urban school boards could not evade their responsibility towards the poorer groups. But this was seen as one of a number of responsibilities, and by some as a necessary evil. In the early years of the London School Board, for example, there was considerable debate as to whether 'street arab' children should be educated promiscuously with the rest. One lady member proposed 'a sort of penal or purgatorial school – something distinctly unpleasant, or at least more unattractive to the unmanageable than the best board schools'.[48] The notion of 'best board schools' enraged the voluntary sector.

The *School Guardian* in 1876 asserted that the poorest children were now worse off than in the days of the ragged schools. Institutions then charging 1d a week were now demanding 3d. The boards were turning away from the neglected, with 'ambitious aims' to educate the upper portion of the working class, showing their primary object was not 'the advancement of the education of the people, but the destruction of the schools which others have provided for that purpose'.[49]

The sense of outrage was maintained throughout the school board period. One of the more redoubtable proponents of the voluntaryist position, Cardinal Manning, complained that poorer children were being thrown more and more onto the voluntary groups, which was certainly true in the Catholic sector.

The poor, therefore, so far, are paying for schools in which their own children are not taught, and the tradesman's children are educated on the rate paid also by the poor.[50]

At this time, voluntaryist opinion on the London School Board was making itself felt, pressing the case of 'unfair competition', accusing the board of discouraging the admission of the poor, and preferring 'to see their schools filled with well dressed and well to do children'. In its riposte, the *School Board Chronicle* ridiculed the 'curious notion of the institution of a poverty-meter at the threshold of every Board school'.[51]

The survey of London elementary education by Charles Booth and his team at the end of the 1880s provided a more objective appraisal. While offering an uncomfortable level of competition at the upper end of the elementary spectrum, board schools were, at the same time, sharing with the Catholic sector the burden of providing for the disadvantaged. Booth's survey made clear the variety of provision offered by the London School Board, more wide-ranging than that of the Anglican, Nonconformist or of the Catholic sectors. He divided the elementary schools of London into six 'Classes', ranging from 'schools of special difficulty' (his Class I), an 'Educational Priority Area'-type compensatory concept introduced by the London School Board, to the Class VI schools, highly regarded by respectable parents. The three upper classes of schools, though taking a minority of the overall scholar total, attracted to themselves large majorities of skilled artisan and lower-middle-class children. At the extremes, the Class I board schools, 99 in number and accommodating 110,000 children, averaged 87.8% in poverty. The Class VI voluntary schools housed 100% of children in comfort, while the three top categories in this sector, with approaching 100,000 children, had over 80% living in comfort.[52]

Crowning the elementary hierarchy came the higher grade schools, most firmly entrenched in manufacturing centres of northern England, where secondary provision was weak (see Chapter 5). These were roughly equivalent in social terms to third grade secondary schools, but educationally were probably superior. The higher grade schools rendered almost obsolete the concept of the third grade secondary school, but were too successful for their own good. They were invalidated by the Cockerton judgement of 1899, which decided that the London School Board was acting illegally in spending public money on education beyond the elementary stage. As in other areas of English education, a combination of official failure to define the upper limit of elementary education clearly, and of local initiative taking advantage of this obscurity, had led to confusion. The social overlaps of schools at this level will be further discussed in the following chapter.

The confusion was an inevitable consequence of that part of the 1870 Act which set as the upper limit of elementary provision a fee of 9d per week. This was a high limit and was determined by administrative (as representing the average per capita cost of maintenance of a child at a grant-aided school) rather than by social criteria.[53] The 9d fee provided plenty of scope for the board sector to replicate the existing voluntary strategy of grading elementary schools by differentiating school fees.

Although in parts of the board school sector, in East Lambeth, for example, low fees were charged, this was by no means the case for London as a whole. By fits and starts, the London School Board set out to cover the whole field, from the 'gutter child' to the aspirant for secondary school scholarships. By 1873, it had provided 28,000 places, of which 23,000 were paying fees of 1d or 2d; 3,670 of 3d; 990 of 4d; and 870 of 6d.[54]

By contrast, about 60% of children in voluntary schools paid 3d per week, and 18% 4d to 9d. This meant that the average fee per child for 78% of pupils in voluntary schools was 3½d, while for 75% of children in board schools it was only 1½d. In addition, in the voluntary sector in particular, fees were graduated according to the different age phases in the school, infants paying the lowest fees.

Clearly there was a social correlation here also, for the more well-to-do children tended to be those staying on into the higher standards. The head-teacher of Newcastle Wesleyan school informed the Cross Commission that his fees were 2d in the infants; 4d in standards I and II; 5d in III; 6d in IV; 7d in V; 8d in VI and 9d in VII. Most of his parents he agreed were skilled artisans.[55] In 1883, in the Ashton Union, near Manchester, the modal fee above the infants level was 4d for standards I and II; 5d for III; 6d for IV; 7d for V; 8d for VI; and 9d for VII.[56] In more general terms, by 1891, 4.8% of scholars were being schooled free; 15.6% were paying 1d and less than 2d; 37.0% 2d and less than 3d; 25.8% 3d and less than 4d; 12.9% 4d and less than 6d; 2.9% 6d and less than 9d; and 0.8% 9d and over, giving an average of about 3d per child.[57]

A crucial correlation was, therefore, between fee level and residential area. The influence of social geography was pervasive. In Manchester, for example, H. E. Oakeley, HMI, identified four categories of elementary schools:

(1) those on the outskirts, where more well-to-do people had moved, and where fees of 6d to 9d per week could easily be paid;

(2) schools in poorer central areas 'whose great and well-deserved

reputation prevented their natural extinction when the homes of their former scholars were replaced by warehouses', and to which 'a good class of scholars attend from considerable distances';

(3) elementary schools 'of the second grade' in stable working-class areas, where fees averaged about 4d per week;

(4) schools attended by the very poor, where the maximum fee would be 2d or 3d per week.[58]

It was in the socially less desirable districts that voluntary schools tended to retain higher status, leaving the board sector to cater for the poorer children, as the following exchange between a Southwark School Board visitor (who was also a trade union official), T. E. Powell, and a member of the Cross Commission on Elementary Education, Canon Gregory, indicates:

52,898. You said that the voluntary schools had higher fees; do you find many parents preferring them on that account? – Yes, some do prefer them, because they are higher fee'd; and some prefer them because the board school is rough. When the parents make an objection at all, it is "Well, I do not care for your board schools; they are so rough; the children are so outrageous"; and, unfortunately, they say they are so dirty; consequently, we have no choice but to send them into this school here; it is a higher fee, but we will send them.

52,899. Then there is a strong class feeling amongst people in your part? – I do not say there is a strong class feeling, but some people prefer the welfare and cleanliness of their children to the 1d and 2d fee; they prefer to pay 3d and keep the children clean.

52,900. Do you think that there is that real difference between the children in the two classes of schools? – Yes, in poor localities. We have board schools equally good, of course.

52,901. Are all the board schools low fee'd? – Immediately surrounding my own neighbourhood they are 1d and 2d fees.

52,902. And in the case of voluntary schools the fees are 6d? – From 3d to 6d.[59]

With the tacit approval of the Education Department, however, school boards established high fee schools in better residential areas. The sifting process is well illustrated in Fig. 4.1, showing the relationship between board school fees and social area differentiation in Bermondsey in the mid-1970s. Based on Booth's social maps (see Chapter 7), they highlight the variations between the poverty-riddled and malodorous 'tanneries' district, where one school charged only a 1d fee; the riverside and other industrialised zones with 2d fees; and less crowded areas to the east and south-east where fees were 3d and

more. Monmow Road (Plate 3) was the prestigious school of this area
from an early stage, and on at least two occasions fees were raised in
reflection of this fact. When the London School Board resolved to raise
fees from 4d to 6d in 1880, radical local groups protested. Local
divisional members of the board agreed with their reasoning, but the
Education Department pointed out that its aim was to secure that fees
be fixed 'so as to suit the particular class of children for which a
particular school may have been erected', relying on local knowledge to
decide on the level of fee suitable to a locality.[60]

Fig. 4.1. Bermondsey 1875: Board School Fees and Social Area
Differentiation (after Booth)

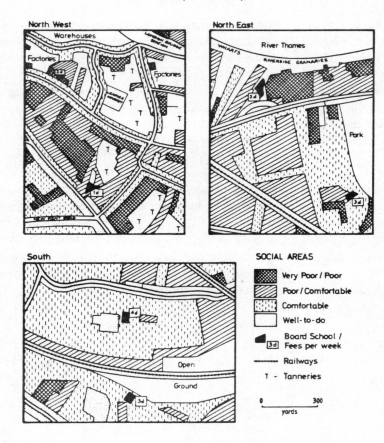

CONCLUSION

So the English public educational system adapted itself to the complex status divisions of tertiary society. Historically there had been a shift from a predominantly rural society, with its impermeable 'orders' or 'estates', in which any concept of an 'education for all' was contested; to, in the late eighteenth and early nineteenth centuries, an industrial society in which aggregate class feeling and vertical antagonism between groups was generated, to which it is tempting to attach the idea of a dual and polarised educational provision; to, in the late nineteenth century, an astonishing growth of tertiary activities, to which came to be attached a more individualistic status-consciousness and a meritocratic ideology. It was this development that was the most characteristically urban, for much early industrialisation had in fact been semi-rural. Many early industrial towns were mere congeries of industrial villages, without typical ranges of urban functions. It was tertiary urban society that predicated more complex schooling arrangements, and overrode the rudimentary split between 'the education of the rich' and 'the education of the poor'.

By the late nineteenth century, an urban revolution was virtually complete. Within cities, anxieties plagued the more respectable groups who, as was noted in Chapter 3, viewed the burgeoning slums as breeding places of revolution and/or racial decay. In response to this threat, at the individual level, segregation of residence became critical in the process of achieving family security and maintaining social status, a sublimated form of a basic human need for survival at an acceptable level of well-being. Propinquity of urban neighbourhoods of differentiated ranking provoked deep-rooted social tensions. Fears became tangible realities when children from 'sub-social units', in Park's terms (see Chapter 1), appeared in the classrooms. The 'enclosure' imperative, which had generated territorially bound, socially homogeneous communities, demanded parallelism in the schools. Such grassroot forces shaped the face of English education, and not least elementary education, in the late nineteenth century. Social stratification, territorial segregation, and educational graduation constituted a powerful trinity of forces seminal, among other things, in the rise of the meritocracy.

REFERENCES AND NOTES

1. J. Nelson, *An Essay on the Government of Children* (London, 1756), p. 33.
2. *Ibid.*, p. 320, p. 330, p. 338, p. 344, pp. 365–7.
3. *Ibid.*, pp. 269–70.
4. Mrs. Trimmer, *The Oeconomy of Charity*, Vol. 1 (London, 1801), pp. 22–3.
5. *Ibid.*, p. 24.
6. *Ibid.*, pp. 27–9.
7. *Ibid.*, p. 24.
8. T. Wyse, *Educational Reform, or the Necessity of a National System of Education* (London, 1836), p. 387.
9. *Ibid.*, p. 49 and p. 380.
10. J. Wade, *History of the Middle and Working Classes* (London, 1833; repr. Cass, 1968), pp. 182–3.
11. *Ibid.*, pp. 496–7.
12. *Ibid.*, p. 497.
13. J. Fraser, *National Education* (London, Salisbury, 1868), p. 7.
14. M. Arnold, 'A French Eton, or Middle-class Education and the State', in G. Sutherland (ed.), *Matthew Arnold on Education* (Harmondsworth, 1973), p. 137.
15. *Educational Reporter*, Vol. 1, No. 3 (1869), p. 1.
16. W. Watson, *Chapters on Ragged and Industrial Schools* (Edinburgh, 1872), p. 9.
17. A Worker (Mary Carpenter), *Ragged Schools: their Principles and Modes of Operation* (London, 1850), p. 3.
18. C. J. Montague, *Sixty Years of Waifdom, or, the Ragged School Movement in English History* (London, 1904; Woburn Press Reprint, 1968), pp. 114–15.
19. W. Booth, *In Darkest England, and the Way Out* (London, 1890), pp. 63–4.
20. 'Results of the Education Act', *Edinburgh Review*, Vol. 139 (1874), pp. 231–2.
21. *School Board Chronicle*, 9 Nov. 1872, p. 397.
22. *R.C.C.E.* (1873–4), pp. 190–1.
23. *School Guardian*, 10 Jan. 1880, p. 15.
24. *M.C.C.E.* (1851–2), p. 730.
25. For the most part, a sympathetic view towards parental opinion was taken. See *Newcastle Commission*, vol. 1 (1861), p. 178.
26. *Newcastle Commission*, vol. 6 (1861), p. 6.
27. M. Arnold, *Reports on Elementary Schools 1852–1881* (London, 1908), p. 3.
28. *Ibid.*, pp. 19–20.
29. *R.C.C.E.* (1858–9), pp. 178–80.
30. *Newcastle Commission*, vol. 6 (1861), pp. 199–204.
31. *R.C.C.E.* (1861–2), pp. 126–7.
32. *Newcastle Commission*, vol. 5 (1861), pp. 384–6.
33. *Newcastle Commission*, vol. 6 (1861), pp. 256–8.
34. *Ibid.*, p. 290.
35. *Newcastle Commission*, vol. 1 (1861), p. 68 and p. 72.
36. *Newcastle Commission*, vol. 6 (1861), pp. 6–7.
37. *Hansard*, vol. 194 (1868–9), Col. 1206.
38. 'Returns of Particulars of All Schools for the Poorer Classes of Children in the Municipal Boroughs of Birmingham, Leeds, Liverpool and Manchester', *British Parliamentary Papers, 1870* (91), LIV, pp. 127–8.
39. H. Mann, 'National Education', *Transactions of the National Association for the Promotion of Social Science*, Bristol Meeting 1869 (London, 1870), pp. 366–8.
40. 'What is the Proper Use for Board Schools', *School Guardian*, 23 Sept. 1876, p. 635.

41. 'For What Class of Children are our Board Schools Intended?', *School Guardian*, 18 March 1876.
42. *School Guardian*, 23 Sept. 1876, p. 635.
43. G. Gissing, *The Nether World* (London, 1928), p. 80.
44. *Reports of the Committee of Council on Education* (1873–4), p. 190.
45. Examples can be found in E. R. Robson, *School Architecture* (London, 1874; Leicester University Press Reprint, 1972), pp. 291–350.
46. *R.C.C.E.* (1875–6), pp. 369–70.
47. *R.C.C.E.* (1878–9), p. 548.
48. *School Board Chronicle*, 9 Nov. 1872, p. 390.
49. *School Guardian*, 18 March 1876, p. 177.
50. Cardinal H. E. Manning, 'Is the Education Act of 1870 a Just Law' (London, 1886), p. 7, reprinted in *National Education* (London, 1889), a collection of Manning's articles and papers.
51. *School Board Chronicle*, 28 July 1883, p. 78 and p. 87.
52. C. Booth (ed.), *Labour and Life of the People vol. II: London* (London, 1891), pp. 477–526 and particularly pp. 478–85.
53. J. S. Hurt, *Elementary Schooling and the Working Classes 1860–1918* (London, 1979), p. 14.
54. *School Board Chronicle*, 11 Jan. 1873, p. 251.
55. *Cross Commission*, 2nd Report (1887), p. 129.
56. *School Board Chronicle*, 24 Feb. 1883, p. 203.
57. *Hansard*, vol. 354, (1890–1), col. 1902.
58. *R.C.C.E.* (1879–80), pp. 246–7.
59. *Cross Commission*, 3rd Report (1887), p. 401.
60. Letter from Education Department to London School Board dated 5 July 1881, printed in *School Board Chronicle*, 16 July 1881, p. 31.

CHAPTER FIVE

Schools for the Urban Middle Classes

... the result is a fierce competition, which constrains the tradesman and artisan to abridge their children's school-time, and also to insist upon their being taught only what can be turned to immediate account ... A boy may be able to discriminate between *nummi* and *pecunia*, but that accomplishment will not get him a clerkship, if he is slow at compound addition.[1] (Clark, 1855)

One of the great social changes of the late nineteenth century was the occupational transition from manufacturing to service industries, resulting in an enormous increase in the 'middling groups' in society. The traditional *petite bourgeoisie* of shopkeepers and others was joined by the advancing ranks of clerks, commercial travellers and elementary school-teachers. As Chapter 4 indicated, just as the upper middle classes effectively colonised the public schools in the second half of the century, so the lower middle discovered and exploited the potential of certain schools in the elementary sector, ensuring selectivity by their willingness to pay higher fees than most, though not all, working-class parents could afford.

The situation was not clear-cut, however. The purpose of this chapter is to explore some of the problems faced by a spectrum of parents, shading from the respectable upper echelons of the working class, to those whose aspirations fell short of the great public boarding schools. It concentrates on two groups of problems. The first relates to the niceties of choice facing late-nineteenth century parents in the fringe zone between elementary and secondary provision, confronted with the paradox that schools that were the most acceptable socially were not necessarily the best educationally. The second concerns the territorial placing of schools for middle-class groups, less thick on the ground and more dispersed than the working masses. Such schools often found themselves misplaced in a time of rapid social change and technological advances in urban transport systems, allowing the flight of more well-to-do groups to the suburbs, as described in Chapter 3. The frequent mismatch of school position and pupil catchment occasioned increasingly long journeys to school, and promoted later in the century the centrifugal movement also of school locations.

CHOOSING SCHOOLS

The lack of suitable schools for the middle classes, and particularly the lower middle class was a recurring lament of mid-century social commentators:

between the serene heights and pure air of Oxford and Cambridge and the swamps and morasses of those peculiar institutions which Lord Shaftesbury delights to honour, lies a long, low, level tract of flat but unexplored country, into which no Inspector enters, and the annals of which are written in no Blue-book. The Central Desert of English Education, is thickly studded with institutions which, being in no sense public property, are exempt from public control, and consequently, for the most part, from public knowledge. The opprobrium of English education is to be found, not in its public schools nor its poor schools – not in its Universities nor its charity schools – but in its middle and private schools.[2]

One of the first attempts to plug the gaps took the form of the urban proprietary school, a somewhat opaque category[3] that covered a multitude of sins as well as some successes. A celebrated example was Liverpool Collegiate, founded in 1843 in what was then a superior location on the fringe of the city. Taking careful and expedient note of the gradations in Liverpool society and the detail of its economy, its controllers created an upper (classical) school, designed for the sons of professional people and merchants, paying the highest fees; a middle school, for the better class of shopkeepers and clerks; and a lower school, for small shopkeepers, clerks and educated artisans. The school was built on three floors, one for each division. But the distinctions were not divinely appointed, in the eighteenth-century sense. As the Headmaster informed the Taunton Commission: 'The defining line of separation between the schools is a pecuniary one: people assess themselves at their own status'.[4] But once assessed, children found it difficult to cross the divides.

The Taunton Commission of 1868 legitimated this by then well-established gradation on a more official basis. The distinguishing criterion between three grades of secondary provision was to be length of stay. Social class was therefore to be measured by parental choice. Lower-middle-class children would be likely to leave at 14, and for these third grade endowed schools were needed. The absence of provision at this level, required by smaller tenant farmers, tradesmen, clerks, and superior artisans, was seen by the Commission as the 'most urgent educational need of the country',[5] while W. E. Forster, Vice-President of the Committee of Privy Council, informed the House of Commons that the third grade issue 'occupied our attention more than any other' comprising 'a large and interesting class of children'.[6] The Commission was clear that National schools were capable of undertaking third grade work, but would not be acceptable to lower-middle and superior artisan parents, on the grounds of the socially suspect status of elementary teachers and children.[7] The board schools were even more dubious:

few who value the future of their children and know the advantages of the superior associations to be found in the best private schools would dream of sacrificing their class distinction – omitting the moral tone – by sending their children to mix up with those who, according to vestryman's notions, should be the 'waifs and strays'.[8]

Such thinking predicated a search for secondary schools willing to undertake third grade provision. But the quality of so many third grade schools, as discerned by D. R. Fearon in his report to the Taunton Commission on the 'middle schools' of London, was low: 'to anyone who has been used to good primary schools under Government inspection, the interiors of these smaller grammar schools are most repulsive'.[9]

While the poorest endowed schools were found wanting, the higher quality secondary institutions did not rush to be designated as third grade. The failure of the endowed sector to provide sufficiently for lower-middle-class children is clear from an 1883 return (Table 1). In the 15 years following the Taunton Commission's report, no first grade and only 13 second grade schools had become third grade, and the latter were accommodating 98 fewer children than in 1868. Five new third grade boys' and over 20 new third grade girls' schools were taking respectively over 1,000 and 3,000 children, while 21 elementary schools turned third grade were taking over 2,000. But the total offering was less than spectacular, and in any case the target groups were demanding quality as much as quantity.

TABLE 1

Table showing increase and decrease of scholars between 1868 (Schools Inquiry Commission) and 1883 (Fortescue Return) in different grades of endowed school.

No. of Schools	Description			Decrease	Increase
34	First Grade,	remaining so			1,940
51	Second Grade,	remaining so			739
35	Third Grade,	remaining so			683
15	First Grade,	changed to	Second		257
13	Second Grade,	changed to	First		300
–	First Grade,	changed to	Third		–
2	Third Grade,	changed to	First	16	–
13	Second Grade,	changed to	Third	98	–
23	Third Grade,	changed to	Second		181
3	New Schools for Boys,		First Grade		222
7	New Schools for Boys,		Second Grade		1,028
5	New Schools for Boys,		Third Grade		1,011
5	New Schools for Girls,		First Grade		822
10	New Schools for Girls,		Second Grade		1,472
25	Schools for Girls,		Third Grade, 22 new		3,111
3	Elementary Schools made		Second Grade		232
21	Elementary Schools made		Third Grade		2,177
				114	14,175
					114
		NET INCREASE			14,061

(Source: *Report from the Select Committee on the Endowed Schools Acts*, PP.191 (1886), Appendix 3.)

There were, however, successes, one of which was the United Westminster School (Table 2). Of approximately 1,750 pupils admitted between 1879 and 1886, nearly 50% had lower-middle-class, 20% skilled artisan, 18% unskilled worker, and 8.5% higher professional parents, representing a considerable social mix. The percentage of exhibitioners is skewed down the social scale, suggesting that the institution was making some contribution to the promotion of social mobility.

The evidence of Chapter 4 suggests strongly that the Taunton Commission was wrong in assuming that the elementary sector would not be acceptable to lower-middle-class and superior artisan parents. The mechanism of the high fee made it possible to build 'select' schools into the system. But the high-fee elementary school did not meet the Commission's definition of middle-class education, namely a

TABLE 2

Socio-economic classification of parents of scholars at United Westminster Schools, 1879–1886

	% Exhibitioners	% Paying Pupils	% Overall
Upper Middle Class (Lawyers, etc.)	3	10	8.5
Lower Middle Class (clerks, etc.)	26	54	47
Skilled artisans	25	18	20
Unskilled (labourers, charwomen, domestic servants, porters, etc.)	35	12	18
Others (e.g. widows, no occupation given)	11	6	6.5

TOTAL PUPILS 1,764

(Based on table of occupation of parents in *Report from the Select Committee on the Endowed Schools Acts*, PP.191 (1886), Appendix 10.)

leaving age of at least 14. At best, elementary scholars left at 13. The dilemma was resolved by the emergence of a new type of school, the *higher grade* school, most notably in the manufacturing districts of the north. Here Robert Morant, the influential Assistant Director of the Board of Education's Office of Special Inquiries, saw a system of natural selection at work[10] in areas where, through meagre endowments, conventional secondary provision was weak.

A perceived advantage of the higher grade school, particularly in the textile towns, was its exclusion of half-time children, regarded as holding back the regular attenders. More positively, it was the gateway to higher levels of education. Two basic types of higher grade school emerged. One could be termed the Bradford model, a selective one, with the fees adjusted, according the Education Department advice of 1879, 'as far as possible [to] the quality of the education given',[11] and attracting 'the children of thoughtful and better-to-do working people, the children of clerks, managers, foremen and artizans, and some of what you would class as small tradesmen – the lower middle class'.[12] Such schools were located peripherally in socially respectable areas, and a scholarship system was introduced to allow children of poorer parents to gain entry.[13]

The second model was exemplified by Sheffield, where a centrally-placed higher grade school, intended for 'deserving and clever children', took pupils from all over the city, an idea which won the

9. St. Alexander's R.C. School: note the signs for St. John's Road Bootle *and* Liverpool, indicating that the school, though mainly receiving Bootle children, was just over the municipal boundary.

10. The staff of Christ Church Higher Grade School, Bootle, about 1900. The headmaster, Mr. A. E. Scott is in the middle of the front row, with D. Munro, Monitor, in front of him. Second from the left at the back is C. F. Nathan, author of *A Schoolmaster Glances Back*.

11. A 'Troublesome Thoroughfare': Derby Road, Bootle, with Mann Street and
Emley Street running off to the right. The photograph was taken in the 1930s. Note
one of the many public houses, a hairdressing saloon and a corner shop.

12. An inter-war 'Lord Street parade', Southport. Note the private schoolboys mixed
in with the high fashion.

13. 'Castles in the Sand': the early years of Birkdale Park. St. James's Church marks
the line of Lulworth Road, which ran behind it. At right angles to this was Aughton
Road (Fig. 10.2) left background, beyond which was the Southport boundary. The
houses in the right background are on York Road. The railway line was behind
these with Birkdale Common beyond. Westcliffe Road was built approximately
along the line of the sandhills in the front of the photograph, which therefore dates
from the late 1850s or early 1860s.

14. The importance of the railways: the prosperity of Southport and Birkdale as
watering places and dormitory settlements, and of course as havens of private
schools, was very much related to their access to the major industrial and
commercial towns of northern England, which this photograph of Southport's
Chapel Street Station illustrates.

15. A Brighthelmston, Birkdale, school photograph of 1899.

16. The Brighthelmston school cricket team in the same year. By this time, the larger private schools, and particularly this one, were ranging well beyond the narrow training in domestic accomplishments and social graces which was characteristic of the smaller and more secluded schools.

'hearty approval' of Forster on a visit in 1874.[14] This pattern, followed later by Birmingham, catered specifically for higher level 'elementary' education, with no standards provided for below the seventh.[15]

There were also elementary schools offering an 'advanced' curriculum, though not actually designated higher grade. There was a close connection between all such schools and a developing scholarship system, one envisaged in the letter from the Education Department which had approved the Bradford pattern.[16] The many London schools of this genre did not become 'higher grade' until the late 1890s, and then somewhat controversially, not least because they were seen as comparing unfavourably with the best provincial examples. They mostly failed on the strict criterion excluding schools which did not appear in the Calendar of the Science and Art Department as having organised science courses.[17] The London School Board's rejoinder was that the nature of the demand in the capital made commercial rather than science schools a more appropriate type of higher elementary provision.

None the less, there were many prestigious board schools in the eyes of London parents, particularly those with a reputation for winning scholarships. Beginning in the 1880s, the London School Board's scholarship scheme was described by Webb as 'one of the most successful developments of the last decade',[18] establishing a ladder, albeit a very narrow one, to secondary education and beyond. Before attempting the climb, however, children had to have reached Standard V.

The most celebrated scholarship school was Fleet Road, East Hampstead, to be discussed in Chapter 7. The school successfully attracted lower-middle- as well as skilled working-class children, and managed to restrict the intake from the lower ranks of society to a minority. Not for the first time, children from this school topped the junior scholarship winners' stakes in the 1896–8 period. Of the scholarship holders in these years, 45% came from lower middle class, 48% from skilled artisan, and only about 4% from unskilled worker families.[19] There was a different mix of winners at Sherbrooke Road school, set amongst the terraced streets of Fulham, a popular residential area for clerks and skilled artisans. Second in the scholarship list in the 1896–8 period, 31% of the school's winners were from the lower middle class, 44% from skilled artisan, and as much as 21% from unskilled worker families. The difference between the two schools seems not to have been to do with catchment areas,

which were not dissimilar, but rather the intake policies of the head-
teachers.

The numbers of scholarships provided by local authorities increased almost tenfold between 1895 and 1906.[20] The extent of the
provision nationally varied greatly between localities, however. The
access of lower-middle- and upper-working-class children to scholarship ladders depended very much on where they lived. Thus entry to
the higher rated 'schools of science' (Fig. 5.1) was predominantly
restricted to certain urban industrial areas. In 1901, for example, the
ratio of scholars in science schools to population was 1:431 in the West
Riding; 1:440 in Tyneside; 1:1016 in south-east Lancashire; 1:1188 in
the west Midlands; 1:1358 in Merseyside; and 1:1463 in London.
The geographical distribution of County Council Minor Scholarship holders in the 1897–1900 period was different again. As Fig.
5.2 illustrates, the leading counties were the West Riding, Derbyshire, Norfolk, Middlesex and Surrey. As late as the beginning of
this century, therefore, some counties, including Lancashire, were
making minimal provision of minor, though they might be offering
other types of scholarship. But in almost all types of scholarship
offering, and at all scales, there were yawning disparities of provision.

Which type of school, therefore, third grade or higher grade, better
served lower-middle-class interests, bearing in mind that their needs
included not only securing for their children steady, non-manual
jobs, but also averting the widely feared prospect of socio-economic
descent? Table 3 compares the backgrounds of pupils in public
secondary and higher grade schools in a selective survey prepared for a
joint conference of head-teachers of the two types of school in 1897. It
adopted a strict definition of higher grade, including only organised
science schools listed in the Calendar of the Science and Art Department. The figures suggest at least the tentative conclusions that both
types of schools were popular with lower-middle-class parents; that
secondary were more popular with upper-middle-class; and higher
grade with skilled artisan. Where the two types coexisted, therefore, lower-middle-class parents had a potentially difficult choice.
It may be surmised that those choosing the secondary schools attached
a higher value to social quarantining, while those selecting higher
grade schools were opting for educational sophistication. It is worth
remembering that one higher grade school, Nottingham, successfully
prepared scholars for the intermediate examination of the London
B.A.[21]

Fig. 5.1. Number of Scholars in Schools of Science, 1899–1900

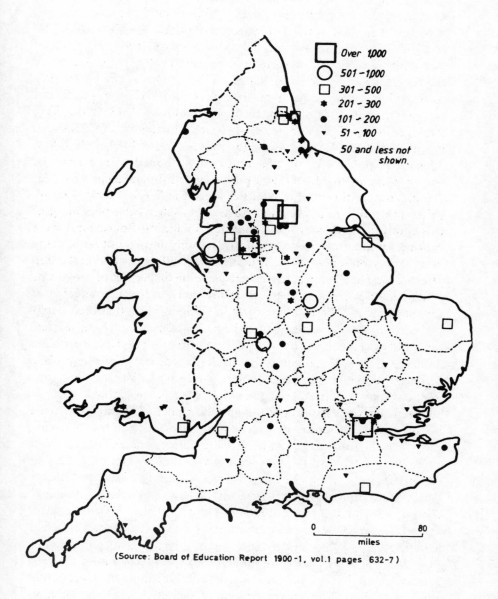

(Source: Board of Education Report 1900-1, vol.1 pages 632-7)

Fig. 5.2. County Council Minor (Junior) Scholarships, 1897–1900

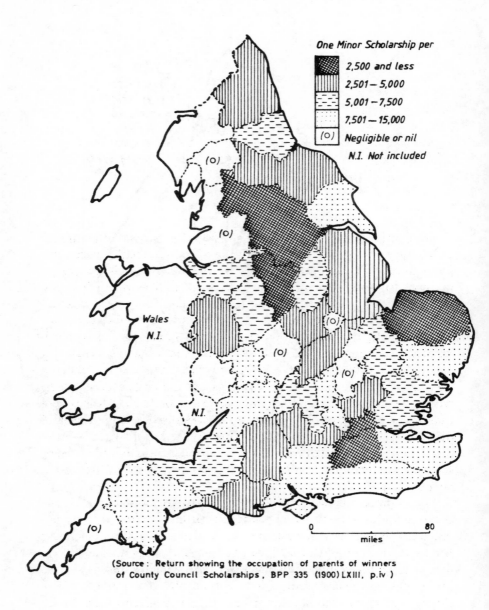

(Source: Return showing the occupation of parents of winners
of County Council Scholarships, BPP 335 (1900) LXIII, p.iv)

TABLE 3

Socio-economic classification of parents of scholars at selected public secondary and higher grade board schools, 1897

| | Percentages in | | |
	Secondary Boys	H.G. Boys	H.G. Girls
Upper Middle Class	38.9	11.0	10.6
Lower Middle Class	46.6	42.0	45.2
Skilled Artisans	8.1	32.7	29.6
Unskilled	1.0	7.3	7.8
Others	4.2	6.2	6.0

(Source: *Return concerning certain Higher Grade Board Schools and Public Secondary Schools prepared for a Conference between the Incorporated Association of Head Masters and the Association of Head Masters of the Higher Grade Schools, held November 1897*: PP.1898, LXX, 10–11.

The contest between third grade and higher grade and other higher elementary schools was not the only one to be found in this particular segment of the social spectrum, however. Lower-middle-class groups merged upwards into the upper-middle as well as down into the upper-working class. While, as Table 3 has suggested, a small minority of upper-middle-class children could be found in higher grade schools, the competition at this level was rather between the 'graded' secondary schools in the Taunton Commission's terms, and smaller scale private schools which the Bryce Commission in its turn classified into five categories, ranging from the large establishment with some boarders, carried on on public school lines, to 'the school that has no particular aim, but exists only because the lady's husband died, or the gentleman's proper venture in life has failed'.[22] A fuller discussion of interaction between these social groups and the smaller scale private sector is provided in the case study of Birkdale in the final chapter.

The competition which had developed by the 1880s and 1890s between middle- and working-class fringe groups was particularly significant. The scholarship system was a vital aspect of the encounter.[23] But for the lower middle class it was a two-edged weapon. There were, for example, many more minor scholarships, which could roughly be said to help in the later acquisition of office jobs, than major scholarships, which provided access for very bright children to the higher reaches of education and the professions. It was thus easier for a skilled artisan child to win a minor scholarship than for a lower-middle-class child to acquire a major. The social process was one of extension of the middle groups of the nation, increasing the blockage on the ladder. This suited the system. While there was a need for large numbers to undertake diligently clerkly tasks, there was equally a desire to limit the supply of candidates for high level positions. The upper classes valued the respectability of the lower middle class, but probably no more than that of the upper working. They were quite happy to see the two fighting it out on the narrow ladder of opportunity.

The 'scholarship school' symbolised the successful lower-middle-class and upper-working-class colonisation of the élite portion of the elementary sector. Success in scholarship winning reflected to some extent the triggering circumstances of the social environment which dictated the intake of the school. But the school itself, as Lindsay later suggested, was a force in its own right, the establishment of a 'scholarship tradition'[24] through perhaps the impetus of a thrustful head teacher, as at Fleet Road in Hampstead, attracting the children of more ambitious parents and more able teachers, combining to make the chief drive of the school winning scholarships.

The development of this system rendered obsolete the concept of the third grade school, though it could be argued that a third grade ethos persisted in the central and then modern schools of the twentieth century. But the new grammar schools of the local authorities, to which the scholarship system became geared, had certainly to be of the first grade, with all the ancestral trimmings, dislodging the higher grade system, one of the most relevant and forward-looking developments in English educational history.

JOURNEYS TO SCHOOL

Anxieties about the access of middle-class children to appropriate schools were brought to the fore by the Taunton Commission in 1868. The emergence of a hierarchical graded system of secondary schools had strong demographic and geographical associations. Thus the 'critical mass' of population for a first grade school was higher than that for a third grade. The issue was also related to other factors such as the existing settlement hierarchy in county areas, and the disposition of endowments in both county and metropolitan areas. J. L. Brereton,[25] a founder of proprietary schools and prominent in the County School movement, was acutely aware of the logistics of the problem, as Table 4 illustrates. The consequences of the Taunton Commission's proposals for graded secondary schools were translated into terms of cost and access. The nation, in Brereton's proposal, would be divided into *provinces*, of 3.5 million people, each with a university. Each province would have three *divisions*, of 1.16 million people, capable of administering a first grade school. The divisions would contain three *counties*, of 390,000 people, administering second grade schools, and these in turn would be divided into *unions*, averaging twenty to a county, and containing nearly 20,000 people, controlling third grade schools.

In practice, there were major disparities over the country. While middle-class children of secondary age could be expected to travel further than elementary school children, there were obvious limits to the distance, not solely spatial distance but also time distance, that pupils could travel. Two contrasting case studies can be taken from the Taunton Commission to exemplify.

Fig. 5.3 shows the situation in Lincolnshire at the time of the Taunton Commission. The Bishop of Lincoln submitted a classification of endowed schools in the county, backed up by a map. Four grades were proposed, which anticipated in general principle the overall classification system recommended by the commission. Grade A schools were the grammar schools, preparing for the universities, learned professions and civil service. Grade B were upper-class commercial schools, teaching Latin, French and perhaps German. Grade C were lower-class commercial schools, excluding Latin, but including mathematics, surveying and book-keeping, while Grade D were a particular type of primary school, defined as 'good National schools', containing an upper department with a higher rate of payment.[26] Figs. 5.3(a) and (b) juxtapose the urban hierarchy of Lincolnshire with the distribution of the county's endowed schools, as graded by the Bishop. Fig. 5.3(b) indicates that the larger part of the county had access to one of the three higher grades of school, with five old-established centres, Lincoln, Louth, Boston, Grantham and Stamford having first grade establishments. The railway system promoted access.

The situation in London, as depicted in Fig. 5.4, based on the map Fearon drew for the Taunton Commission, was of high degree of concentration in the centre, with the clientele moving more and more out to the suburbs. Again railways and urban transport systems came

TABLE 4

CAPITAL OF SCHOOLS.

Per Average Province, &c., with Specimen.

AVERAGE (*Educational*).	Population.	Middle Schools—Capital estimated at 10s. per head of population. £	1st Grade.	2nd Grade.	3rd Grade.
PROVINCE = ⅓ of Rural Districts, with a University Centre providing teachers and examiners ...	3,500,000	1,750,000	Day Scholars, 3,500 × 20 = £70,000 Boarders ... 3,500 × 100 = £350,000 £420,000	Day Scholars, 14,000 × 15 = £210,000 Boarders ... 10,500 × 70 = £735,000 £945,000	Day Scholars, 21,000 × 10 = £210,000 Boarders ... 3,500 × 50 = £175,000 £385,000
DIVISION = 3 to a Province, administering 1st Grade Schools ...	1,166,666	—			
COUNTY, or Associated Counties 3 to a Division, administering 2nd Grade Schools ...	390,000	—			
UNION, average 20 to a County, administering 3rd Grade Schools ...	19,500	—			

For the above—No. of Boys estimated at 16 per 1,000 of Population.

Assigning 1 Boy in 16 to 1st Grade Day Schools, paying £12 10s. Annual Fees.

    " 1 "   "   Boarding   "   £52 0s.
    " 4 Boys " 2nd Grade Day Schools   "   £7 16s.
    " 3 "   "   Boarding   "   £32 4s.
    " 6 "   " 3rd Grade Day Schools   "   £3 14s.
    " 1 Boy "   "   Boarding   "   £15 16s.

SPECIMEN.

DIVISIONS.	Population.	Capital (Total for 3 Grades).	1st Grade Schools.
Group A, containing—1. Lincolnshire ... 2. Derby and Notts ... 3. Leicester and Rutland ...	436,165 700,495 290,835	1,427,495	713,747	Day Boys, 1,427 × 20 = 28,540 Boarders, 1,427 × 100 = 142,700
EASTERN PROVINCE, with its Educational Council and County College for supplying Masters centered in *Cambridge*...	3,689,700	1,844,850	

" B,	"	1. Cambridge and Hunts ...	280,035	
		2. North Hants and Beds ...	890,165	1,008,785 } 604,392
		3. Bucks and Herts ...	388,595	
" C,	"	1. Norfolk ...	488,510	
		2. Suffolk ...	848,480	1,253,420 } 626,710
		3. Essex ...	466,430	

2nd Grade Schools.

Day Boys, 1,008 × 20 = 20,160
Boarders, 1,008 × 100 = 100,800
Day Boys, 1,253 × 20 = 25,060
Boarders, 1,253 × 100 = 125,300

£442,650

	£	£
Group A	Day Boys, 5,710 × 15 = 85,650	
	Boarders, 4,281 × 70 = 299,670	
Group B	Day Boys, 4,032 × 15 = 60,480	
	Boarders, 3,024 × 70 = 211,680	
Group C { Norfolk	Day Boys, 1,752 × 15 = 26,280	
	Boarders, 1,314 × 70 = 91,980	
Suffolk	Day Boys, 1,392 × 15 = 20,880	
	Boarders, 1,044 × 70 = 73,080	
Essex	Day Boys, 1,864 × 15 = 27,960	
	Boarders, 1,398 × 70 = 97,860	

£996,520

SAMPLE COUNTIES.

	Population.	Capital.
		£
Norfolk ...	488,510	219,255
Suffolk ...	848,480	174,240
Essex ...	466,430	233,215

3rd Grade Schools.

SAMPLE AVERAGE UNION.

	£	£
Day Boys, 132 × 10 = 1,230		
Boarders, 20½ × 60 = 1,025		

£2,255 × 180 = £405,900

Population	...	...	...	...	20,500
Capital ...	...	...	...	...	£10,250

from J. L. Brereton, *County Education* (1874)

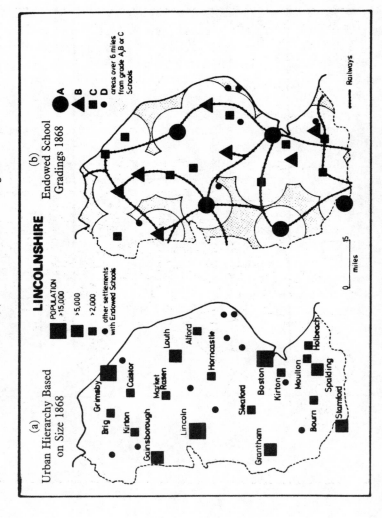

Fig. 5.3. Lincolnshire, 1868: (a) Urban Hierarchy based on
size and (b) Endowed School Gradings

Fig. 5.4. Endowed 'Middle' Schools in London, 1860

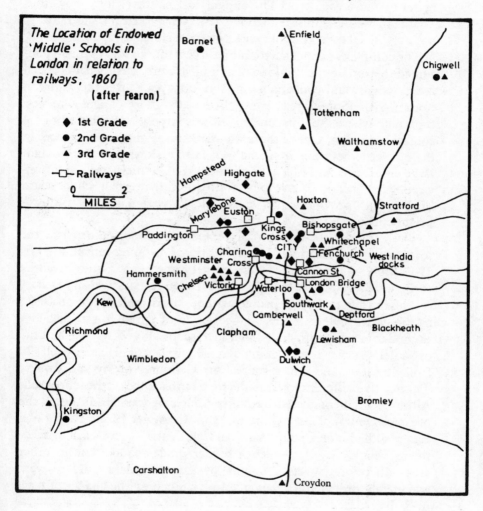

to the rescue, but at a price. Fearon analysed the time taken for boys to reach the City of London School and the amount it cost. A few journeyed from as far away as Southend and Chelmsford, taking three hours or more each day. The annual cost of travel for a boy from Southend was 17 guineas. Schools less well placed for the railway, such as St. Olave's at Southwark, faced decline.[27]

The complex of issues surrounding access to secondary schools continued to exercise the thinking of administrators, members of official commissions, and consultants for the forty years after the Taunton Commission. Some areas were chronically short of endowments, especially where rapid urban growth was imposed on the traditional county landscape. One of these was Yorkshire, where many places in the old settlement hierarchy had access to endowments, but certain large cities, such as Hull, Huddersfield and Sheffield were ill- or un-supplied (Fig. 5.5). It was in such situations that urban school board initiatives to provide higher grade schools were particularly appropriate and successful.

The 'critical mass' problem prompted some counties to engage the services of Michael Sadler as an educational planning consultant. His 1905 study of Derbyshire[28] exemplified some of the issues explored earlier by Brereton. He found a tract between Chesterfield and Derby, containing about 100,000 people, without third grade provision as late as the early 1890s. In 1893, however, local initiative established a Secondary and Technical School in Heanor (Fig. 5.6). At the time of Sadler's survey it was taking over 30 pupils from Heanor itself, 20 from Ilkeston, and ten or more from Codnor, Shipley and Ripley. Twenty-five different settlements were represented on the school roll. Although well-connected by railway, Heanor was by no means the obvious 'central place' to plug this gap. Ilkeston, Alfreton and Long Eaton all had larger populations and, in Sadler's view, each of these towns should have provided a higher grade school.[29] As in other areas, therefore, whether or not lower-middle-class children were adequately provided for depended very much on the chance of local initiative.

The situation found by Fearon in London in 1868 became typical of other conurbations. Thus on Merseyside, Merchant Taylors' School Crosby, a seventeenth-century foundation for the education of poor children in Sefton parish (Fig. 5.7) was taken over, as were so many other old grammar schools, to provide for the needs of the middle classes.[30] As well-to-do Merseysiders moved north during the late

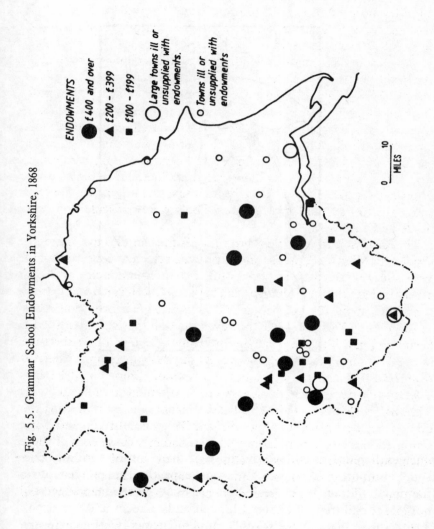

Fig. 5.5. Grammar School Endowments in Yorkshire, 1868

ENDOWMENTS

● £400 and over
▲ £200 – £399
■ £100 – £199

◯ Large towns ill or unsupplied with endowments.

○ Towns ill or unsupplied with endowments

0   10
MILES

Fig. 5.6. The catchment area of Heanor Secondary and Technical School, Derbyshire about 1900 (after Sadler)

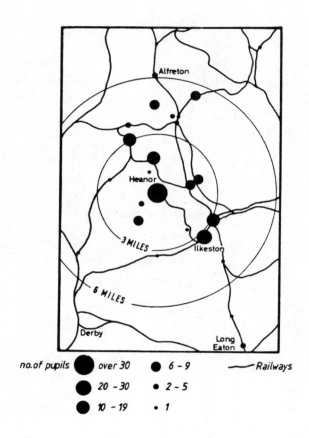

nineteenth century, taking advantage of the commuter railway line from Southport to Liverpool, the school expanded, and moved into a fine new building, which sealed its success.[31] As the map suggests, most of the children came from Blundellsands, Crosby and Waterloo. One of the outliers of the school's catchment was Bootle, currently under invasion from dockland development (see Chapters 8 and 9). But residual enclaves of middle-class housing remained, and the intake of Bootle boys to Merchant Taylors' school was related to highly-rated areas of the borough, conveniently close to railway stations.

Fig. 5.7. Merchant Taylors' School, Crosby, 1888: Catchment Area and the Liverpool–Southport Railway

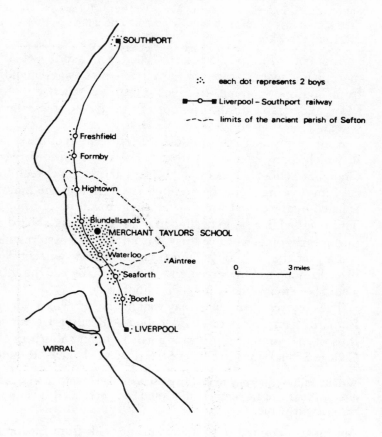

There rapidly grew a hierarchy of provision in this élite sector. Well-regarded though Merchant Taylor's became, for example, affluent parents in places such as Southport might well prefer to send their sons to small, socially select private schools within the town, or, if prioritising a high level academic provision, might select alternative grammar schools further afield. In his report to the Bryce Commission on Secondary Education in 1895 on the Hundreds of Salford and West Derby in Lancashire, Assistant Commissioner F. E. Kitchener made special mention of the 'train boys' of Manchester Grammar School, and illustrated the extent of their daily journeys by an elaborate dot distribution map:[32]

The most remarkable tribute to the efficiency of the Grammar School is the distance from which boys come to school. Wherever I went in the Hundred of Salford, and, indeed, in most of West Derby, I did not fail to recognise by their school caps the Manchester Grammar School boys on their way by rail to and from school.[33]

About one-third of the boys travelled from a radius of six miles or more, while over 30 came from over 20 miles away, including three from Southport, about 40 miles distant. Kitchener thought such travel undesirable on the grounds of time lost for recreation, cost to parents and wear and tear on the boys.[34]

Another problem was the social disintegration of the central areas in which many of the old town schools were placed. Manchester Grammar School, for example, formed an island between the chemical fumes rising from the polluted river Irk and the moral poisons exhaled by the casual street-sellers and prostitutes of Long Millgate. This resulted in a rapid decline in its attractions as a boarding school in the early nineteenth century,[35] from which it was rescued by the coming of the train boys. Westminster School was similarly badly placed among narrow streets and courts, seen by parents as 'no longer a suitable environment for their children'.[36]

The children themselves may well not have been so worried. H. C. Barnard, later Professor of Education at Reading University, wrote thus of his commuting from a north London suburb to University College School, then in Gower Street, via the L.N.W.R. and Euston:

A daily railway journey to and from school may involve a waste of time and energy, but there are compensations and I do not think that I ever found such travelling irksome.

But he also pointed to problems in the walk from Euston to Gower Street:

The neighbourhood of Bloomsbury and the Euston Road had in those days (about 1897) its special dangers for adolescents, and it was by no means unknown for older boys to be solicited in the streets on their way home in the evening.[37]

Girls were seen as specially unsuited to exposure to urban journeys to school. Sadler remarked that the central location of Liverpool Girls' College was a disadvantage, with parents as a rule unwilling 'to expose their daughters to a long tram journey'.[38] Their daughters may have been less inhibited. Thus Molly Hughes, in an autobiographical trilogy about a London family in the school board period, describes her first journey to her 'grand new school', the North London Collegiate:

> I was as proud of my season ticket from Highbury to Camden Town as any girl of later years with her latch key . . . With this talisman in my pocket I was able to pass the booking-office as though I didn't exist, and mutter 'season' in an off-hand manner at the barriers: a taste of life indeed.[39]

Another London girls' school, Notting Hill, illustrates well the impact of social change and urban transport systems on prestigious town grammar schools in the late nineteenth and early twentieth centuries. It was established in Norland Square to serve the populous middle class district around Holland Park, an area with, according to Booth's survey, less than 10% in poverty (Fig. 5.8). By the 1880s the school had forged a good social and academic reputation, and was fed by a series of more or less hand-picked preparatory schools. But it was not too well served by railway stations, and its early intake was mostly from the immediate vicinity of Holland Park, with some from adjacent parts of Shepherd's Bush, Hammersmith and Bayswater. Later groups were drawn from the West End and Bloomsbury. One girl travelled from Great Portland Street, then walked down the hill from Notting Hill Gate station to the school, a considerable journey for one of the younger children. The Latimer Road Station alternative would have been unthinkable, for the final trek to school would have crossed the notorious Notting Dale area (see Chapter 7). Other children alighted at Kensington High Street and Hammersmith stations, to be left with quite lengthy walks to school (Fig. 5.8).

A productive catchment developed in west London, increasing numbers travelling in from Ealing, Chiswick and Acton, utilising the bus services which focused on Shepherd's Bush. Some of these children were later able to use the Central Line from Ealing Broadway to Holland Park. It was the strength of this westward tie and a perception of social descent in the Notting Hill area that led to the school moving out to Ealing in 1931.[40] Many similar schools had made the change long before, and such locational shifts were the stuff of the adjustment of the middle-class day school system to social change.

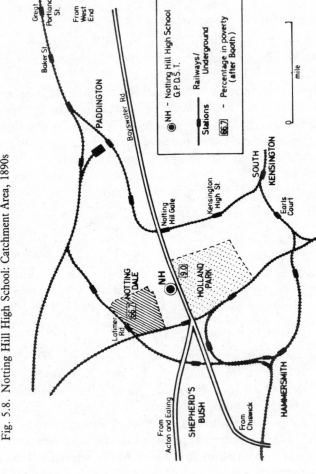

Fig. 5.8. Notting Hill High School: Catchment Area, 1890s

CONCLUSION

In the 27 years between the Taunton and Bryce Commissions, considerable aggregate advance had been made in educational provision for the urban middle classes. But there remained disconcerting variations in access, both geographically and in quality of provision. The problem of the ambiguity of the legislation and the obscure lines of demarcation between elementary and secondary education which emerged was far from resolved. The situation was not helped by the parallel and perhaps inevitable lack of consensus among middle-class groups as to what was wanted. The upper middle classes were by this time well established in the expensive part of the private sector. But the lower middle classes faced multiple choices of whether to send their children to less exclusive, but still protective, private schools; to National, British or Wesleyan schools in the more selective part of the voluntary elementary sector; or to some of the strikingly advanced higher grade or higher elementary schools which progressive urban boards had provided. Here they would mix with children of the respectable working classes in the main, a not entirely alien prospect in a sector in which many families contained both white and blue collar members.

Proponents of the higher grade schools saw them as the model secondary schools of the future, leaving to the endowed schools the strictly limited task of providing a classical education. But the hope of some that the school boards would in the twentieth century be given responsibility for a unified system of popular elementary and secondary education was not realised. Their existence was terminated, and an alternative model chosen, an event which subsequently provoked much discussion of the 'might have beens'. As the sociologist Olive Banks has indicated:

The higher grade schools, in their technical and scientific curricula, as in their close association with the elementary schools, offered a challenge to the traditional grammar school education. Moreover, in their welcome to children of all grades of ability from all social classes, they looked forward to the twentieth-century conception of secondary education for all.[41]

While the detailed evidence does not suggest that Banks was accurate in suggesting that the higher grade schools took children of all grades of ability from all social classes, the general drift of her argument can be accepted. The higher grade schools were socially better balanced, as Table 3 indicates, were based on meritocratic principles, and pointed a way forward to a system that would have been likely to be less exclusive, more connected as between phases, more varied in curriculum, and more vocationally orientated than the model that was to dominate in the century to come.

REFERENCES AND NOTES

1. W. G. Clark, 'General Education and Classical Studies', in *Cambridge Essays 1855* (London, 1855), p. 282.
2. 'Middle and Private Schools', *Saturday Review*, 15 June 1861, p. 610.
3. For an attempt at definition and classification see D. Leinster-Mackay, 'English Proprietary Schools: a Victorian Marriage between Commerce and Education', *Educational Research and Perspectives*, vol. 8 (1981), pp. 44–56.
4. *Taunton Commission*, vol. 4 (1868), pp. 265–6. For further detail of the social make-up of the three divisions of Liverpool Collegiate see J. S. Howson, 'Statistics of the Liverpool Collegiate Institution', *Transactions of the National Association for the Promotion of Social Science*, vol. 2 (1858), p. 242. The standard history of the school is D. Wainwright, *Liverpool Gentlemen* (London, 1960).
5. *Taunton Commission*, vol. 1 (1868), p. 19 and pp. 78–80.
6. *Hansard*, 3rd Series, vol. 194 (1869), col. 1357.
7. *Taunton Commission*, vol. 1 (1868), p. 90.
8. 'Editorial', *Camden and Kentish Towns, Hampstead, Highgate, Holloway and St. Pancreas Gazette*, 7 June 1879.
9. *Taunton Commission*, vol. 7 (1868), p. 305.
10. *First Morant Memorandum* (1897), 'The Higher Grade Schools in England, their Origin, Growth and Present Condition', reproduced in full in E. Eaglesham, *From School Board to Local Authority* (London, 1956), Appendix A, p. 184.
11. *Ibid.*, p. 185. See also A. B. Ellis, *Higher Grade Schools in Bradford before the 1902 Education Act* (Unpublished University of Durham M.Ed. Dissertation, 1965); and Bradford Corporation, *Education in Bradford since 1870* (Bradford, 1970).
12. *Cross Commission*, 2nd Report (1887), p. 739 and pp. 746–7.
13. A. B. Ellis, *op. cit.* (1965), pp. 4–5.
14. *School Board Chronicle*, 24 July 1880.
15. Morant in E. Eaglesham, *op. cit.* (1965), p. 189.
16. *Ibid.*, p. 185.
17. See J. D. Mellor, *The Policy of the School Board for London in Relation to Education in and above Standard V* (Unpublished University of London M.A. Dissertation, 1954), p. 213.
18. S. Webb, 'London Education' (1903), in E. J. T. Brennan (ed.), *Education for National Efficiency: the Contribution of Sydney and Beatrice Webb* (London, 1975), p. 116.
19. For a contemporary account of the Headmaster of Fleet Road School, Mr. W. B. Adams, see *Practical Teacher*, vol. 15 (1894), pp. 1–7.
20. P. Gordon, *Selection for Secondary Education* (London, Woburn Press, 1980), p. 167.
21. *Second Morant Memorandum* (1900), 'The Proposed Minute of the Board of Education establishing Higher Elementary Schools', also reproduced in full in E.

Eaglesham, *op. cit.* (1956), Appendix B, p. 191.
22. *Bryce Commission*, vol. 6 (1895), pp. 224–5.
23. See P. Gordon, *op. cit.* (1980), pp. 85–124.
24. K. Lindsay, *Social Progress and Educational Waste* (London, 1926), pp. 88–9.
25. J. L. Brereton, *County Education* (London, 1874).
26. *Taunton Commission*, vol. 2 (1868), p. 37.
27. *Taunton Commission*, vol. 7 (1868), pp. 240–6.
28. M. E. Sadler, *Report on Secondary and Higher Education in Derbyshire* (Derby, 1905).
29. *Ibid.*, pp. 85–9.
30. See, for example, F. G. Gomez, 'The Endowed Schools Act 1869 – a Middle Class Conspiracy? The South-west Lancashire Evidence', *Journal of Educational Administration and History*, vol. 6 (1974), pp. 9–18.
31. See H. M. Luft, *A History of Merchant Taylors' School, Crosby, 1620–1970* (Liverpool, 1970), pp. 204–8.
32. *Bryce Commission*, vol. 6 (1895), inset at back.
33. *Ibid.*, p. 119.
34. *Ibid.*, p. 120.
35. J. A. Graham and B. Phythian (eds.), *The Manchester Grammar School, 1515–1965* (Manchester, 1965), pp. 28–9.
36. T. W. Bamford, *The Rise of the Public Schools* (London, 1967), pp. 13–14.
37. H. C. Barnard, *Were those the Days? A Victorian Education* (Oxford, 1970), pp. 92–3.
38. M. E. Sadler, *Report on Secondary Education in Liverpool* (London, 1904), p. 53.
39. M. V. Hughes, *A London Family, 1870–1900* (Oxford, 1981 edition), p. 162.
40. J. E. Sayers, *The Fountain Unsealed: a History of Notting Hill and Ealing High School* (London, 1973), pp. 11–16, p. 34, pp. 53–6, pp. 73–4 and p. 148.
41. O. Banks, *Parity and Prestige in English Secondary Education: a Study in Educational Sociology* (London, 1955), p. 29.

CHAPTER SIX

Variations in Local Decision-Making: Comparative Studies of Lancashire Town and Country during the School Board Period

> The position of Manchester compared with Liverpool needs some explanation and suggests some thoughts. It is at first sight disappointing to find a large and influential board behind another of similar importance in results (of attendance) which it would seem to have equal means of attaining. But there is something fairly to be urged in explanation.[1]
> (Reports of the Committee of Council on Education, 1891–2)

The publication in 1973 of Stephens' monograph *Regional Variations in Education during the Industrial Revolution, 1780–1870*[2] was a timely reminder of the need to take account of the historical presence of spatial disparities in educational provision, disparities which were by no means eliminated, though they were reduced, in the 30 years which followed the 1870 Act: the School Board period. The intention here is to explore the disparities which continued to exist in a major industrial county, Lancashire, during this period. Lancashire was in general in its nineteenth-century educational arrangements an atypical county, where the voluntary agencies exerted more than their average share of influence,[3] as discussed in Chapter 2. As late as 1896, with 9% of the inspected elementary schools in England and Wales, Lancashire contained about 30% of Catholic and Wesleyan, nearly 8% of Anglican, but less than 5% of board schools.[4] Lancashire stands out as an area seemingly under-provided with school boards (Fig. 6.1). At the time of the Cross Commission it had only one school board to over 30,000 people, a proportion exceeded only, and for obvious reasons, by London. This was in stark contrast to the pattern in Wales and the south-west, where Nonconformity was strong,[5] and to much of rural southern and eastern England. Over the larger proportion of the country, there was one school board for less than 15,000 of the population.

This does not in itself imply weakness of elementary provision in Lancashire where, as has been noted, voluntary agencies were relatively strong. In addition, areas with a higher proportion of school boards were in many cases rural districts with small, and often inefficient and/or apathetic boards. Fig. 6.2 indicates the proportion of population under school boards to the total population, in which Lancashire comes much higher up the list, because its boards, though few in number, were comparatively large in size.[6] In terms of size, three of the Lancashire boards (Fig. 6.3) had the maximum membership of 15 (for populations over 100,000): these were Liverpool, Manchester and Salford. Blackburn, Bolton and Oldham (populations between 70,000 and 100,000) had 13 members, and Rochdale and Wigan 11. The map does not in fact do full justice to the enormous size continuum that was present. In the 1890s, for example, Liverpool and Manchester had incomes of over £100,000, as compared with £15 for Egton-cum-Newland.

The size factor had important consequences in terms of economies of scale. Many of the smaller boards needed large rate precepts per head of population. Hence the precepts at Shevington were constantly above 6d in the £ for a population of 1,800, to keep going two small board schools which the School Board had not built, merely taken over.[7] Those of Prescot, from the late 1870s, were always 6d and often over 10d (Fig. 6.4). On the other hand, despite the daunting social problems they had to face, Manchester's precepts did not rise much above 5d until the early, and Liverpool's until the late, 1890s. The large city boards possessed the resources to become pacemakers, if they so decided.

An intriguing feature of Fig. 6.3 is the presence of quite large towns which did not have school boards. There would seem no apparent logic behind the variations which existed, whether geographical, demographic, economic, social, religious or political. Of

Fig. 6.1. Ratio of School Boards per head of population, 1885

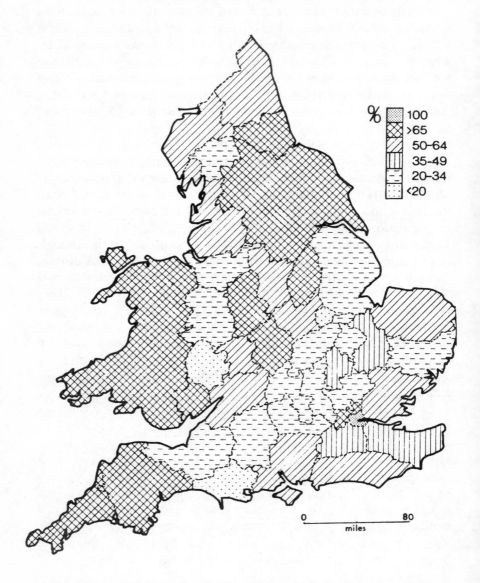

the cotton towns, for example, Blackburn, Bolton, Burnley, Oldham and Rochdale established school boards; Bury and Preston did not. Of other industrial towns, Barrow, Bootle, Salford, Widnes and Wigan formed school boards; St. Helens and Warrington did not. Of the

Fig. 6.2. Proportion of population under School Boards to the total population, 1885

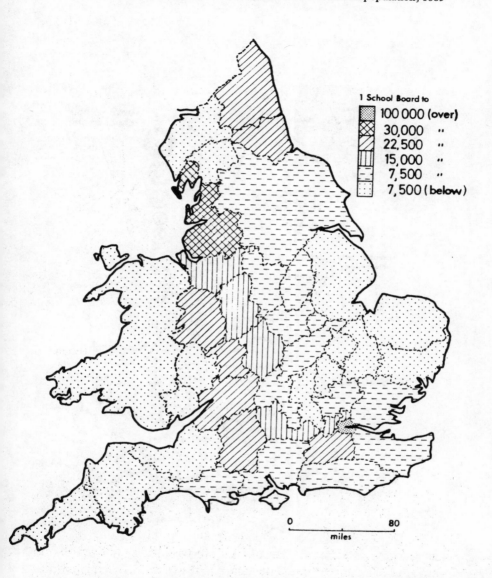

resorts, Morecambe (in the shape of Poulton) and Blackpool (but not until 1899) had school boards; Southport did not. Of strongly Catholic towns, Bootle and Liverpool elected school boards; St. Helens and Preston did not. Of towns whose main population growth

UEP-F

Fig. 6.3. Lancashire School Boards 1870–9

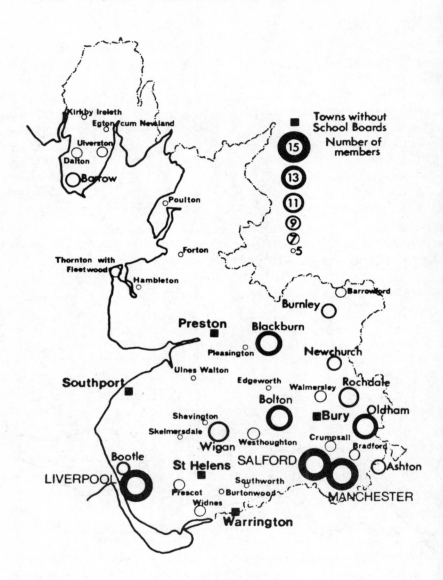

was in the earlier part of the century, and whose voluntary agencies had by 1870 kept up with accommodation needs, Wigan had a school board, but Preston did not. Possible explanations would seem most likely to result from an investigation of the complex of relationships

Fig. 6.4. The burden on the rates of selected Lancashire School Boards

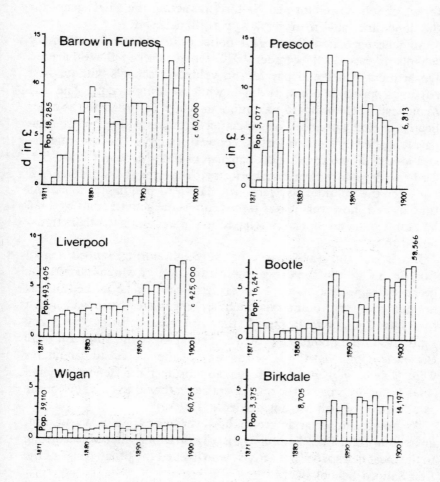

between the energy of voluntary agencies, the size of the problem which had to be faced, and perhaps especially the nature of local power groupings and ideologies, and their judgements as to the best strategy with which to cope with the new legislation.

The behaviour of boards of similar size in not dissimilar socioeconomic situations could thus be quite diverse. Fig. 6.5 illustrates that while Bolton was by 1874 providing relatively large sums of money for building and maintaining elementary schools, the function for which it had been formed, Salford was acting as a relief agency for the denominational managers,[8] as was Manchester.

Manchester School Board gave notice of its support for voluntary schools as early as December 1870, when it asked the Education Department if it could pay fees in voluntary schools without first passing a special bye-law. It did so while awaiting a reply. The first Manchester School Board paid more in school fees than all the other boards of England and Wales together. Dominated by the Anglican party, headed by Herbert Birley, a powerful supporter of voluntaryist and industrial interests, and Chairman of both Manchester and Salford boards, it gave clear initial priority to acting as an 'Education Aid' body for the voluntary system rather than to building schools.[9] As time passed, however, it was forced into some activity, and by 1886 had built sixteen schools, purchased ten more, and had others transferred to it.[10]

But it was the performance of the neighbouring Salford School Board, one of the three biggest in the county, which excited the greatest disapproval. One of the earliest boards to be formed, it was dominated by the voluntaryist interest, represented by seven Church of England and two Roman Catholic members. Birley was a key figure, as in the Manchester Board. The editor of the *Salford Weekly Chronicle* noted that the large majority of the successful candidates were 'solemnly pledged to foster and protect the denominational schools and to prevent the ratepayers being forced to build out of the rates schools which are not needed'.

Among the unsectarian group, however, was William Warburton, an uncompromising 'champion of irreligion in our schools', according to the local newspaper, an activist who livened the proceedings of the first Salford School Board.[11]

As Fig. 6.5 indicated, much of the early expenditure of the Board took the form of paying the fees of children attending voluntary schools. Warburton refused to pay rates for this purpose, and was summonsed. In a speech to the bench he presented an eloquent case:

I appear here today with considerable regret. I come here, not as a martyr, though, possibly, as a victim. No one in Salford is more anxious to promote education, or more willing to pay rates used for legitimate purposes, than myself; but I cannot ... conscientiously pay a rate to support sectarian schools ... Not only are the rates in Salford used for the support of sectarian schools,

Fig. 6.5. Salford and Bolton: School Board Spending, 1874

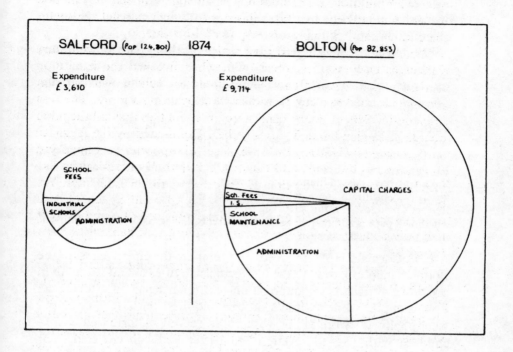

but the majority of the Board persistently refuse to allow a single Board School to be established. The result is that all those inhabitants who belong to denominations not having day schools, and also that very large section of the people not connected with any denomination, are compelled to send their children to the schools of sects with which they conscientiously differ, and are also compelled to pay rates for the support of such schools.[12]

He was regarded by the *School Board Chronicle* as the first martyr under the 1870 Act.[13] Though his furniture was confiscated to pay his fine, Warburton continued to protest, arguing that the fees being paid were not necessarily to children in the poorest districts. It was here that board schools were badly needed.[14] No doubt to the relief of his opponents, Warburton's bankruptcy in 1874 led to his dis-qualification from the Board.[15] He was to reemerge in a similarly active capacity on the Birkdale School Board in the 1880s (Chapter 10).

In this early period, there was some sympathy from the inspectorate for the Salford policy. Thus HMI Brodie, while agreeing that Salford had aroused great controversy over the fees issue, felt the charges 'groundless and unreasonable', explaining the absence of board school building by the presence of sufficient existing voluntary accommodation.[16] The Board was grateful for this support.[17]

The harmony which prevailed on the Salford Board following Warburton's removal, however, appears to have led to stagnation, and from the early 1880s the inspectorate joined the *School Board Chronicle* in a devastating series of attacks.

To the negligent and thriftless Salford offers many inducements. There is a large choice of houses with facilities for frequent change. The standard for full-time exemption is one standard lower than in Manchester, and children of 10 who have passed Standard III may run the streets for half their time, and those who have passed Standard IV for all their time. As the two boroughs are virtually continuous, and, where the Irwell is the boundary, are joined by frequent bridges, it is not surprising that a large proportion of the children, who hawk papers and matches about the streets, live in Salford but do most of their business in Manchester.[18]

F. F. Cornish, HMI, proceeded to compare the effectiveness of the Bolton School Board with the ineffectual activities of Salford, both in providing efficient accommodation and securing good attendance. For example, while Bolton's officers required ten attendances per week, Salford's were happy with eight, merely exhorted parents of children with five to seven to do better and concentrated their attentions on those with less than five. While Salford had less than a third as many half-timers as Bolton, it nevertheless made repeated application to reduce the standard for part-time exemption from III to I, with II as a possible compromise.[19] Cornish returned to the attack in 1885:

When I reported in 1882 the percentages of children on the books in average attendance were, allowing for half-timers, Bolton 82.6, Salford 70.9. This year the quarterly returns gave Bolton 86, Salford 73. Anyone who wished to realise the difference in the results produced need only visit both towns in school hours. He would hardly find a child of school age in the streets of Bolton, whilst in those of Salford they swarm.[20]

In the 1890s, Cornish was again to contrast the 'public spirit and vigour' of Bolton, with the 'persistent improvidence to the wants of the future of Salford'.[21] During this time, the *School Board Chronicle* similarly drew attention to the shortcomings of Salford which, among other things, after the Sandon Act, sought to take advantage of the ambiguities of the Factory and Workshops legislation. A 'reasonable excuse' for non-attendance was 'that the child is employed otherwise to the satisfaction of the board'. This involved the Salford School Board in the late 1870s and early 1880s in complex legal wrangling with the Education Department. The *School Board Chronicle* was predictably upset by Salford's ploys. It pointed out that so long as parents, possibly in good circumstances, saw fit to cause their children to work half-time in the factory, it was counted a reasonable excuse for non-attendance at school. The Board was apparently only concerning itself about the Standard III partial exemption clause for those children whose employment was *not* in factories. The *Chronicle* found the motivation obvious:

It may appear uncharitable to hint that the powerful interest of the employers in factories is at the bottom of this petition from Salford [against Clause 4 of the 1880 Bill], but since it seems impossible to find any other reason for wishing to place factory children in a position different from that of other children, we are driven by force of logic to this explanation.[22]

The *Chronicle* was also inflamed by Salford's attempts to reduce the standard for half-time exemption, so that children passing Standard II could work in and out of factories. Salford was concerned about those children reaching the age of ten after the critical date of 26th August 1880 when the new and more restrictive clause of the 1880 Act came into effect. Before this, on reaching ten, the child could be employed in a factory, whether or not any standard had been passed. This could now no longer happen. The *Chronicle* was convinced that Salford was worried because it had so many children who could not pass Standard III, their existing standard of exemption, and thus qualify for factory life at about the age of ten. 'What have you been doing all these years with the children who are now reaching the age of ten?'[23] The Board was thus reaping the fruits of previously allowing parents to think their children could go to work at ten without any educational qualification. It was understandable that the Education Department was unwilling to lower the age of exemption for half-timers to Standard II for children who after five years at school should have without difficulty been able to pass Standard III.[24] But of course Salford had not been rigorous about attendance.

Cornish supported the arguments against the Board, reinforcing the decision of the Department.

I have met with no one outside the board, either manager or teacher, who did not fully share your Lordships' opinion, and I wish to add my own conviction that any such relaxation as the board advocated would have destroyed one of the most valuable inducements to early and regular attendance that could be devised.[25]

After this reactionary period, however, Salford gradually brought its standard into line with that of other authorities. In 1889 it adopted Standard VI for full exemption, a position Bolton had achieved in 1871. During the 1890s the age of exemption was raised to 12, and standards for partial and total exemption to VI and VII respectively. By 1903, only 91 out of 41,093 on the registers were employed half-time under the Factory Acts, and only 37 were specially exempted by the Board.[26] But the improvement came late. The opportunities offered to children in two nearby cotton manufacturing centres over a period of nearly 20 years were so diverse as to constitute almost differences in kind.

Bolton and Salford were not the only Lancashire towns in which such variations in effort were identifiable. As we have seen (Fig. 6.3), some towns successfully resisted having to establish school boards. Those most able to escape this fate were places which by 1870 had long since experienced their greatest population spurt, and had managed to match supply to demand at a time where the expected standards of provision were lower, and thus the cost less. Preston was a good example. Its largest inter-censal increases were in the first half of the century, peaking at about 50% between 1830 and 1840, as against 0.6%, 9.7% and 8.3% respectively in the decades between 1861 and 1891. The first National and Catholic schools had been built as early as 1814.[27] By 1851, the town had 15 elementary schools: nine National, four Roman Catholic and two Nonconformist; and by 1871, 27, divided 14, six and seven respectively among the religious groups. There was at this time an excess of accommodation over demand in all types of school.[28]

Yet this initial strength was related to longer term weakness. The school stock gradually became obsolete. Preston remained the largest of the nation's towns, with a population of 99,000 in 1891, not to have a school board. The *School Board Chronicle* wrote scathingly of such places as 'much more discreditable and more mischievous' than rural areas not establishing boards.

Take the case, say, of Chester, or Warrington, or Preston, each with its tens of thousands of inhabitants, its flood of daily newspapers, its eager watching of the political events of the world. The education of the children of the people in these places is still entirely in the hands of the sects. Every public elementary school in Preston, in Chester, in York, in Cambridge, in Peterborough, is a Church school, a Wesleyan, a British, or a Roman Catholic school. There is not even the leaven of a single school belonging to the people: the sects have it all their own way. With a certain difference, due to the Reformation, the system is that of the Dark Ages.[29]

While the *Chronicle* had approved the initial burst of activity of Preston's School Attendance Committee, it pointed out that already a generation of school children since 1870 had suffered 'grievous and permanent' injury through lack of enforcement of attendance, producing an ignorant young group who would be unable to move from the town owing to their poorer educational qualifications than those of peers elsewhere.[30]

In 1893, similarly, Cornish commented that the educational spirit of Preston suffered 'from the want of the impulse towards improvement, which in other towns was supplied by a school board'. Worse still, Preston, as a regional centre, instead of taking the lead in educational initiative, was lagging behind, with a consequent deleterious influence on the whole district.[31] In the adjoining Preston 'union' the local HMI had in fact complained in 1885 that the area had forty schools, but employed only one officer, working in tandem as a sanitary inspector. 'No one in authority appears to possess any interest in education, and no serious effort has been made to carry out the law'.[32]

The problem of obsolete accommodation was not confined to Preston. Here and in other towns many schools dated back to the first half, and some to the first quarter, of the century. In Bury, another Lancashire town without a school board, F. A. S. Freeland HMI was in 1891 dismissing some of the old denominational buildings as 'of wretched quality'.[33] Similarly W. H. Brewer had been critical of Blackburn, a town with a school board but relying on its old stock of voluntary schools, for being 'content with doing very little school building' and accepting as adequate buildings which did not compare with those of other towns.[34] It would seem that by this time the opinions of the inspectors had progressed to a stage when they were very ready to make comparisons between voluntary and board sectors to the discredit of the former, a situation different from the early 1870s when Brewer had complimented the Blackburn board for running its operations 'with an economy that commends itself to the ratepayers'.[35]

Though Preston excited the disapproval of the *School Board*

Chronicle, in general it kept a low profile, unlike another Lancashire industrial town, Warrington, whose adequate stock of voluntary schools in 1870 had enabled it thereafter, in the opinion of the
Chronicle, to neglect 'the national duty cast upon it by the legislation
of 1870'.[36] Warrington was seen as particularly culpable on three
counts. On the first, in a place in which, as the *School Guardian* was
quoted as describing, voluntaryism was 'doing a noble work', the
School Attendance Committee was proposing to build a school for
ragged children, 'treated as outcasts by the Voluntaryism of Warrington', in other words, refused entry to denominational schools.[37] In a
deputation to Mundella, the Warrington delegates made it clear that
schools were refusing to admit dirty and ragged children, to which
Mundella replied: 'If any voluntary schools refuse to receive ragged
children I shall at once cut off the grant'.[38]

The second point was of course that the Town Council were asking
Mundella to treat the Attendance Committee, seen by the *Chronicle* as
'faltering and inefficient', a 'mere subservient sub-committee' of 'a
Town Council of a somewhat antediluvian and eccentric type', as a
School Board, able not only to enforce attendance, but in this case to
build a 'special difficulty' type of school, described by the *Chronicle* as
a 'novel and eccentric thesis', though one regarded as quite reasonable
by the Warrington Town Council,[39] a body 'proud of its educational
appliances'.[40]

The third issue was an attempt to reduce the half-time exemption
standard from III to II. The delegation was apparently upset by
its treatment by Mundella. The *Chronicle* made the most of its
embarrassment:

The figure made by Warrington was amusing. We have often had occasion to
comment upon the absurd, the prejudiced and the discreditable position
which the town of Warrington occupies in connection with the great work of
national education, but we did not expect that members of the Warrington
Town Council would be so innocent as to aid their benighted notions and
prejudices before the authorities at Whitehall. Mr. Mundella, as a matter of
course, had a very short answer for the foolish suggestion that power should
be placed in the hands of the Warrington Town Council to build Board
schools. He told them to apply for an order for the election of a School Board,
and he threatened to cut off the grant of any school in Warrington which
refused to take in the poorer class of children.[41]

Some evidence in support of the *Chronicle*'s predictably jaundiced
view of such proceedings came from the Inspectorate. Once again a
distinct change of attitude between the early 1870s and the mid-1880s

is discernible. In 1873, for example, W. S. Coward HMI had spoken well of denominational provision in the Warrington district.[42] The situation in 1885 was less positively regarded, the inspector finding a sprouting of private schools, at a time when they were dying out in other places:

> their presence is accounted for very easily, viz. by the *laissez faire* of the local authorities respecting them, or by the scandalously lax action of the magistrates. The borough of Warrington with 19 adventure schools comes under the former category ... The great majority of these schools I gather to be wholly bad.[43]

A separate group of towns in Lancashire were those which established boards, notwithstanding adequacy of accommodation in 1870. These were manifestly established for strategic purposes, as already noted at Manchester and Salford, and in general kept their rate precepts very low. Thus Blackburn's remained below 2d in the £ until 1891, while those of Wigan (Fig. 6.4) and Ashton-under-Lyme continued below 1½d. Burnley also managed to keep its rates under 1½d until 1890, at which stage demand exceeded supply of accommodation and there was a sharp increase.

Wigan, meanwhile, was attacked by the *School Board Chronicle* for its low standards of exemption, and for taking advantage of the ambiguities of the Factory and Mines and educational legislation.[44] HMI Mr. Phelps found in 1880–1 a very low percentage of children in the Wigan area reaching the upper standards, only 16.7% being examined in Standard IV, 6.4% in V and 1.5% in VI,[45] with the loopholes referred to by the *Chronicle* being taken advantage of. Nearly ten years later, Phelps remained disenchanted with the Wigan district. While the Wigan School Board had raised standards for partial and full exemption to III and V respectively, II and IV were more common in the district in general, the local authorities often 'lukewarm and indifferent about the matter, their principal object being to keep down the rates'. A considerable number of children were still appearing at school for the first time at six, seven or eight years, and sometimes even at nine or ten.[46]

The Burnley Board's ability to avoid having to build schools largely depended on the continuing existence of the half-time system.[47] Its activities were managed, as Hawkes puts it, to the 'mutual advantage' of the cooperating denominational bodies for over twenty years.[48] But the introduction of free places in 1891 caught up with Burnley, and the consequent need to build schools led to a rapid rise in the rate burden.

By contrast, there were a number of Lancashire boards which set about their task more energetically. Widnes, Barrow and of course Bolton came into this category. The level of their rate precepts was testimony to this activity. For much of its existence, Widnes' rates were over 7d in the £. Within a year of its foundation in 1874 it had opened up two temporary schools, and within five years three large board schools. In a town in which the population in ten years had grown from 14,000 to 25,000, it was providing by 1879 43% of the elementary school accommodation.[49] Scott-Coward's view was that the Board had been 'of the greatest benefit to the place', even though he was at the same time praising the voluntaryists of St. Helens, Southport, Warrington and Wigan for their 'local effort and zeal'.[50]

The demographic growth facing Barrow was even more acute. The town's population had risen from 16,000 in 1866 to 35,000 in 1874 and 50,000 by 1883,[51] as a result of the growth of iron mining in the Furness district and shipbuilding in Barrow itself. Though fluctuations in trade made attendance records suspect, the 'energetic and enlightened' school board was seen by HMI Tremenheere as addressing itself 'to its heavy task' with 'zeal', building schools almost without intermission.[52]

The Barrow-in-Furness School Board has hardly enjoyed a moment's respite from building operations since its formation; and little wonder, for besides overtaking heavy arrears, they have had to meet the demands of a population which well-nigh trebled itself.[53]

Although by 1884 it had only 9,000 places for a reported 12,000 child population, two-thirds of these were in board schools.[54] The penalty paid by the ratepayers was quickly apparent. Passing the 5d in the £ mark in 1880, the rate rose to a norm of over 8d in the 1880s and over 10d during the 1890s, with one year above 15d (see Fig. 6.4).

Southport was another town without a school board, but in general kept out of the headlines until the Free Education Act of 1891. This purported to introduce free education, but in the event was another compromise piece of legislation, prompting idiosyncratic responses. It allowed school boards to remit fees without investigating the means of parents, and also demanded sufficient free accommodation in an area for children between three and 15. Failing this, a school board would be necessary. The Act led to new outbreaks of religious confrontation in some places. As it entitled parents to demand free education, Nonconformists in areas of shortage made maximum capital, and encouraged local parents to insist upon their rights.

Sectarian strife reached new heights in Southport, which had for twenty years provided enough accommodation to avoid the need for a school board. The trouble here resulted from the rapid growth of population in a working-class suburb known as High Park (see Fig. 10.1). As early as 1892 the local Trades Council had forwarded a resolution to the Vice-President of the Committee of Council claiming that serious hardship was being caused by voluntary agencies restricting free education to infant schools, and then under conditions suggesting pauperisation.[55] Following the emergence of this problem in the High Park district, local Nonconformists alleged that parents were generally over the town being questioned about their income when applying for free places. A local vicar inflamed the situation by asking parents to pay as to their ability, appealing to Nonconformists not to cripple existing schools by demanding free education and 'claiming a legal right at the expense of their church neighbours'. The Education Department was meantime being inundated by applications from Nonconformist parents for free places.

In January 1897 the Northern Counties Education League issued a pamphlet entitled 'Educational Tyranny in England, as illustrated at Southport', accusing school managers of refusing to grant free places, and local Nonconformist parents of 'selling their rights for a mess of pottage' by allowing their children to attend Catholic schools. It was reported that fifty Protestant children were being educated at a Roman Catholic school in the High Park area, the only alternative being to pay for an education elsewhere. The Church party argued that the Nonconformists were themselves to blame, for closing schools while the Catholics were opening schools. One Anglican spokesman referred to

the shame which I feel when I contemplate the practical outcome of the zeal of the Romanist, and the miserable outcome of the 'zeal' of the Puritan for the education of the children of the rising generation.

Hurst Hollowell, Secretary of the Northern Counties Education League, addressed a mass meeting in the town in the same year, which culminated in the overwhelmingly successful resolution:

That this meeting condemns the policy of the Government in granting vast sums of public money to schools that are sectarian and under clerical or irresponsible control.

Despite the anti-school board feeling which had long characterised the town, Southport's School Attendance Committee surprisingly proposed that a school board be formed to meet the deficiency in High Park, a decision hastily though narrowly averted by the Town Council. But it admitted to a shortage of accommodation in this area, and that Protestant children were being taught in Catholic schools. In 1898 the foundations of a new school, under Church auspices, were laid, which held off the threat of a school board until this finally passed with the 1902 Act.[56]

Another category of school board, adding to the variety of response, was the rural, though clearly not present in Lancashire in similar quantity as in counties such as Norfolk and Devon. Almost by definition, the small rural boards were expensive to operate. Where they had to build a school, albeit a single one and small at that, rates were high, commonly over 5d. At Shevington (Fig. 6.4) the building of a school resulted in rates over 10d for five successive years. Others were intent on keeping their rates down and were formed in order to take over a pre-existing school.

The budget for Egton-cum-Newland in Furness (Fig. 6.4) was round about £15 per annum. Seymour Tremenheere found its members' 'intervention in the educational affairs of mankind ... imperceptible ... the only action I ever knew them to take was to resist the demand for a school at Spark Bridge and to petition ... for their own dissolution'.[57]

An interesting study[58] of differential local responses to national legislation exists in the case of Hambleton, in 1871 a small village of about 350 people across the Wyre estuary from Blackpool (Fig. 6.4). The district inspector visited the area in 1871, estimated that there was a need for 68 places, and found the existing accommodation quite inadequate. The first notice of deficiency was issued in February 1873, but the voluntary agencies showed no disposition to act. Though no permanent educational provision was made at the condemned National School through the 1870s, the final notice from the Education Department arrived as late as May 1877. A School Board was formed with five members, the vicar, a tailor and three farmers. A one-unit school building, with a school room and adjoining classroom and a teacher's house, was opened in March 1880, leading to annual demands on the rates, in an area of only £12,800 rateable value, of

6d and over in the £.[59] Once established, Hambleton Board School came under 'subtle pressure' from the Manchester Diocesan Inspectorate, which culminated in the Creed and probably the whole of the Diocesan syllabus being taught, for Diocesan reports became more and more enthusiastic until 1898, when 'the highest possible mark' was given to the School, which by then was presumably 'Anglican in all but name'.[60]

CONCLUSION

While the Education Department in Whitehall thus undeniably exercised gross supervision over local affairs, the room for manoeuvre which was left was exploited to the full by areas which, reacting to local pressures, were not disposed to cooperate. They fought effective delaying actions before either being forced to form school boards, as at Birkdale (see Chapter 10) or build board schools, as at Bootle (see Chapter 8). While local diversionary tactics, manipulating the statistics, prevaricating over definitions, pleading poverty and special social difficulties, may ultimately not have subverted national aims, to particular groups of children and parents at the time, they may have been 100% influential. The Lancashire towns illustrate a variety of responses of local provision to national legislation in the late nineteenth century. This variety demonstrates the need to deploy a multi-layered framework of study, building on the institutions and actors in the drama, the unfolding and resolution (or heightening) of tensions which made up the interaction between the local, regional and national units. Thus while on the face of it some places had comparable demographic and socio-economic problems, equivalent quality of school board membership, faced similar voluntaryist and ratepayer pressures, and a need to relate to Whitehall, no single one had quite the same mix. And it is the mix which helped to determine the nature and the timing of the decisions that were made. Population pressure caused Barrow, Bootle and Burnley, for example, to decide to build board schools, but Barrow's were started in the 1870s, Bootle's in the 1880s and Burnley's in the 1890s. The composite values of the Salford, Bootle and Birkdale board members were very similar. In none of them was the majority enthusiastic about building board schools. But Bootle did not, like Salford and Birkdale, have a committed *agent provocateur* on its board, such as William Warburton, whose catalytic personality directly or indirectly led to Salford and Birkdale, at different times and for different reasons, attaining some national notoriety. Though such individuals might not have changed national policy, they completely changed the local colour.

While Whitehall provided the same overall parameters for all boards, it was not wholly untuned to local idiosyncracies. It was either inefficiency, overwork, or a spirit of compromise that allowed boards such as Bootle (see Chapter 8) to sail so close to the wind, and even transgress the bounds of legality. At the same time, the Department at critical moments stamped down on the Board's more airy speculations about what it was providing. But it might fairly be concluded that Whitehall had local decision-making under only partial control.

REFERENCES AND NOTES

1. *R.C.C.E.* (1891–2), p. 341.
2. W. B. Stephens, *Regional Variations in Education during the Industrial Revolution 1780–1870: the Task of the Local Historian* (Leeds, 1973).
3. See, for example, M. Sanderson, 'Literacy and Social Mobility in the Industrial Revolution in England', *Past and Present*, 56 (1972), pp. 75–103; E. C. Midwinter, 'The Administration of Public Education in Late Victorian Lancashire', *Northern History*, vol. 4 (1969a), pp. 184–96: also M. Sanderson, 'The National and British School Societies in Lancashire 1803–1830: the Roots of Anglican Supremacy in English Education', in T. G. Cook (ed.), *Local Studies and the History of Education* (London, 1972), pp. 1–36; and M. A. Cruikshank, 'The Anglican Revival and Education: a study of School Expansion in the Cotton Manufacturing Districts of North-West England, 1840–1850', *Northern History*, vol. 15 (1979), pp. 176–90.
4. E. C. Midwinter, 'The Administration of Public Education in Late Victorian Lancashire' (unpublished M.A. Dissertation, University of Liverpool, 1969b), p. 53.
5. See J. D. Gay, *The Geography of Religion in England* (London, 1971), pp. 309–11.
6. *Ibid.*, p. 271. It is tempting to point to the similarities between areas with a low proportion of school boards and Gay's areas with a high index of Church of England attendance.
7. E. C. Midwinter, *op. cit.* (1969b), p. 126.
8. F. Adams, *History of the Elementary School Contest* (London, 1882), p. 255.
9. See D. Bickerstaffe, 'Educational Opportunity and Achievement – the Manchester Area 1833–95' (unpublished University of Durham M.Ed Dissertation, 1968), pp. 232–3.
10. J. Watts, 'Fifteen Years of School Board Work in Manchester', read at Manchester/Statistical Society, 14 April 1886; reprinted in *Journal of Sources in Educational History*, vol. 1, no. 3 (1978), pp. 85–6.
11. See I. R. Cowan, 'School Board Elections and Politics in Salford, 1870–1900', *The Durham Research Review*, vol. 5 (1969), pp. 408–11.

12. *School Board Chronicle*, 10 Feb. 1872, p. 399; see also *School Board Chronicle*, 28 Dec. 1872, p. 207; and 20 Sept. 1873, pp. 276–7.
13. Quoted in I. R. Cowan, 'The Work of the Salford School Board' (unpublished Durham M.Ed. Dissertation, 1965), p. 81.
14. *Ibid.*, pp. 81–5.
15. *Ibid*, p. 90.
16. *R.C.C.E.* (1872–3), p. 55.
17. *School Board Chronicle*, 12 April 1873, p. 204.
18. *R.C.C.E.* (1882–3), p. 293.
19. *Ibid.*, pp. 295–6.
20. *R.C.C.E.* (1885–6), p. 271.
21. *R.C.C.E.* (1893–4), pp. 23–4.
22. See *School Board Chronicle*, 31 July 1880, p. 111.
23. *School Board Chronicle*, 24 Sept. 1881, p. 277.
24. *School Board Chronicle*, 29 Oct. 1881, p. 435.
25. *R.C.C.E.* (1882–3), p. 298.
26. For a fuller account see I. R. Cowan, *op. cit.* (1965), pp. 310–35; see also I. R. Cowan, *op. cit.* (1969), pp. 415–21.
27. For a general account, see W. Baldwin, 'The Development of Elementary Education in Preston from 1815–1902' (unpublished University of Liverpool M.Ed. Dissertation, 1970).
28. P. J. Dixon, 'School Attendance in Preston: some Socio-Economic Influences', in R. Lowe (ed.), *New Approaches to the Study of Popular Education 1851–1902* (History of Education Society Occasional Publication No. 4, 1979), pp. 43–4.
29. *School Board Chronicle*, 6 Sept. 1884, p. 235.
30. *School Board Chronicle*, 8 Sept. 1877, p. 230.
31. *R.C.C.E.* (1833–4), pp. 23–4.
32. *R.C.C.E.* (1885–6), p. 268.
33. *R.C.C.E.* (1891–2), p. 349.
34. *R.C.C.E.* (1887–8), p. 283.
35. *R.C.C.E.* (1874–5), p. 503.
36. *School Board Chronicle*, 8 Sept. 1887, p. 230.
37. *School Board Chronicle*, 17 Jan. 1880, p. 63.
38. *School Board Chronicle*, 24 April 1880, p. 426.
39. *Ibid.*, pp. 425–7.
40. *School Board Chronicle*, 14 Feb. 1880.
41. *School Board Chronicle*, 16 July 1881, p. 39; and 23 July 1881, p. 65.
42. *R.C.C.E.* (1873–4), pp. 88–9.
43. *R.C.C.E.* (1885–6), p. 270.
44. *School Board Chronicle*, 27 April 1878 and 8 June 1878.
45. *R.C.C.E.* (1881–2), pp. 374–5.
46. *R.C.C.E.* (1889–90), p. 301.
47. *R.C.C.E.* (1874–5), p. 195.
48. G. I. Hawkes, *The Development of Public Education in Nelson* (Nelson, 1966), p. 55.
49. J. R. Hunt, 'The Widnes School Board, 1874–1903', *Transactions of the Historic Society of Lancashire and Cheshire*, Vol. 106 (1954), pp. 145–7.
50. *R.C.C.E.* (1877–8), pp. 444–5.
51. J. F. Chadderton, *Barrow Grammar School for Boys, 1880–1960* (Barrow, 1964), pp. 1–2.
52. *R.C.C.E.* (1883–4), p. 413.
53. *R.C.C.E.* (1885–6), pp. 266–7.
54. *R.C.C.E.* (1884–5), p. 534.
55. See H. J. Foster, 'The Influence of Socio-Economic, Spatial and Demographic

Factors on the Development of Schooling in a Nineteenth-Century Lancashire Residential Town' (unpublished University of Liverpool M.Ed. Dissertation, 1976), p. 84.

56. See W. E. Marsden, 'The Development of the Educational Facilities of Southport, 1825–1944' (unpublished M.A. Dissertation, University of Sheffield, 1959), pp. 35–9.

57. *R.C.C.E.* (1883–4), p. 418.

58. W. Bentley, 'A History of Elementary Education in the Fylde area of Lancashire during the Period 1870–1903' (unpublished M.A. Dissertation, University of Liverpool, 1961).

59. *Ibid.*, pp. 68–71.

60. *Ibid.*, pp. 136–7.

PROVISION AT THE GRASSROOTS: EDUCATION IN SLUMS AND SUBURBS

CHAPTER SEVEN

Charles Booth's Surveys and Educational Disparities in Slum and Suburban London

The attendance is poor compared with other Schools; but under the circumstances, fault can scarcely be found with the Teachers.[1]

The order and tone are excellent ... Many of the girls are of a class superior to that usually found in Board Schools.[2]
(London School Board Inspectors' Reports, October 1884 and December 1889)

Among the many impressive aspects of the social surveys of London by Charles Booth and his team was the meticulous identification of great territorial variations in poverty and comfort.[3] Of particular interest to the educational historian is the fact that the units by which the information was classified were London School Board blocks. Fifty of these blocks had ratios of over 55% poverty, and parts of Bermondsey, Southwark, Bethnal Green and South Lambeth rose to over 75%. At the other extreme, about 75% of the people of the School Board Divisions of Marylebone, Chelsea and Westminster were living in comfort.

Even in relatively prosperous areas, there would be individual black spots, with blocks of streets suffering grave hardship. Thus the desperate Notting Dale slum, in which the school mentioned in quotation 1 was located, lay 'cheek-by-jowl' with prosperous North Kensington suburbs, which included the school referred to in quotation 2. Similarly, Marylebone's overall 26% in poverty covered a range of from 13.5% to over 30%. As Fig. 7.1 illustrates, parts of Highgate and Kentish Town contained over 35% in poverty, while in adjacent Belsize Park there was virtually none. Even in affluent Hampstead, pockets of distress could be found in the old and congested village area.

Another of the major achievements of Booth's survey was the probing of urban community life in what were in effect ecological micro-studies. The scale at which these were pursued is best illustrated in the detailed street-by-street maps. In the first edition of *Life and Labour of the People of London* four of these appeared, covering inner areas of the metropolis, while in the Third Series this was extended to suburban areas. A colour-coding scheme was employed, ranging from the black and blues of poverty, through the purple of mixed poverty/comfort and the pink of working class comfort, to the red and yellow of affluence.[4] The detail embodied, together with the revisions of later maps, enabled Booth to interpret closely the ecological, centrifugal forces at work in urban society, impulses from the centre pushing people out into the inner ring, thence to the outer, changing the social maps of the city.

The red and yellow classes are leaving, and the streets which they occupied are becoming pink and pink-barred: whilst the streets which were formerly pink turn to purple, and purple to light blue.[5]

Probably the most neglected aspect of subsequent appraisals of Booth's work has been any consideration of the educational element, which figured so prominently in certain sections of the surveys.[6] One reason for this was no doubt the use of School Board visitors to collect the data:

Most of the visitors have been working in the same district for several years . . . They are in daily contact with the people, and have a very considerable knowledge of the parents of the school children, especially of the poorest among them, and of the conditions under which they live.[7]

The information acquired made possible the consideration of educational provision at two levels: the metropolitan level, and the detailed community level.

VARIATIONS AT THE METROPOLITAN LEVEL

Variations at this level can best be examined by taking the major School Board divisions, marked on Fig. 7.2, which illustrates the crisis facing the London School Board in 1871. Only the City and Westminster came anywhere near to matching supply with demand.

Fig.   7.1. North   Marylebone: Ratios   of   Poverty   in   School   Board
       Blocks, 1887–1889

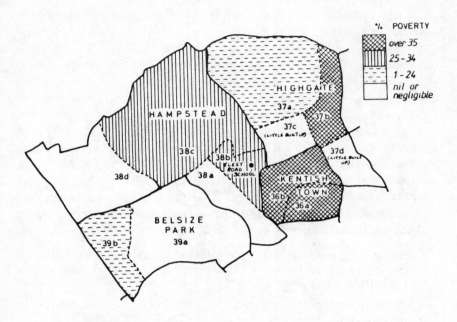

Marylebone and Chelsea just about met the needs of junior boys.
Provision for girls was in most cases less than adequate, and that for
infants critically short. Fifteen years later, the compensatory provision of the Board had improved the situation in areas such as Tower
Hamlets, Southwark, Hackney, Lambeth and Greenwich.

The responsibility of the Board was relatively small in the well-
endowed Cities of London and Westminster, while the voluntary
resources of north-west London lessened the demands made on the
Board in these areas also. The 'filling in the gaps' principle can thus be
redefined in considerable part in terms of the resolution of spatial
inequalities.

Within Booth's broad poverty–comfort classification was a series of
sub-categories. This included people in distress (Category A); in
chronic want (B); and those who were poor because of 'intermittent'
or 'small regular' earnings (C or D). A and B, about 8.4% of the
population of London, formed the 'residuum'. While not chronically

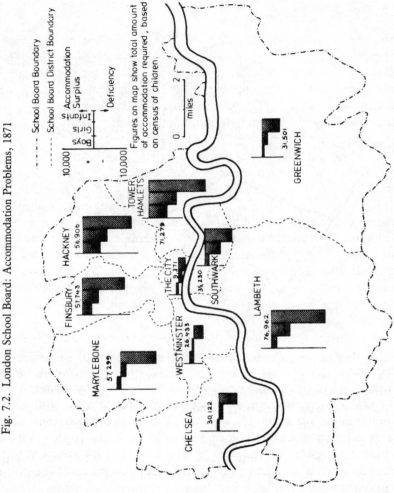

Fig. 7.2. London School Board: Accommodation Problems, 1871

'in want', the lives of the C and D groups comprised 'an unending struggle'.[8] Categories E and F were consistently above the poverty line, and existed in 'working class comfort'. F formed the labour aristocracy. Category G was essentially the lower middle class of shop-keepers, clerks and small employers, while H constituted the true middle class: the servant-keeping class.[9]

This social classification was translated by Booth and his team into a graded hierarchy of elementary schools, assessed according to the proportion of children they contained in each of the social groups. There were thus in the elementary sector six classes of school, whether board or voluntary. They were collapsed into three grades, a lower, a middle and an upper, as shown in Table 1.

TABLE 1

	Characteristics	*Grades of Elementary*
I.	Accommodating the 'poor' and 'very poor', with a sprinkling of the lowest semi-criminal class.	
II.	Accommodating the 'poor' with but a slight mixture of 'very poor'.	*Lower*
III.	Accommodating the 'poor' and comfortably off together.	
IV.	Accommodating the comfortably off with but few 'poor'.	*Middle*
V.	Accommodating the comfortably off and some fairly well-to-do.	
VI.	Accommodating those who are fairly well-to-do only.	*Upper*

Having classified the schools numerically in a series of tables,[10] Booth and his team described the situations of different types of school, and especially those in the lower categories, more fully. His assistant, Mary Tabor, was appreciative of the work of the *upper grade* schools, 'planted where the better trades abound', and largely taking children of social groups E and F.

The great bulk of the children are wholesome, bright-looking, well-fed, well-clad, eager for notice, 'smart', and full of life. 'Smartness' is much cultivated in schools of this class, and the superiority in nervous power is often very noticeable as compared with those of the lower grades.[11]

Middle grade schools took between 26% and 37% of children from groups E and F, only a sprinkling from A, about 10% from B, and the great majority from C and D. A key factor in the success or otherwise of this grade of school was seen to be the quality of the head-teacher. Under good leadership, a middle grade school would show as many open intelligent faces among the boys, as much refinement and decision among the girls, as one of quite the upper grade that has been managed by a mere mechanical driver for 'results'.

Critical was the knowledge of childrens' homes, and the capacity to win the confidence of parents. Where this happened such schools, generally in mixed neighbourhoods, were seen by Tabor as civilising agencies 'of the highest kind'.[12]

The *lower grade*, and particularly the Class 1 schools (Table 1) provoked more detailed attention. These included the *schools of special difficulty*, such as Orange Street in Southwark (Plate 1). There were twenty-two such schools at the time of Booth's survey, taking about 21,000 children. They had been established by the London School Board in 1884. Criteria for designating special difficulty schools were 1d fees; few children in attendance over school exemption age; a transitory school population; and parents of children of such a character as to impose special difficulties on the teachers.[13] In these schools head-teachers were paid £20 and assistants £10 per annum extra.

The type locale was

usually on the skirts, or standing in the midst of a crowded, low insanitary neighbourhood. The main streets, narrow at best, branch off into others narrower still; and these again into a labyrinth of blind alleys, courts and lanes; all dirty, foul-smelling, and littered with garbage and refuse of every kind. The houses are old, damp and dilapidated ... Few families in the neighbourhood occupy more than a couple of rooms.

The children spent as little time as possible at home.

Their waking hours are divided between school and the streets. Bedtime is when the public houses close. The hours before that are the liveliest of all the twenty-four, and they swarm about undisturbed till then. They have no regular meal times.[14]

Tabor found a certain variety in the slum schools, with children from 'fully half the homes ... decent in their way. A few of the children were clean and tidy, and even wore collars, but most were ... ragged, ill-kept and squalid in appearance ... filthily dirty ... sickly looking, with sore eyes and unwholesome aspect'.[15] A small minority stayed on above Standards III and IV, but generally no more than 6% of the intake, and in some schools only 2 to 3%. In the very worst schools, there was no leaven at all.

The slum look is everywhere. It penetrates like a slimy fog into the school itself. 'Slum-born' seems written on the faces of the children, hardly one of whom impresses us as well up to the average ... We see numbers of half-imbecile children throughout the school; big boys in low standards who cannot learn, try as they may; children of drinking parents chiefly ... Two-thirds of them have their fees remitted. About the same number have free meals as often as the funds allow. A full fourth of the children on the rolls are seldom seen at school ... These irregular children add enormously to the labour of the teacher. Sometimes a boy is running wild for weeks together. When he returns he must be coached somehow to the level of the others. If this is not done the school is discredited ... the Government grant ... lost. They, or their parents for them, present to the baffled officer ... a front sometimes of sturdy defiance, more frequently of masterly inactivity or infinite evasiveness.[16]

VARIATIONS IN LONDON SLUMS AND SUBURBS

As previously indicated, a uniquely useful feature of Booth's surveys so far as the urban historian is concerned is the opportunity they offer for establishing links between particular schools or groups of schools and the neighbourhoods they served. Methodologically, connections can be established between the social analyses of Booth and contemporary school records, such as admissions registers and log books.

A case in point is the St. George's-in-the-East area of the East End of London (Fig. 7.3). In his report to the Newcastle Commission Josiah Wilkinson reported St. George's as an area of deteriorating character, and quoted the Medical Officer of Health describing its people as 'cowed in mind and exhausted in body'.[17] Twenty-five years later, Booth found no improvement.

Of all the districts of that 'inner ring' which surrounds the City, St. George's-in-the-East is the most desolate. The other districts each have some charm or other – a brightness not extinguished by, and even appertaining to, poverty and toil, to vice, and even to crime ... a rush of human life as fascinating to watch as the current of a river to which life is so often likened. But there is nothing of this in St. George's, which appears to stagnate with a squalor peculiar to itself.[18]

Of all the districts of London, St. George's was worst in terms of poverty, domestic crowding, death rate per thousand, and on a combined position based on all the variables of social difficulty considered by Booth, on the basis of information in the 1891 census. As an example of extremes, St. George's could only be compared with Hampstead, at the other end of the scale, last in five of the six indices of difficulty.[19]

Fig. 7.3. St. George's-in-the-East, 1890s: Selected Catchment Zones and Social Area
Differentiation (after Booth)

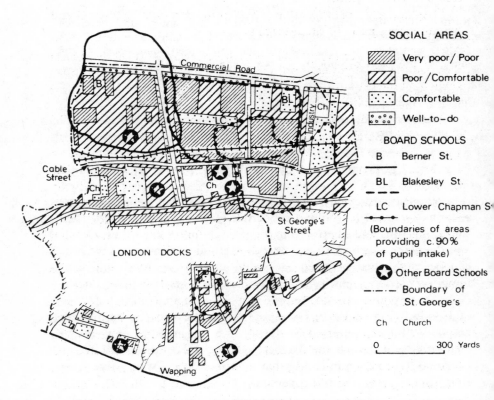

One concern peculiar to Whitechapel and adjacent parts of St.
George's was the influx of European Jews at this time, which Booth
saw as an important cause of over-crowding.

The German Jew is coming into St. George's in large and increasing numbers.
They can live under conditions and so close together as to put to shame the
ordinary overcrowding of the English casual labourer ... There were at one
time only Irish colonies in St. George's but these are slowly giving way before
the German Jew who occupies their quarters and supplants them in other
ways.[20]

The influence of this almost unique example, aside from the Irish,
of significant foreign immigration, was seen by Booth's secretaries
as mixed, in that although the Jews contributed to appalling over-
crowding, they presented a 'favourable contrast to the promiscuity

of many of the English poor', and could be seen 'as cleaners or scavengers of districts of Irish poor'. But in better districts they were said to hasten decline.[21]

They had a major impact on school provision in Whitechapel and neighbouring parts of St. George's:

I can remember when even at Chicksand Street school [in Whitechapel] less than half the children were Jewish and now there are hardly any Christian children in the place. Bink's Row, Rutland Street, Lower Chapman Street [Fig. 7.3] and Betts Street schools are all now Jewish or being Judaized.[22]

At the time of the formation of the London School Board, St. George's-in-the-East was a classic area of educational under-provision. Fig. 7.2 demonstrated the inadequacies of accommodation available for boys, girls and especially for infants in the Tower Hamlets division of which St. George's was a part. The situation was gradually improved by the Board's energetic school building programme, and by the time of Booth's survey St. George's had been provided with large board schools, accommodating over 1,000 children in each, such as Berner Street and Lower Chapman Street.

Fig. 7.3, showing board schools only, illustrates how thick on the ground schools had to be to service so densely packed an area. By the end of the school board era, apart from the three board schools whose catchments are shown on the map, there were also Betts Street, Cable Street, Christian Street, the 'Highway' (a 'school of special diffi-culty' in St. George's Street) and, in Wapping, Brewhouse Lane and Globe Street. With the exception of that of Lower Chapman Street, fractured as it was at this time by the presence of London Docks, the catchment areas were very compact. Blakesley Street appears to have catered for the most concentrated area of serious poverty, to the south of Commercial Road, though the 'Highway', for which the appro-priate information is not available, would no doubt have been worse.

The relatively homogeneous social nature of the area does not appear to have generated a clear-cut hierarchy of elementary schools based on differentiated fees, as described in Chapter 4. In 1877, for example, the two board schools then in existence in St. George's, Berner Street and Lower Chapman Street, had fees of 1d and 1d or 2d respectively. Of all the board schools of St. George's only Cable Street, small for a board school with accommodation for 400 only, attained higher grade status. They were conspicuous by their absence in the lists of successful London scholarship schools (Chapter 5).

The Sultan Street area of Camberwell[23] was a more confined slum area but one which stood out like a sore thumb in the context of more respectable working-class areas which surrounded it. In sharp social decline in the second half of the century, the influence of the slum eroded the reputable status of surrounding areas. In Sultan Street, the mean figure of persons per house rose from nine in 1871 to fifteen in 1881.[24] The district was picked out in Booth's notebooks as one of London's blackest slums (Fig. 7.4):

West of the Camberwell Road is a black patch of poverty and drunkenness. Here there are many Irish and costermongers and the houses are very dilapidated and in bad repair ... The children sleep upon the floor and the place is infested with rats. Streethawkers and costermongers live in these streets which have a very bad character. The rest of the population is com-

Fig. 7.4. Camberwell: Social Change and Catchment Areas in the late nineteenth Century

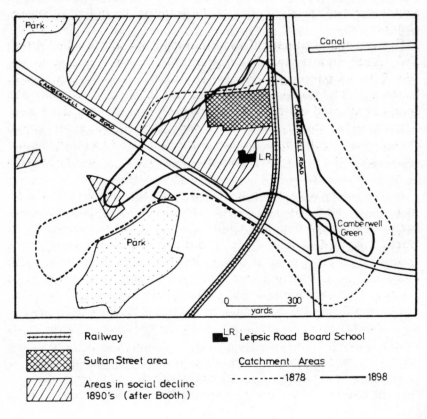

posed of a very poor and miserable class ... who are just on the brink of pauperism ... In the two-storied houses two families generally live, but there is a good deal of sub-letting, and some overcrowding in the poorer streets.[25]

The school chiefly responsible for the non-Catholic children of this district was Leipsic Road board school (Plate 4). The social decay of the area is faithfully reflected in its intake. Of the boys' entry in 1879, roughly 60% came from homes in streets later marked as of working-class comfort, 10% from mixed areas of comfort and poverty, and 30% from poor. Almost all of this last group lived in the Sultan Street district. By 1898, however, on the basis of the later social area maps in the 3rd series of Booth's survey, less than 20% came from 'comfortable' areas, 33% from mixed and almost 50% from poor areas. Fig. 7.4 illustrates the particular areas which Booth showed had declined.

The slight attenuation in the school's catchment area between the two dates is perhaps symptomatic of the fact that the school was losing some of the children from the more salubrious neighbourhoods to the south-west and the south-east as the result of the influx of poorer children.

Even more dramatic social disparities stood out between the Notting Dale area[26] and surrounding suburbs of North Kensington (see Fig. 5.8), its poverty of 'as deep and dark a type as anywhere in London'.[27] The board school serving it, St. Clement's Road, was seriously affected by the poverty, over 70%, in its immediate area. The school fee was 1d, half the fees were remitted and, at the time of Booth's survey, 500 children received free meals. As with the Sultan Street area, the vicious reputation of Notting Dale affected streets around, which gradually slid down the social scale.

It also distorted the catchments of surrounding board schools. The map of the intake of two board schools (Fig. 7.5) is particularly interesting. Large numbers of the children of St. Clement's Road Board School, a 'school of special difficulty', were drawn from the slum, and others from poor though less notorious areas to the north and north-west. Its catchment broke off abruptly at the well-to-do Ladbroke estate to the east, and Holland Park to the south. No other school was happy to take children from the Notting Dale 'special area'. Notice how the catchment of nearby Saunders Grove school neatly skirts the area, its own intake coming predominantly from somewhat more respectable working-class streets surrounding it.

Similarly, the vicar of St. Clement's church pointed out to Booth that the children attending his own National school were not of the

Fig. 7.5. North Kensington 1892: Pupil Intake by Area of two Board Schools

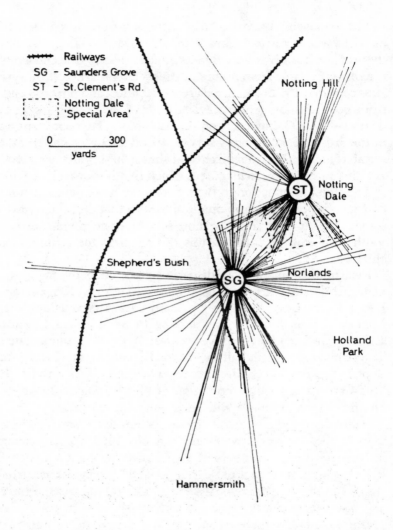

lowest class, and that his parents did not wish their children to mix with those of the Notting Dale area.[28] Just to the north, in a middle-class fringe area (Plate 2), the Oxford Gardens Board School, built in 1884, was shielded by fees of sixpence, and later of ninepence, per week, local tradesmen having petitioned that such fees should be charged to keep the school select.[29]

The extreme range in the socio-economic spectrum of London was, in Booth's estimation, exemplified by St. George's-in-the-East and Hampstead. St. George's topped all but one of Booth's indices of poverty, while 'in Hampstead, happy Hampstead, there is neither poverty nor crowding, or at least much less than anywhere else in London'. As Booth remarked, in these two districts 'we have our alpha and omega'.[30] Notwithstanding pockets of poverty in old Hampstead village, most of the area was prosperous. The inhabitants of districts 38c and 39a (Fig. 7.1) discerned no need whatsoever for board schools and successfully resisted attempts to introduce them until the very last years of the London School Board.

Of particular interest, however, is the transition zone between Hampstead proper and Kentish Town, marked by 38b. In this block the London School Board built Fleet Road School in 1879. Fleet Road was appropriate territory for the construction of a board school. It was at the end of a tram route. Trams were the low status form of transport at the time and had been excluded from Hampstead proper.[31] It was the site of a smallpox hospital. Close to the working-class housing of Kentish Town, creeping north-west and threatening the slopes of Hampstead itself, Fleet Road, described by Besant as 'this dreary street',[32] represented very much the 'fag-end' of Hampstead. The intention was that the school should cater for the escalating population of West Kentish Town and Gospel Oak.

This was a socio-economically mixed urban zone, as Booth described:

Many find employment in the railways and in Brinsmead's and other piano makers ... Wives of working-class work in the laundries round about. Not much distress but majority live from hand to mouth ... some shopkeepers, mixed with labourers, some of the latter in struggling poverty.

In the immediate neighbourhood of Fleet Road, Booth referred to 'modern roads containing decent artisans and their families',[33] an area with nearly three-quarters of the population living 'in comfort'.

In the seven years between the opening of the school, and the sittings of the Cross Commission on Elementary Education, the Headmaster, Mr. W. B. Adams, had established Fleet Road as one of the most celebrated board schools in London. In the evidence he gave to the Commission, he insisted that his catchment area was not especially privileged:

The population is a very mixed one; we have the children of bricklayers and labourers: a considerable sprinkling of the parents of the children are employed on the Midland and North-western Railways. The great industry of the neighbourhood is pianoforte making ... and a great number of the parents of the children are employed there. Then we have a new neighbourhood springing up of small villas, which are occupied by people engaged in city warehouses, and so on.[34]

It would seem that Mr. Adams spotted the potential in this 'new neighbourhood' from an early stage. Just to the north of the school, on the fringes of blocks 38b and 38c (Fig. 7.1), this was essentially a lower-middle-class area. The esteem of the school was quickly established by expert public relations. The successes of the school in the London School Board scholarship stakes and choral competitions were given maximum publicity through prize days and school concerts, to which influential educational and political figures were invited, and through entries in the local press. Competition for places at the school became intense, as the catchment area was pivoted towards Hampstead proper, and more and more children were entered from other parts of London, making use of the railways which focused on Gospel Oak for daily transport. Unlike the situation in other areas, where board school head-teachers complained of voluntary schools foisting on them difficult children, the opposite seems to have occurred in the case of Fleet Road.

CONCLUSION

Booth's surveys are thus an invaluable basis for tracing the links between territorial segregation of differentiated social groups and the related educational provision in London in a situation in which, as we have seen also in Chapter 4, the wide range of fees that could be applied made possible a close adjustment of the school system to the social pretensions of the area it served. On what amounts to a regional scale, they are a mine of information on the range of variations in poverty and comfort across the metropolis, to which a useful general classification of schools was attached. At the same time, they sensitise the social historian to the problem of scale: the existence of minute street by street variations within the broader groupings, which can form the basis of detailed ecological case studies of relationships between schools and their communities.

On the fringes of the 'Hampstead of the villas', Fleet Road School provides a vintage case study of the interpenetration of residential and school choice, in the peopling of an area closely associated with the 'great age' of three major social developments: railways, domestic music and popular education. Parents who worked as engine drivers and stationmasters, skilled piano craftsmen, and as clerks travelling by the North London line to offices in the city, were at one with the aspirations of a headmaster who made Fleet Road the best-known, if not the best, of the London board schools.[35] It was a school at the cutting edge of the rise of the meritocracy, an attack on privilege of the kind which Galton had anticipated would be beneficial in improving the character of the population:

where incomes were chiefly derived from professional sources and not much through inheritance; where every lad had a chance of showing his abilities, and, if highly gifted, was enabled to achieve a first-class education and entrance into professional life, by the liberal help of the exhibitions and scholarships he had obtained in his early youth.[36]

REFERENCES AND NOTES

1. *GLRO*, SBL 1590, Board Inspector's Report, Oct. 1884, St. Clement's Road School, North Kensington.
2. *GLRO*, SBL 1596, Government Inspector's Report, Dec. 1889, Oxford Gardens School, North Kensington.
3. See particularly C. Booth (ed.), *Labour and Life of the People, Vol. I: East London; Vol. II: London continued* (London 1891), the Appendix to Vol. II containing detailed tables and maps.
4. Some of the Booth maps have been reprinted. See D. A. Reeder, *Charles Booth's Descriptive Map of London Poverty 1889* (London Topographical Society, 1984), which provides an introduction.
5. C. Booth (ed.), *Life and Labour of the People in London, Third Series: Religious Influences*, Vol. 5 (London, 1902), p. 194.
6. See C. Booth (ed.), Vol. II, *op. cit.* (1891), pp. 477–588.
7. C. Booth (ed.), Vol. I, *op. cit.* (1891), p. 5.
8. *Ibid.*, p. 131.
9. *Ibid.*, p. 60.
10. See M. C. Tabor, 'Elementary Education', in C. Booth (ed.), Vol. II, *op. cit.* (1891), pp. 515–26; also pp. 478–85 in that volume.
11. *Ibid.*, pp. 507–8.
12. *Ibid.*, pp. 504–5.
13. See T. Gautrey, 'Lux Mihi Laus': School Board Memories (London, 1937), pp. 93–4.
14. M. C. Tabor, *op. cit.* (1891), pp. 491–2.
15. *Ibid.*, p. 497.
16. *Ibid.*, pp. 500–2.
17. *Newcastle Commission*, Vol. 3 (1861), pp. 323–4.
18. C. Booth (ed.), Vol. I. *op. cit.* (1891), p. 66.
19. C. Booth, 'Life and Labour of the People in London: First Results of an Inquiry

based on the 1891 Census', *Journal of the Royal Statistical Society*, vol. 56 (1893), pp. 557–96.
20. In *Notebooks* (Booth Collection, London School of Economics), Group B, vol. 333, p. 3.
21. In *Reports by Secretaries* (Booth Collection), A39, pp. 8–9.
22. *Ibid.*, p. 6.
23. See C. Booth (ed.), Vol. 6, *op. cit.* (1902), pp. 15–20.
24. See H. J. Dyos, *Victorian Suburb* (Leicester, 1961), p. 112; also H. J. Dyos and D. A. Reeder, 'Slums and Suburbs', in H. J. Dyos and M. Wolff (eds.), *The Victorian City: Images and Realities*, Vol. 1 (London, 1973), pp. 373–6.
25. In *Notebooks* (Booth Collection), Group B, vol. 317, p. 19.
26. For a fuller account of the Notting Dale area see W. E. Marsden, 'Residential Segregation and the Hierarchy of Elementary Schooling from Charles Booth's London Surveys', *The London Journal* (1986).
27. C. Booth (ed.), Vol. II, *op. cit.* (1891), pp. 419–20.
28. In *Parish Notes* (Booth Collection), Group A, vol. 43, p. 26.
29. See L. C. B. Seaman, *Life in Victorian London* (London, 1973), p. 117.
30. C. Booth, *op. cit.* (1893), pp. 569–74.
31. See F. M. L. Thompson, *Hampstead: Building a Borough 1650–1964* (London, 1974).
32. Sir W. Besant, *London North of the Thames* (London, 1911), p. 386.
33. C. Booth (ed.), Vol. II, *op. cit.* (1891), Appendix, pp. 15–16.
34. *Cross Commission*, 2nd Report (1887), p. 45.
35. The writer is engaged on a full-scale ecological study of this 'flagship' of the London School Board.
36. Quoted in G. Jones, *Social Darwinism and English Thought: the Interaction between Biological and Social Theory* (Brighton, 1980), p. 36.

CHAPTER EIGHT

Bootle in the School Board Period: School Supply, Status, and Achievement

Not only in the construction of the docks, but in the
carrying on of the work which their existence has
created, a large amount of unskilled labour has from time
to time been attracted to the Borough, with the
consequence that the character of the district has been
completely changed, and its people have become strictly
urban ... The casual nature of the employment ... tends
to encourage habits of idleness and its concomitants.[1]
(Bootle School Board Triennial Report, 1888)

POPULATION AND URBAN GROWTH

During the third quarter of the nineteenth century Bootle became
an integral part, geographically if not administratively, of the growing Merseyside conurbation. In addition to the original agricultural
village, set back from the river, a separate resort and residential area
developed along the Mersey shore in the first half of the century. The
northward encroachment of Liverpool's dockland reached the Bootle
boundary in mid-century. The resort and residential functions were
displaced northwards, to be replaced in Bootle by a marked intensifi-
cation of land use, dominated by warehouses, factories and railway
sidings, interspersed with working-class terraced housing. The population grew steadily in the first half of the century and thereafter very
rapidly.

The town was roughly divided, both physically and socially, by the
Leeds and Liverpool Canal and the Liverpool–Southport railway line.
A middle class enclave grew on the inland side of the railway, its axis
running along Merton Road and into Breeze Hill (Figs. 8.1 and 9.3b).

TABLE 1

POPULATION GROWTH OF BOOTLE, 1801–1901

1801	500	1871	16,200
1841	2,000	1881	27,400
1851	4,000	1891	49,200
1861	6,400	1901	58,600

By contrast, a sea of working-class dwellings dominated the urban landscape between the canal and the docks, forming the most disadvantaged social area of the town, to be considered in the next chapter. Working-class zones later spread east of the railway (Fig. 9.3a) and northwards to the Seaforth boundary (Fig. 8.1).

The rate of population growth and the changing social nature of the population profoundly agitated those charged with the responsibility of providing school accommodation and regulating attendance for enlarged numbers and a new breed of children. Table 2 indicates that the proportion of Bootle's child population to the total remained fairly constant over the 1851–71 period. The 3–15 group formed about 27–28% of the total and the 5–13 about 20%. Even if the smaller percentage is chosen, however, it suggested that one in five rather than one in six was in need of school accommodation, an embarrassing prospect for the agencies of provision, whether the churches or the School Board. Information collected locally at the time of the formation of the School Board confirmed the extent of the problem. Taking the child population itself, the figures of 'scholars' in the occupational returns reveal a steady growth from 45.4% to 56.9% in 1871 for the 3–15 population, or from 51.5% to 68.1% for the 5–13 population, the more realistic figure.

TABLE 1

BOOTLE: CHANGING CHILD POPULATION, 1851–1871

	Total Population	Children 3–15	% Scholars	Children 5–13	% Scholars	% Children in Population	
						3–15	5–13
1851	4,106	1,149	45.5	823	51.5	27.9	20.0
1861	6,414	1,759	53.8	1,235	63.0	27.4	19.3
1871	16,203	4,691	56.9	3,271	68.1	28.9	20.2

Fig. 8.1. Bootle: Nineteenth-Century Urban Growth and School Provision

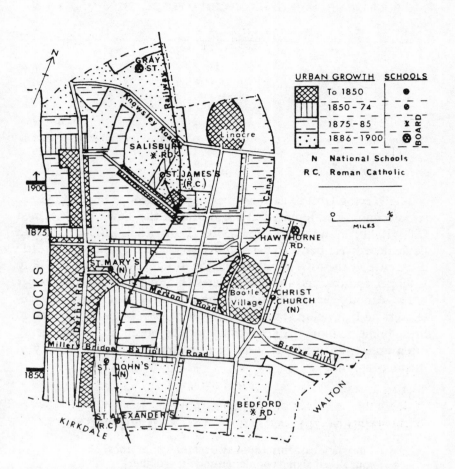

Table 3 shows the changing socio-economic grouping (SEG) of the child population of Bootle between 1851 and 1871. It is based on a well-known though controversial categorisation by Armstrong, in which I and II are the professional groups, III covers clerical and shopkeeping groups and skilled manual workers, and IV and V semi-skilled and unskilled manual workers respectively.[2] Here category III is split into non-manual (A) and skilled manual (B) employees. The 'child population' is that in Mann's school age range at the three dates. The socio-economic categories here of course relate to the parents or guardians of the children.

TABLE 3

BOOTLE: CHANGING SEG OF CHILD POPULATION, 1851–1871

	I	II	IIIA	IIIB	IV	V
1851	10.5	21.1	7.5	23.8	11.7	25.4
	31.6		31.3		37.1	
1861	8.7	17.7	10.1	27.5	12.7	23.3
	26.4		37.6		36.0	
1871	3.2	11.7	12.3	24.6	20.2	28.0
	14.9		36.9		48.2	

The varying level of earnings between the groups highlighted the socio-economic differential. Thus in Bootle the Town Clerk earned £800–1000 per annum, while in SEG II salaries of £200–£400 could be achieved. As between IIIA and IIIB there may have been little difference in the total amount, but the former had salaries of £40 to £100 per annum, and the latter wages from perhaps 35/- to 55/- per week. Among the dock-workers the labouring elite, such as coal-heavers and stevedores, might earn 35/- to 40/-, but were reputed to bring home no more than the casual dock labourers and 'scavengers', often on less than £1 per week, and suffering from irregularity of earnings as well.[3]

SCHOOL SUPPLY:
THE BOOTLE SCHOOL BOARD AND WHITEHALL

> The whole case turns upon two sets of figures, those of your Board giving population and those of the Department giving present school accommodation. Unless your board can point out a flaw in either set of figures they may surely accept the conclusion drawn from them, that there is a grave deficiency of school accommodation which they should at once proceed to supply.[4]

Prior to the period of rapid urban growth which followed dockland extension into Bootle, the borough was served by one inspected public elementary school, St. Mary's. This was followed in the 1860s by St. John's and Christ Church for the Anglican sector, and St. Alexander's and St. James's for the important Catholic element (Figs. 8.1 and 9.3a). Even this increased voluntary provision was far from sufficient. The Bootle School Board, however, one of the first to be formed, soon demonstrated its intention to give priority to protecting the rate-payers. A consequence was a number of skirmishes with the Education Department over problems of school supply, the most intense taking place in the 1880s.

In the early 1870s a preliminary exchange occurred, ending with honours not far from even, the Education Department having fired warning shots across the bows, the Bootle School Board having bought time, helped by the provision of voluntary accommodation in the late 1860s and supplemented by timely extensions in the 1870s (Table 4). As we have seen, a critical issue related to the theoretical one-sixth figure requiring schooling, based on Mann's calculation in the 1851 Education Census. In Bootle, however, the census of 1871 showed 3,820 children aged 3–13, more even than a one-fifth index (Table 3). The impact of the youthful age structure of the borough (Fig. 3.1) and accelerating population and urban growth (Fig. 8.1) on educational provision seems at this stage not to have been fully appreciated.

TABLE 4

GROWTH OF SCHOOL POPULATION AND ACCOMMODATION
IN BOOTLE

Year	Total popn.	One-fifth	One-sixth	No. of* Schools	On Rolls	Average Attendance	Accomm.
1861	6,400	1,280	1,065	2V	–	–	–
1871	16,000	3,200	2,700	5V	2,528	1,174	2,274
1881	27,000	5,400	4,500	5V	4,532	2,841	4,053
1887	45,000	9,000	7,500	5V/2B	7,508	6,009	7,615
1895	52,000	10,400	8,650	5V/3B	9,382	8,092	10,100
1901	58,000	11,600	9,650	5V/4B	**10,708	9,221	10,759

*	Public Elementary Schools only.
**	Figures for one month only.
V	Voluntary
B	Board

Between 1881 and 1885, the most rapid population surge in Bootle's history occurred, numbers rising from 27,000 to over 40,000. In July 1883, a letter was received from the Educational Department requesting a careful review of the accommodation situation, in view of the increasing population. The Board had been anticipating problems, for in February they had sponsored a report which indicated that 671 children from outside the boundaries were attending Bootle schools. Reports followed of children being refused admission because schools were full. The Board resolved to enquire into the possibility of persuading managers to expel children not resident in the borough from the church schools, even though traditionally the voluntary sector had ignored administrative boundaries.

Following receipt of the returns from schools, the Board informed the Education Department that on the basis of an estimated 33,000 population there were 5,500 children requiring accommodation. This was, of course, a one-sixth estimate, invalid in the light of the demographic structure of Bootle. Using a one-seventh reduction for those 'unavoidably absent' the 5,500 were reduced to 4,715. Accommodation at the five inspected schools was now 4,056. Although this constituted an apparent deficit of about 700 places, the Board claimed a surplus of 1,256, arrived at by compensating for average attendance (still well below numbers on the rolls), and for numbers of children from outside the borough attending Bootle schools. The newly-revealed surplus was increased to 1,696 to cover building additions pending. Not yet finished, the Board enumerated 857 places in private adventure schools 'under the Board's supervision', bringing a further credit of 77 places, and giving an overall surplus of 1,773. In addition, it pointed to accommodation in 'dissenting congregations' of 1,705, and in mission rooms 'capable of being used as day schools' for 996. By various sleights of hand the Board had blithely turned a large deficit into a surplus of 4,474 places.

Even the local newspaper, ever ready to condemn extravagant expenditure, was nonplussed at the 'guileless simplicity' of this 'remarkable composition', intended as it was to help the ratepayers, and anticipated it would be received by the Education Department 'with some amusement'.

Imagine any humane man, let alone a school inspector who has his departmental regulations to guide him, condemning children to spend the greater part of every day in the garret in Lincoln-street (in the dockland slum area), or in the cellar under the Bootle Baptist Chapel.

In any case, this accommodation belonged neither to the Board nor the ratepayers, and was in effect 'as much private property as the drawing-room of any of the members of the School Board'.[5]

Seemingly slow to have appreciated the gravity of the impending situation in Bootle, the Education Department now moved quickly. In a predictably forthright reply to the Board's calculations, it refused to countenance the one-seventh deduction for children unavoidably absent, already taken account of in the one-sixth calculation, an estimate in any case 'not often applied by the Department, and in a population such as that of your Borough my Lords doubt whether it would be applicable'. The Board's statement of accommodation in inspected schools of nearly 4,200 was disputed, figures from the managers showing it to be 3,927. This gave a clear deficiency of 1,573 school places. The Board was put in its place over its other calculations in terms brooking no further prevarication:

It is of course quite impossible for the Department to take into account as you do Sunday Schools which might, if necessary, be used as Day Schools, Mission Rooms capable of being used for the purposes of elementary education, and Private schools 'under the Board's supervision' – an expression which my Lords do not clearly understand ...

It is urgently needed that your Board should take prompt measures to prevent the educational requirements from greatly outstripping the supply, and my Lords hope that after your next meeting they may have satisfactory assurances from you upon the matter.

A request from the Board for an interview with Scott-Coward, the Inspector, was rejected, the Department indicating that it was relying not on the Inspector's figures but on those received from the school managers. Later in the month, the Board received an equally dusty reply from the trustees of the Nonconformist Sunday schools, refusing to cooperate on the grounds that their buildings were ill-adapted for use as day schools, and because the feeling in the congregation was in any case in favour of board schools.

At its September 14th meeting the Board at last resigned itself to appointing a Sites Committee, to take immediate steps to provide one or more board schools. A further overture was made to the Education Department to take into account at least Bootle College, which was far more than an average private adventure school, accommodating over 100 boys. The Education Department's reply pointed out that had they taken into account middle-class schools of this type, they would have used a one-fifth estimate (one more appropriate to the situation in Bootle, which would have pushed the accommodation need up to 6,600 places). Having introduced this veiled threat, the Department suggested new schools should be built in 'needful localities'. 'If two such localities be selected a proposal to build a school for 600 in each would be favourably entertained by your Lordships as giving evidence that your Board were really alive to their responsibilities.'

Sites were eventually selected in Bedford Road and Salisbury Road, to cater for rapidly growing areas near the southern and northern boundaries of the town (Fig. 8.1). So rapid was the rise in population, however, that the Board itself suggested that the schools should be for 1,000 pupils each.

The Department belatedly realised that even 2,000 new places would prove inadequate. It calculated that of the population of 40,147, 35,922 were living in houses of rateable value under £20, taken as an index that such households would require elementary school places for their children. Even excluding middle-class parents, a one-fifth requirement was confirmed, i.e. for 7,182 places. Even with voluntary additions and the two new board schools, a deficiency of 690 places would remain. Though shocked at this new demand, the Board resolved to look for a third site.

Notwithstanding continued population increase, now concentrated at the northern end of the borough (Fig. 8.1), it was six more years before it was finally agreed that a third board school was needed. Eventually a site in Hawthorne Road was selected. By 1891 there were 300 more children on the rolls of Salisbury Road than the level of accommodation. Even more serious, there were more children in average attendance than there were places, a situation still in existence in 1895 (Table 5). While waiting for Hawthorne Road, temporary use was made of Bootle Institute in Knowsley Road as a means of relieving the frightening pressure on Salisbury Road.

In April 1893 the Education Department sent a strongly worded letter requesting reasons for the excess of average attendance over accommodation. The following month the Department was forced to agree to the expedient of reducing the square footage required per child at Salisbury Road, on condition the building of a new school was pushed ahead as fast as possible.

Hawthorne Road opened in March 1895, with nearly 1,000 children enrolled from the start. Table 5 shows the accommodation in the borough at this time to have been 10,020, and illustrates two of its planning problems. First, overall accommodation was ostensibly sufficient, but the surplus was largely confined to the Catholic sector which could not be taken up by children from outside it. Second, accommodation was crucially short at the northern end of the town.

TABLE 5

BOOTLE PUBLIC ELEMENTARY SCHOOLS (1895)

	On Rolls	Average Attendance	%	Accomm.	
C. of E					
St. Mary's	869	775	89.2	823	(+)
Christ Church	849	742	87.4	910	(+)
St. John's	1,000	861	86.1	980	(−)
	2,718	2,378	87.4	2,713	
R.C.					
St. Alexander's	881	676	76.7	1,450	(+)
St. James'	1,519	1,380	90.8	1,986	(+)
St. James' Select	255	233	91.4	320	(+)
	2,655	2,289	86.2	3,756	
Board					
Bedford Road	1,174	1,027	87.8	1,157	(−)
Salisbury Road	1,787	1,541	86.1	1,437	(−) (−)
Hawthorne Road	982	857	87.3	957	(−)
	3,943	3,425	86.9	3,551	
Grand Total	9,316	8,092	86.8	10,020	

(+)   Surplus.
(−)   Deficiency.
(−) (−) Deficiency even in terms of average attendance.

The *in toto* adequacy of accommodation was nevertheless used in reply to another complaint from the Education Department that Salisbury Road was overcrowded. As the borough was geographically compact, children could travel to school, the Board argued. It should not be expected to provide another school until all accommodation was utilised.

The Board had again to submit to the battering-ram of numbers, however. It was agreed in 1896 to build a further board school on the northern fringe of the town in Gray Street (Fig. 8.1). In 1900, it was resolved to erect an additional board school in Linacre, opened as a Council School just after the demise of the School Board. In 1902 Bedford Road was enlarged by three classrooms.

It is fair to reinforce the point that the period of the Bootle School

Board coincided with an escalation in numbers of people, changes in demographic structure, with an increasingly youthful and socially descending population, and radical changes in economic geography and land use, as port and industrial development imposed itself upon the borough. But similar changes were taking place, for example, in Barrow-in-Furness (Chapter 6), where even more pressing demands were met by positive reaction. What were the reasons for Bootle's tardy responses to local population pressures and demands from Whitehall? These may in part be explained by looking at three related questions. Who were the members of the Board? What were their perceptions of the situation they had to face? In a situation of conflict of interests, who were they trying to please most?

TABLE 6

OCCUPATIONS OF THE MEMBERS OF THE BOOTLE SCHOOL BOARDS

	The Changing Composition of each Board, 1870–1903											
Occupation	*1*	*2*	*3*	*4*	*5*	*6*	*7*	*8*	*9*	*10*	*11*	%
Commerce	6	7	6	4	4	1	2	0	1	1	1	33
Professions	1	1	1	3	2	4	3	6	6	7	7	42
Maritime/Industry	2	1	1	2	1	2	2	1	0	0	0	12
Gentlemen	0	0	1	0	2	2	2	2	2	1	1	12

THE BOOTLE SCHOOL BOARD

Table 6 shows the occupations of the members of the eleven Bootle School Boards, and their changing composition. Six of the members of the first Board were merchants or brokers, six lived in the main middle-class enclave of the borough (Fig. 8.2) and two more in a 'residual' middle-class area on the north-western shore. Four represented Anglican, three Nonconformist and two Catholic interests. After the first election, amicable 'arrangements' were made, and no further elections took place until 1891. By the 1880s there was evidence, however, of a shift of membership interests from commerce towards the professions. This trend surfaced in the 1890s, when the clergy entered the election fray. By this time, the local voluntary agencies had become alarmed by what they saw as competition from the board schools which had appeared in the mid-1880s, while the school fees issue determined the churches to exert a more direct influence. The elections of the 1890s suggested the Catholics had been deprived of their fair share of representatives, and the balance of power between the three religious groups changed to 3–3–3.

Fig. 8.2. Bootle, late 1890s: Pupil Intake by Area of five Elementary Schools

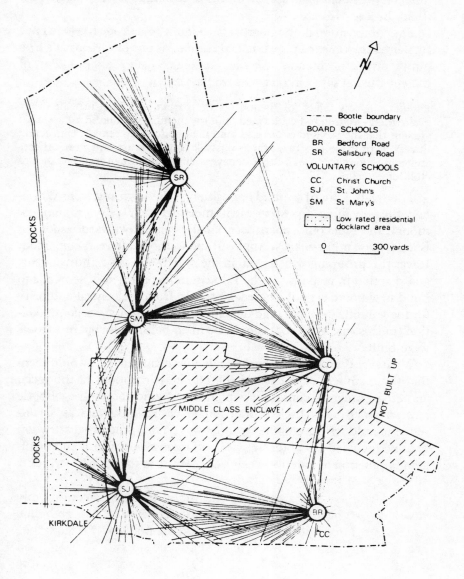

Of those elected to the 1894–7 Board, two were categorised as 'gentlemen', six were professional people, including two 'clerks in Holy Orders' and one was in commerce. Three of the members, the two clergy and the physician, lived outside the truly middle-class area of Bootle, an unusual feature in the light of the previous almost universal residential preference of Board members for the Merton Road–Breeze Hill area.

The composition of the Board does not impress as one likely to have furthered the cause of rate-aided education, as one of the Board's first public pronouncements, over the attendance issue, suggests. Part of the conclusion of a circular to parents read:

Parents can now select for themselves the particular school in which they desire their children to be educated, and the members of the Board are most anxious that they should do so, and send their children to school at once, and thus prevent the necessity (as far as possible) for the appointment of officers and consequent expense of the Ratepayers, for compelling the attendance of children at school.[6]

Though the Board aroused opposition in the town and from Whitehall, the prevailing atmosphere in its meetings was rarely acrimonious, though the Nonconformists occasionally raised awkward issues. In Bootle, as on other boards, Anglican and Catholic interests coincided. It was this grouping which even in the mid-1890s was fighting a rearguard action in response to the Education Department's demands to build new board schools, beseeching help from the central authority for the voluntary system, and demanding that voluntary accommodation (in this case Catholic) should be filled before new board schools were built.

Whatever their occupational or religious affiliations, it would seem that the members of the Board shared like perceptions of the social and environmental context in which they found themselves. Bootle had an abnormally high proportion of casual labourers as a consequence of dock development, and it was on this group that attention became focussed (Chapter 9). The notion of a recalcitrant and negligent population of parents became an *idée fixe* in the pronouncements of the School Board.[7]

In so compact an area as Bootle the abyss was uncomfortably close. As we have seen, a formerly attractive suburban shoreline had disintegrated both socially and environmentally over the last four decades of the century. On the more ventilated slopes of Merton Road and Breeze Hill (Figs. 8.1 and 9.3b), in encastled seclusion, the

School Board members and their peers experienced little contact with the recipients of attendance enforcement and later of board school provision. But they learned about it at second hand, from the spicy reports of street disturbances, police court proceedings for assault and child neglect, and in the 1890s from accounts of industrial unrest at the docks (Chapter 9). Members of the Attendance Sub-committee were among the few to meet at first hand certain members of the dockland community, appealing for fees from the Board (until 1876) or summonsed for non-attendance of their children. Attendance enforcement was seen as the critical issue, and became coercive enough to impress all but the hard-liners. Between 1879 and 1891 nearly 10,000 irregularities were dealt with. Approaching 3,000 parents were brought before the magistrates, and over 200 children committed to industrial schools.[8]

In exerting this authority, the Board was not merely exercising a modicum of social control. It was also giving precedence to the attendance over the accommodation issue, thus serving the voluntary interest as well as an accepted educational priority issue. Paradoxically, increasing success in this role exacerbated the problem of finding accommodation.

The peers and masters of the Board were the influential ratepaying interests. The rates were there legally to be drawn on, if the Board so willed. It was reluctant to do so. Significantly, in its Triennial Report of 1891, the Board congratulated itself on the cordial relationships established with the voluntary managers, and also on its success in being 'impartial', advancing the cause of elementary education while remembering its duty to the ratepayers.[9] Protection of ratepayers' interests made it certain that supply of accommodation always lagged behind demand.

The Board had thus a difficult task in steering a course between competing pressures. Looking charitably upon its efforts, it may be argued that it made pragmatic decisions in accordance with what it thought prevailing influential local opinion would stand. Its policies evolved slowly. Attendance enforcement was given priority. This brought Bootle's figures up to national standards by the mid-1880s and surpassed them from then on.[10] Its negative and then gradualist approach to board school provision, needing a hefty push from Whitehall, did not run too far ahead of ratepayer tolerance, and the ratepayers seem eventually to have become resigned to the principle of providing funding for schools. By 1900 even the *Bootle Times*, almost

for the first time, was complimenting the Board on its efforts, allowing it the liberty of 'keeping pace with the requirements of the
borough' so long as it showed a 'good educational return' in terms of
the efficiency of its schools.[11] Bootle had suddenly woken up to the
fact that its board schools could be counted as a municipal achievement.

CATCHMENT AREAS AND SCHOOL STATUS

> The School Board Visitor brought two boys . . . as new
> scholars. I declined however to admit them today as they
> were barefooted, but promised I would do my best to
> procure them shoes and stockings and thus make them
> presentable before the rest of the boys. Were we to admit
> such children, unclad as they are, we should alienate
> many of our best boys. I take this to be a 'reasonable
> excuse' for refusing admission.[12]

While the Bootle School Board was agonising over the problems of
reconciling ratepayer interests with the imperatives of population
growth and the demands of the Education Department, the managers
of the voluntary schools were grappling not only with the difficulties
of finding places, but also with satisfying the aspirations of parents in
search of an appropriate school for their children in a situation of
social change and territorial shifts in residential status. Within this
spatial-ecological framework, as noted in Chapter 1, the catchment
area provides the vital linking concept between the school and local
community.

Fig. 8.2 indicates the catchment areas of five Bootle schools, two
board and three voluntary, in the late 1890s. In the 1870s, the catchment zone of St. John's had been more compact than it appears in the
1890s, largely confined to the dockland area, but extending over the
municipal boundary into the Kirkdale district of Liverpool. But
the construction of a road under the Liverpool–Southport railway
(Fig. 8.1) improved access for children wishing to attend the school
from about 1875. The catchment of Bedford Road was more compact and socially homogeneous, reflecting the increasingly bureaucratic policy of the School Board which, in response to pressure on
accommodation, and to discourage unnecessary flitting from school
to school, zoned the town rigidly so far as intake to its own schools
was concerned. Children from over the municipal boundary were
expressly excluded.

The catchment zone of Christ Church was much more extensive than either of these schools, and encompassed more differentiated social areas. The school had by the 1890s achieved prime status among Bootle's elementary institutions, where parents from respectable districts all over the borough, including some from the middle class enclave, were anxious to enrol their children. As we saw in London (Chapter 4), an elementary hierarchy of schools emerged.

Ambitious parents had become skilled at 'working the system'. While no doubt many removals from one school to another were 'capricious', in this particular social sector the more appropriate descriptor is 'calculated'. Fig 8.3 illustrates the transfer of children between five Bootle schools during the 1896–1900 period. The three dominant directions of transfer were from Salisbury Road to St. Mary's and to Christ Church; and from St. Mary's to Christ Church. By contrast with the high status of Christ Church, St. Mary's, another Church of England school, had lost prestige as dockland development and associated social decline affected its immediate intake area. Salisbury Road was swathed in a sea of dockland slum housing from the time the Bootle School Board established it in the mid-1880s and its catchment was largely confined to this area (Fig. 8.2). By the 1890s Christ Church was as already noted an elite establishment of its type, 'a wonderful school for its time', according to an ex-teacher.[13] To some extent, this status reflected the school's favourable catchment area, but to capitalise on this advantage meant excluding poor-looking children who strayed through the doors, or at least keeping their numbers to a minimum. Difficult pupils were offloaded on to the board schools as they were built. The headmaster of Salisbury Road Board School referred to the well-known 'weeding' process of the voluntary schools. 'The children admitted at the present here consist wholly of outcasts from other schools'.[14] Similarly, in justifying to the Education Department the opening of a new 'Select School', in a quite different location from the main schools, the priest of St. James's explained that 'our shopkeeping class wish to have their children educated in separate schools from the poorer children'.[15]

Fig. 8.3. Transfer of Children between Schools in Bootle 1896–1900

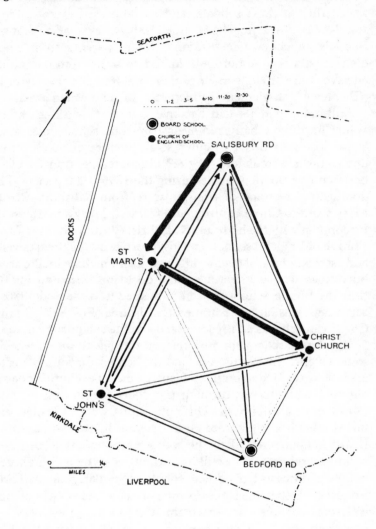

SCHOOL ACHIEVEMENT

Every lesson is now a species of examination.[16]

Another way of attracting respectable custom was to achieve good results in the government examinations, and publicise successes through prize days and accounts in the local newspapers.

Whether there was in fact some correlation between social background and elementary school achievement at this time is an important question. An earlier survey[17] tentatively offers less than clear-cut
answers, but possible lines of further enquiry. What does seem
apparent is that children coming up through the infants' section of
an elementary school in a socially disadvantaged area tended to
achieve higher standards than those entering, for example, from
private adventure schools, often of poor academic credentials. The
same did not happen in the case of Christ Church, whose intake from
other schools presumably was helped by the fact that these had
provided a competent educational foundation.

Another finding was the obvious, but important, one that children
who stayed in school longer achieved generally higher standards,
suggesting the vital task of the elementary school was to keep its
children on the books, especially in a school in a socially difficult area
such as St. John's, where by the 1890s 60% of the children were
staying for less than two years, as against only 28% in the 1870s, an
indication of the highly mobile state of the catchment area at the later
period. Head-teachers were convinced that length of stay, combined
with good attendance, were crucial factors in school achievement. In
general, there appeared *within* individual schools little correlation
between socio-economic grouping and educational achievement as
measured by standard reached, which appears surprising in view of
the stereotype of Victorian working-class parents being hostile or at
least apathetic towards schooling.

By way of explanation, two technical points must be made. To
begin with, the samples used in the survey were necessarily socially
attenuated, containing virtually no children from the upper middle
classes, and probably a less than representative sample from the 'low
poor'. In addition, the children were, if need be, given more than one
opportunity to sit for each standard. Indeed, each standard was
prerequisite for the next. There are many examples in the registers of
children repeating the same standard, though rarely more than once.
Hence a slower child could move up the standards by extending the
length of stay.

There are also two more general factors. It is well known that the
'payment by results' system encouraged rote learning, which must
have lowered the power of the examination to discriminate. Discrimination was not in any case its purpose. In these circumstances,
the perceived frailer aptitudes of the socially disadvantaged children

would be less than clearly exposed. The innate ability and imagination of brighter children would constitute a kind of overkill for which there was no tangible reward in the shape of better results.

Perhaps more important, there is evidence of positive discrimination in the schools on behalf of the slower children. As the headmaster of Christ Church revealed, 'The teachers have been examining one another's classes during the week' (a tactic designed to simulate the inspector's visit, accustoming the children to 'a variety of voice and manner'). 'There is of course a backward division in each standard, upon which they are bestowing great pains'.[18] Government grant depended as much on the results achieved by less able as more able children. Far from considering that less able pupils merited less able teachers, a head might well find it expedient to put an experienced teacher in charge of a small group of slower children, leaving pupil teachers to attend to the rest, and particularly in the critical period after Christmas which in Bootle led up to the annual examination. Expectation of success must needs be the same for all but a small minority of children, who were excluded from the examination on grounds of excessive ill-health and/or absence, or extreme 'dullness'.

On the other hand there were significant differences *between* schools of markedly different social composition. For example, in the 1870s Christ Church had 36% of its children in socio-economic groupings I–III as against 14% at St. John's, but only 21% as against 40% in SEG V. This social differentiation was paralleled by the better results achieved at Christ Church, where 65% of them had achieved Standard III or over, as against 44% at St. John's. Parents were apparently correct in seeing choice of school as a means of improving opportunity. Clearly other factors need to be considered, including teacher quality. It would seem likely that the higher status schools were able to attract more readily able and experienced teachers and, as the Christ Church log books indicate, were quick to dismiss those not gaining satisfactory results in the government examinations.

Bootle classically illustrates the ecological forces impinging on education identified in London by Booth's surveys of the 1880s and 1890s (Chapter 7). Thus the close proximity of the middle-class zone of Merton Road and Breeze Hill in Bootle with the dockland slum ghetto almost immediately on the other side of the physical barrier of the canal and railway line, is reminiscent of the juxtaposition of the Notting Dale slum and the Ladbroke Grove estate in North Kensington, and the Sultan Street area and its more respectable surroundings in Camberwell. In areas such as these, parents had to respond to the cosmetic and moral realities of contact with the destitute and the dire warnings of such as Mary Carpenter and William Booth (Chapter 4) of the consequences which might ensue if their children were not protected by a socially hierarchical arrangement of schooling.

The Headmaster of Salisbury Road Boys' School found his school overtaken almost from the start by a new surge of dockland development to the northern boundary of Bootle (Plate 8) and recorded its consequences for the school, in the loss of

a number of our most respectable children, whose parents are leaving the district, their reason being that the neighbourhood is sadly deteriorating. This is unquestionably the case. Our admissions, with a very few exceptions, were never of a very high stamp as regards educational qualifications, but those which are now being admitted are of the 'gutter-snipe' class.[19]

The educational impact was a thinning of the older children: 'Standard V is the fence over which comparatively few will leap',[20] and a deterioration in attendance, seen as crucial to academic improvement: 'excellence of attendance and efficiency seemingly go hand in hand ... the base of the pyramid is lowest both in attendance and in proficiency'.[21]

The problems he was facing in the late 1880s and 1890s had, however, already been heralded in an even more notorious dockland slum in the south-west corner of Bootle, to which we now turn.

REFERENCES AND FOOTNOTES

1. Bootle School Board, *Triennial Report*, 1888.
2. For a fuller discussion of the problems relating to Armstrong's classification, see W. E. Marsden, 'Social Environment, School Attendance and Educational Achievement in a Merseyside Town 1870–1900', in P. McCann (ed.), *Education and Socialization in the Nineteenth Century* (London, 1977), pp. 196–7.
3. For a fuller discussion, see *ibid.*, pp. 197–8.
4. This quotation is drawn from the dialogue between the Bootle School Board and Whitehall, and is taken from the Minutes of the School Board. Hereafter reference will not be made to this source in the context of this particular debate.
5. *Bootle Times* (hereafter *B.T.*), 18 July 1883.
6. *Bootle School Board Minutes*, 16 March 1871.
7. See, for example, Bootle School Board, *Triennial Report*, 1888.
8. W. E. Marsden, *op. cit.* (1977), pp. 208–14.
9. Bootle School Board, *Triennial Report*, 1891.
10. See W. E. Marsden, *op. cit.* (1977), pp. 211–12.
11. *B.T.*, 7 April 1900.

12. *Christ Church (Boys) Log Book*, 9 Feb. 1877.
13. C. F. Nathan, *A Schoolmaster Glances Back* (Liverpool, 1946), p. 79.
14. *Salisbury Road (Boys) Log Book*, 12 Aug. 1887.
15. Public Record Office, *Education File*, 21/9080.
16. *Christ Church (Boys) Log Book*, 7 Jan. 1881.
17. Reported in W. E. Marsden, *op. cit.* (1977), pp. 214–24.
18. *Christ Church (Boys) Log Book*, 7 July 1881.
19. *Salisbury Road (Boys) Log Book*, 29 April 1887.
20. *Salisbury Road (Boys) Log Book*, 27 April 1888.
21. *Salisbury Road (Boys) Log Book*, 5 Oct. 1888.

CHAPTER NINE

'Troublesome Thoroughfares': Schooling and Communities in Bootle's Dockland

> Deer Mr. Heditor,
> ... I've allwus cent my childer to skool and allwus
> will, till they hort to go to a trade, but there is times you
> wud like to keep the oldest at ome a bit we'n the muther's
> bad or wen you want him to go for a fu errands without
> them inspektors coming to se wats the matter and give
> you all sorts of cheak and may be sum-muns you in the
> bargain. Wone time I keeps my lad at ome to go with my
> diner, we sends him to skool in the hafternoon. 'Wel' the
> master says were wus you this morning my lad tells him
> he ad bin with a message, he says 'hold yer and out' and
> kanes him never comes to se if the lad was telling a lie.
> (Bootle Times, 25 July 1885)[1]

Officially obliging children to attend school is a social phenomenon of considerable interest to the historian in that the responses to it of both providers and recipients of educational facilities are testimony to their attitudes to popular education in general. There are major problems of interpretation, however, for expressed motives cannot always be taken at face value on the one hand, while on the other so much of the evidence is circumstantial. The attempt is important, however, to combat the stereotyping of the slum community, both by its contemporaries and later commentators, as a homogeneous, subversive and alien social force. Here newspaper records provide some limited evidence of alternative perspectives to those of the officials, whether school board members and agents, magistrates, medical officers of health, or school managers and head-teachers.

The term 'community' is in itself problematic, suggesting both a geographically discrete territory and a group of people with a common economic and social life and sets of values. As will be shown, the Merseyside dockland slum of southwest Bootle was territorially bounded, but by no means socially homogeneous. Indeed it contained a Catholic and non-Catholic community; a casual labouring group and one with more stable employment. There was also a subtle residential segregation in that while all streets were predominantly working-class, different streets and even different parts of streets enjoyed varying social ratings. Apart from the disparities at the micro-scale, a coarser level of resolution existed, which inevitably delineated the slum as different and internally undifferentiated, distinguishing it from more desirable residential parts of the borough. A further complication in this case was the fact that what emerged as an 'instant slum' was located in a district which had within living memory been a middle-class suburb. The 1870 Education Act thus caught the area in a state of rapid social and environmental transition.

But as late as 1872 the Clerk to the Bootle School Board felt able to inform the Education Department in Whitehall that the apparently large number of Bootle children attending private schools outside the borough reflected the high proportion of middle-class residents as compared with other towns.[2] In fact these had long fled this part of the Mersey shore, which by 1872 was overwhelmed by an invasion of warehouses, factories and high-density terraced housing adjacent to the docks.

The impact on local institutions was dramatic, not least in a period of increasing demand for schooling. The churches were still primarily responsible for educational provision. In a letter to the National Society in 1866 the incumbent of the recently established dockland parish of St. John's appealed for funds:

In the large district over which I have been placed containing 6,500 souls there are no schools save a temporary one in a shed. I am about to erect large and convenient schools but require extraneous help.[3]

In the following year, he asserted that the population had increased from 2,000 to 20,000 (something of an exaggeration) through dock extension, and that

whereas the middle classes who some fifteen years ago settled in Bootle as a suburb of Liverpool have now removed, there remain only the 6,500 poor who are unable to erect schools unless very mainly helped from without.[4]

As indicated in Chapter 8, the middle classes had migrated either north to the suburbs which had grown along the line of the Liverpool–Southport railway, or across the canal and that railway within Bootle (Fig. 9.3a), into a new enclave, which developed in the 1860s, 1870s and 1880s along the Merton Road–Breeze Hill axis (Figs. 8.1 and 9.3b).

The census returns of 1851, 1861 and 1871 tell of inexorable social descent in Bootle as a whole. On the basis of the *socio-economic grouping of parents or guardians* (i.e. not the total population) of Bootle children aged 3–15, the situation in 1851 was well-balanced, with just over 30% in each of Groups I/II and III respectively, and 37% in Groups IV/V. The advancing dock development was largely responsible for a shift by 1871 to 15% in Groups I/II, 37% in III, and no less than 48% in IV/V. A sample of the *total* population of Bootle in 1871 suggests an even starker picture, with only just over 8% in SEGs I/II, 43% in III, and nearly 49% in IV/V.

The censuses and associated enumeration districts help to delineate the boundaries of this particular slum, which fitted neatly Enumeration Districts 5, 6 and 7 of Bootle (Fig. 9.2). The clarity of definition was the result of the presence of the Leeds and Liverpool Canal, crossed only by one road bridge and a foot bridge in this area. Inland of the canal was a transition social area, Enumeration District 4, slotted in between the canal and the Liverpool–Southport railway, a useful buffer zone between the slum and the middle-class Merton Road–Breeze Hill enclave (Figs. 9.1 (a) and (b) and 9.3 (a) and (b)).

THE DEMOGRAPHY OF THE SLUM

The association of the slum with three enumeration districts makes fairly precise identification of its aggregate population and housing characteristics practicable.[5] A diagnostic feature of this and other slums was high population density, in gross terms 108.4 people per acre, as against 12.6 for the rest of Bootle, in 1871. The highest densities were in Districts 5 and 6, east of Derby Road, with 132.6 and 117.2 respectively, but District 7, with 75.5 per acre, was undoubtedly equally crowded, the actual density being obscured by the presence of riverside industry and warehousing in this area. Of other parts of Bootle, only District 4, between the canal and railway, was nearly as heavily populated, with 42.6 people per acre. As the century progressed, more and more of Bootle was built up. By 1901,

Fig. 9.1. Spatial Variations in the Socio-economic Grouping of Children aged 3–15 in Bootle, 1871.

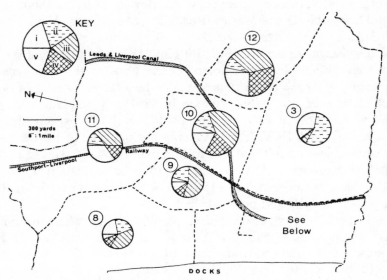

(a) Spatial variations in the socio-economic grouping of children aged 3–15 in Bootle, 1871.

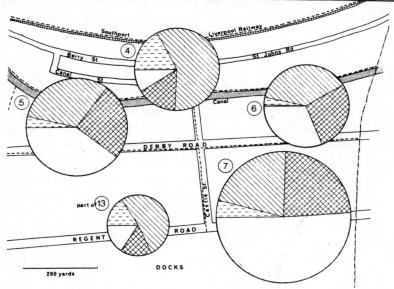

(b) Socio-economic grouping of children in the South-West corner of Bootle, 1871.

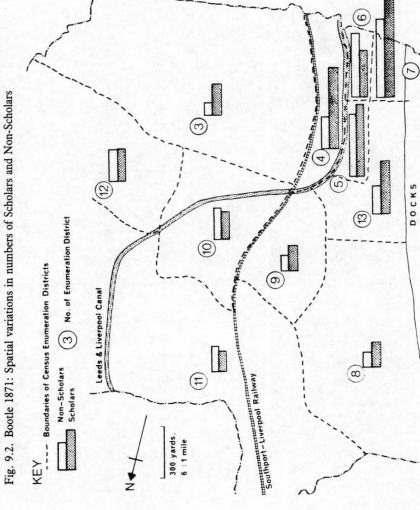

Fig. 9.2. Bootle 1871: Spatial variations in numbers of Scholars and Non-Scholars

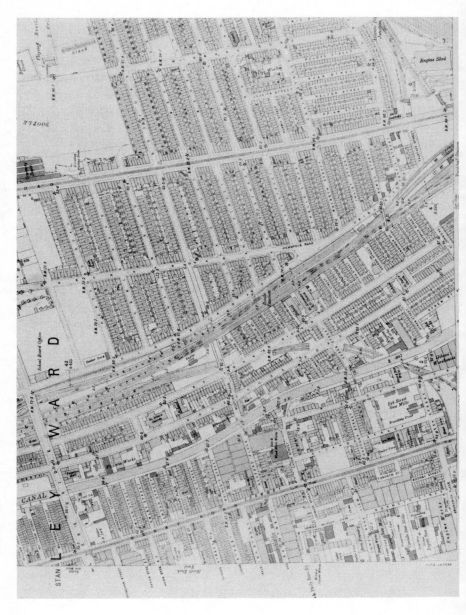

Fig 9.3(a) South-west Bootle and Kirkdale, 1890s: 25″ O.S. map extract

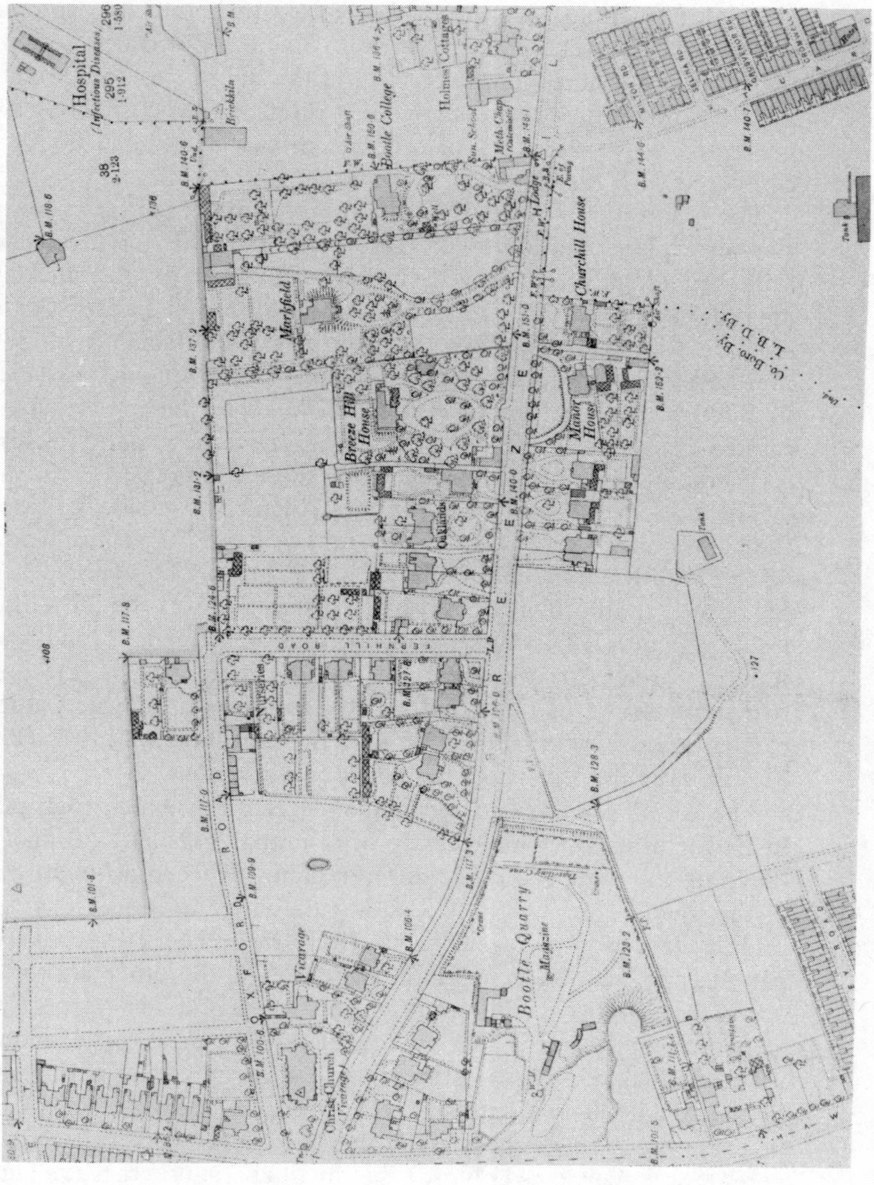

Fig 9.3(b) Breeze Hill, Bootle, 1890s: 25" O.S. map extract

there were 58,556 people on the town's 1,576 acres, giving over 37 per acre, as against 8 per acre in Southport and Birkdale (Chapter 10).

Bootle as a whole had a youthful age structure both at the beginning and end of the School Board period. Fig. 9.1 illustrates just how many children there were to educate in this south-western corner of Bootle, while Fig. 3.1 shows how the overall age structure inevitably generated larger numbers of scholars in places such as Bootle as compared with resorts such as Southport and Birkdale.

The sex ratio was another important differentiating measure. Lawton's pioneer study of the 1851 census returns for Merseyside indicated a high proportion of single men in a comparable dockland area of Liverpool.[6] The situation was replicated in Bootle's waterside areas in 1871. Taking a baseline of 100, the female–male ratio averaged 93.71 in Enumeration Districts 5, 6 and 7, as against 128.98 in Bootle as a whole, and rising to 180.28 in the predominantly middle-class District 3, with its spinsters, governesses and domestic servants, a comparable situation again to Southport and Birkdale.

The most striking feature of the population born outside Bootle was the high proportion of Irish immigrants, with in 1871 a concentration of 17.6% of the population of Districts 5, 6 and 7 as against 7% for the rest of the borough. Even more distinctive was the 35% figure for Enumeration District 7, with its notorious Lyons, Dundas and Raleigh Streets. It was the Irish element which led to the negative stereotyping of this area, and the building of a large Catholic elementary school in connection with St. Alexander's Church (Plate 9), just over the Liverpool boundary in Kirkdale.

The social descent and residential segregation which took place in Bootle after 1851 has already been noted. Figs. 9.1 (a) and (b) illustrate the socio-economic differentiation between different parts of the town. Thus Districts 3 and 8, the latter in its last days as a middle-class suburban zone, had in 1871 82% and 44% respectively of parents and guardians in SEGs I and II. At the other end of the spectrum, in Districts 5, 6 and 7, 65%, 59% and 74% respectively were in SEGs IV and V. The vast majority of the male population was in the manual working category in these areas, and much of this semi- or unskilled. These figures may well overestimate the population in these areas in categories III and above, for they relate to the parents and guardians only. It is highly likely that there was a higher percentage of unskilled labour among the many single males who crammed the common lodging houses which abounded in the dockland streets. There is ample evidence that between two-thirds and three-quarters of the working population of this dockland slum was in the semi- or unskilled manual categories, as against less than half for Bootle as a whole, at the opening of the School Board period.

HOUSING

Housing density is another useful index of the crowded nature of Bootle's first dockland slum. Districts 5, 6 and 7 had an average density of 16.7 per acre, as against 2.8 for the rest of Bootle, admittedly not at this stage fully built up. Of other Districts only adjacent 4, with 7.8, came anywhere near these figures. By 1881, Bootle had about 5,000 houses on its 1,600 acres; by 1891, about 9,000, and by 1901 over 10,000, giving a density of well over six houses to the acre, as against 1.5 in Southport and Birkdale.

The raw density is only the first index of overcrowding, however. More critical were the numbers inhabiting each house. In south-west Bootle there was an average of 7.1 persons per house in Districts 5, 6 and 7, as against 5.9 for the rest of the borough. Were the actual sizes of houses to be taken into consideration, the distinction would be much greater, as comparison of the Ordnance Survey maps, contrasting the south-western slum with the pleasant slopes of Breeze Hill, makes clear (Figs. 9.3 (a) and (b)). The ground space of Lyons Street would have fitted neatly the garden area of Bootle College.

The number of households per house, multiplying by 100, was 145.3 in Districts 5, 6 and 7, in comparison with 111.3 for the rest of Bootle. The percentage of lodgers was 11.4 in Districts 5, 6 and 7, rising to 18.3 in District 7. The figure for the rest of Bootle was 7.8. Thus this south-western corner was the leading area for both multi-occupancy of dwellings and for common lodging houses.

The case of Lyons Street highlights the overcrowding endemic in this area. In its 118 occupied houses there were 154 households and 857 people. These included 140 lodgers and 390 children of 15 years and below, giving this age group a colossal 45% of the population of the street. The average household size was 7.12 persons. 16% of the inhabitants were recorded as lodgers, but of the 45 houses in which there were lodgers, 38 were 'family' houses as well. A not untypical example of a multiply-occupied house was 83 Lyons Street, shown in Table 1, a simplified extract from the enumerators' returns of 1871.

On this evidence, the type pattern would seem to have been one of

TABLE 1

Name	Relation to Head of Family	Condition	Age M	F	Profession or Occupation	Where Born
John McGawvern	Head	Married	34		Labourer at Coal	Ireland
Elizabeth	Wife	ditto		30	–	ditto
Mary Ann	Daughter	Unmarried		10	–	Liverpool
Margaret	ditto	ditto		7	–	ditto
Charles	Son	ditto	14months		–	Bootle
Patrick Morgan	Boarder	Widower	52		Labourer at Cargo	Ireland
Mary Ann Morgan	ditto	Unmarried		11	Domestic Servant	Liverpool
William Morgan	ditto	ditto	15		Blacksmith	ditto
Hugh Kelly	ditto	ditto	20		Labourer at Coal	Ireland
Richard Cannon	ditto	ditto	21		ditto	ditto
Patrick McNully	ditto	Married	45		Labourer at Cargo	ditto
Catherine McNully	ditto	ditto		34	–	ditto

immigration from Ireland to Liverpool, followed by a northward move into Bootle with the extension of the docks; a dependence on the docks for casual labouring employment; with place of work and national origin the prime channels of communication for those looking for lodgings. No scholars were recorded at this particular house.

From their unenviable origins as instant slum-dwellings, the houses of Raleigh, Dundas and Lyons Streets fell into an increasingly dilapidated state over the next forty years. An eye-witness of 1890 described Dundas Street thus:

From the front, the places present a bad enough appearance. Each house, standing three stories in height, shows blackened and decayed walls; broken windows – some with the holes papered up; others left just as they have been shattered for the cold damp air to blow through at night. The doors seem to be the only intact pieces of furniture about the place. Even the chimney pots and holes in the roof are chipped and broken, as if the hand of destruction had gone through the dwelling, passing the door only because it stood open and presented no barrier to its evil progress.[7]

As late as 1902, cellars in Lyons Street were still being used as dwelling-places.[8]

Conditions were little better on the opposite side of Derby Road. Thus the two- and three-storeyed dwellings of Mann Street were described as standing 'like rows of black spectres'.[9] Plate 7 illustrates the density of the built-up area, as here between Mann Street and

Emley Street, with postage stamp backyards and outbuildings, the narrowest of alleyways, and washing waging an unequal struggle against the prevailing grime. The area was subject to slum clearance in the inter-war period, when the photograph was taken.

Some of the most telling narratives of the privations experienced in south-west Bootle appear in courtroom accounts of child neglect. Thus in one case in Mann Street in 1892, the police witness reported a mother, with a husband at sea, going out drinking with other women, and neglecting four boys of nine years and under, found 'huddled together, lying on a bed not fit for anyone to use, the smell arising from it being fearful'.[10]

That this slum area was 'terra incognita' to the well-to-do citizens of the town was noted by a local newspaper columnist, 'Penanink', who wrote of Derby Road being Bootle's 'Temple Bar, and few who wear cloth and silk are found to frequent that thoroughfare' (Plate 11).[11]

The bad publicity associated with child neglect was supplemented by the notoriety of the lodging houses, whose keepers were perennially summonsed for not abiding by the regulations. Thus in 1878 Patrick Donnelly of 24, Mann Street was brought to book for having more lodgers than the three the house was registered to take. Of the eight adults found there by the police inspector, one was a man 'stark naked hiding in a cupboard'.[12] There was equal worry over the unregistered cellar dwellings of Lyons Street, where a reformist Councillor declared in a Council debate in 1902 that 'he had never been in a more filthy, disgraceful place than the cellar in Lyons Street he visited ... and the man and woman he saw there looked less like a man and woman than any he had ever seen'.[13]

Over Bootle as a whole, rent and rateable values changed little in the late nineteenth century, but provide an invaluable index of the spectrum of poverty and comfort in the borough (Fig. 9.4). Overall, the rateable values of Districts 5, 6 and 7 averaged less than £12 in 1900, as compared with over £24 in the more affluent parts. At the grass-roots, the levels of rent provide more pertinent measures. In the slum areas, rents for the poor quality housing were from 4/- to 5/- per week. Sub-letting of rooms at about 2/- per week was endemic. In respectable working-class areas six-roomed houses would fetch about 6/6d per week.[14] For the best working-class accommodation, with perhaps eight rooms, up to 10/- per week might be sought. In the middle-class zones, rents upwards of £1 per week could be expected.[15] At the other extreme, a few pence per night would find a bed in a common lodging house. One of the pre-dock era middle-class villas on Derby Road was referred to in 1884 as having 'fallen on evil days', having been 'converted into a common lodging house' at 4d per night.[16]

By 1900, the dockland slum had spread over much of the waterfront (Plate 8), with other neighbourhoods than the south-western corner carrying rateable values of less than £12. There had certainly been no appreciable improvement in housing conditions over the existence of the School Board. If anything, the slum areas were not only more extensive, but also in deeper distress.

HEALTH

The pervasive overcrowding and poor sanitation created serious health hazards. Of particular concern were the high infantile mortality rates. The local Medical Officer of Health regularly pin-pointed the districts of the town most at risk. In reviewing his 1880 Report, the leader writer of the *Bootle Times* drew special attention to the south-west dockland slum:

The report points significantly to the unhealthiness of Dundas Street, one of the most troublesome thoroughfares in the borough. The street is conspicuous for a large mortality ... and also, we may be permitted to add, for squalor, broken heads and inebriety ... The people are negligent; they take no sufficient precaution for the protection of themselves from disease, and when infectious cases are known to exist, the recklessness of the lower class of inhabitants in allowing their children to mix with other children during the period of desquamation is astonishing.[17]

The frightening infantile mortality rates were not confined to this area, however. In 1878 the overall rate was 22.32 per thousand, with deaths of infants (less than five years old) 55.5% of total deaths, and rising to 59% in March and April as a result of a measles epidemic, and 74% and 75% in July and August owing to an outbreak of infantile diarrhoea.[18]

The impact of such hazards on school attendance was apparent in late 1902, when in fact the south-western corner of the borough was less badly hit than other areas. In the week ending 27 September, 724 cases of measles were identified. Some infants departments were closed for two weeks. While the outbreak was most evident in the first two weeks of September and was most apparent in St. John's school, it became concentrated in this instance on Hawthorne Road, Salis-

Fig. 9.4. Bootle: Residential Rateable Values about 1900

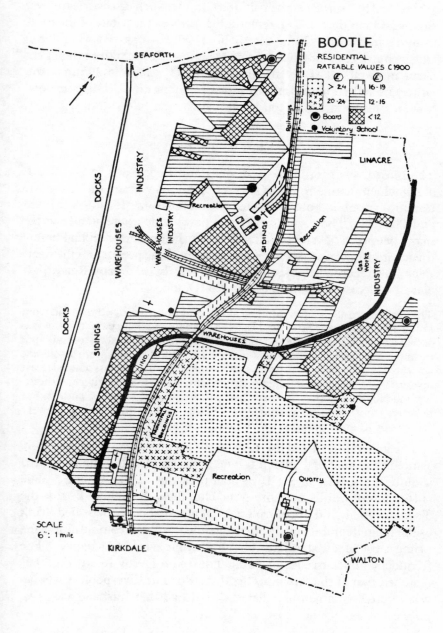

bury Road and Gray Street board schools, and on Christ Church, St. James' and St. Mary's in the voluntary sector. Such diseases leapt over the social boundaries. The remarkable fact was that none of the cases came from the Day Industrial School, which took truant children from some of the more disadvantaged homes. Here children were kept clean and well-fed. They attended from 8.00 a.m. to 5.30 p.m., and largely used their homes as dormitories.[19] In the crowded day schools, however respectable, the outbreak had spread like wildfire.

STREET LIFE

The most lively thoroughfare of dockland Bootle was Derby Road, along which ran the trams to Liverpool, and low-grade shops and the ubiquitous public houses formed the street front (Figs. 9.3 (a), 9.5 and Plate 11). The corner stores and pawn shops were stand-bys for many people in the community, tick and the broker providing barely the means to eke out existence between one wage packet and the next. Penanink recorded the scene on a 'brilliantly lit' Derby Road, past eleven o'clock on a Saturday night in October 1890:

The shops were all open as I walked along, and women crossed the road from Dundas Street, Lyons Street and Raleigh Street to purchase penn'orths of tea, stale loaves of bread, quarter pounds of sugar, and such like accessories before business was suspended for the night ... The public-houses were all closed, and the thoroughfare was thronged by the members of that class which is least favoured by fortune. Men three-quarters intoxicated were singing and shouting and laughing as they wended their way homeward. Though nothing but poverty – miserable, abject poverty – stared them in the face, they were careless of it, and, perhaps, for the nonce, happy.[20]

The general tenor of local newspaper accounts was less favourably slanted than that of Penanink. The borough resented the tag it had acquired, not least in the Liverpool press, of 'Brutal Bootle'.[21] The custodians of public morality – the churches, the School Board, the Town Council, and of course the local newspapers – identified drink as the main demoralising influence in the dockland communities, the prime cause of low standards of living, crime, vice and truancy.[22] The frequency of occurrence of public houses on Derby Road (Fig. 9.5) matched that of the infamous Scotland Road in Liverpool. A woman was quoted as lamenting that she could get her husband past two public houses but not past six.[23]

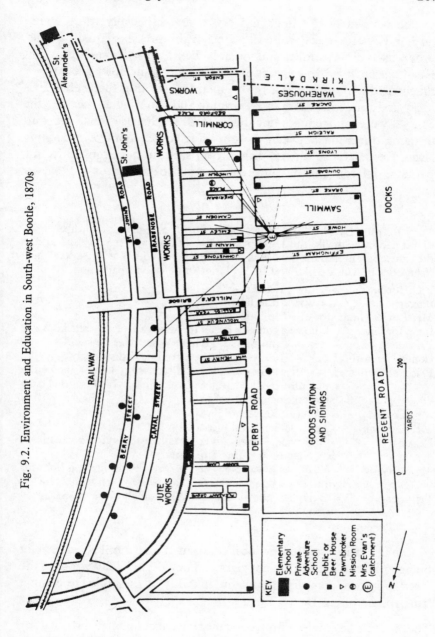

Fig. 9.2. Environment and Education in South-west Bootle, 1870s

The women of the dockland areas, and especially those whose husbands were at sea, were depicted in the press as equally drink-prone as their menfolk, and notably bellicose when in this state. Headings such as 'The Lyons Street Viragoes', and spicy accounts of raucous courtroom scenes, the women 'conducting themselves in a noisy and unseemly manner by singing and shouting as they left the court', were of frequent incidence.[24] Of such occasions, the gulf in communication between the opposing forces loomed impossibly large. Responses to official disapproval seem to have ranged from a pathetic deference to uncomprehending stupefaction:

A Voluble Prisoner

Mary Barrett, Lyons Street, was charged with being drunk and disorderly.
    'I'd had some drink, but not much: I was not drunk', she now said, and as the constable entered the box, 'Ask him. He will tell you, if he doesn't tell lies. If he does he will be like you.' This latter to no one in particular.

P.C. Jordan	– 'I saw prisoner' –
Barrett	– 'I was in the beerhouse' –
Mr. Lewes (Magistrate)	– 'Be quiet' –
P.C. Jordan	– 'She was going to break the windows of a public house' –
Prisoner	– 'Go on, you liar ... (Later) What does he say?' –
Constable in the Dock	– 'He says you were drunk and disorderly' –
Prisoner (vehemently)	– 'I was not drunk and disorderly. He took me by the hand, and I walked as straight as himself. It's because I have been talking about religion.'
Mr. Lewis	– 'What's the record?' –
Mr. Cumming	– 'This is her 32nd offence.'
Prisoner	– 'I got some drink given to me yesterday, and because it was New Year's Day I took it.'
Mr. Glasgow	– 'Well, as it was New Year's Day we will make it light for you. 2/6d (fine?) and 2/6d (costs?) or seven days.'
Prisoner	– 'I haven't got the money. Will you allow me till Saturday to pay it?' –

Removed below.[25]

The law was regarded by local tradesmen and shopkeepers as not being enforced with sufficient rigour. They periodically wrote to the *Bootle Times* to complain about the inability of the police to combat 'ruffianism' along Derby Road:

The road between Miller's Bridge and the boundary is infested night and day with the very worst class of youths and high rippers, also females of the very worst type ... I assure you, sir, it is having a most disastrous effect upon the shopkeepers ... the tradesman lives in daily dread of these vagabonds ...

Even on a Sunday afternoon these wretches congregate under the windows, their language being filthy and disgusting. The magistrates should be located here with their families, probably they would then take the necessary steps to deal with these villains.[26]

The perception of a perennially drunken slum population was translated down to an equally generalised stereotype of its children: the 'street arabs', urchins who inconveniently did not confine their activities to the dockland streets, but were found 'begging from door to door in the roads leading from Hawthorne Road' (a middle-class fringe zone) and infesting 'Stanley, Merton, Trinity and Balliol Roads, pestering passers-by for coppers, which they spend on cigarettes, etc.'.[27] Like the law, the school system was indicted for not taking such children off the streets.

THE PROVISION OF SCHOOLING

The timing of dockland extension into Bootle more or less coincided with a national anxiety about gaps in educational provision in the large towns and cities, and with moves towards universal schooling. Though racked with poverty and the need to cater for an unusually large number of children, at no stage was there pressure to plug the gaps in this south-western corner of Bootle with a board school. All the Bootle board schools were established, after Whitehall intervention (Chapter 8), to cover later working-class growth points in the north and east of the town. This was in part the consequence of the slum invading a former middle-class suburb in which there were three Anglican churches (including one adjacent in Kirkdale) and one Roman Catholic, with resources just sufficient to provide schools in the period before the full enormity of the problems created by rapid population growth were realised. In addition, school accommodation of sorts was to be found in the many small private adventure schools which sprang up in the area.

THE PRIVATE ADVENTURE SCHOOLS

As Fig. 9.5 indicates, the terraced houses of Enumeration Districts 4, 5, 6 and 7 were a popular location for private adventure schools in the 1870s. The largest number was in District 4, a social transition area, largely occupied by respectable working-class people. It may be that some of the schools catered for children of parents not wishing their

UEP–H*

offspring to be contaminated by association with the urchins of the slum. But the houses shown in Plate 9, in St. John's Road, make it clear that these schools were hardly being conducted in commodious and purpose-built accommodation. As the following list suggests, most were for girls. Many of them were short-lived.

TABLE 2

Private Adventure Schools in Enumeration District 4 in the 1870s

Berry Street

66	Mrs. Clarke's	(Mixed)	18 in attendance on inspection, 1875 24 on registers, 1876
108	Misses Lloyd's	(Ladies)	55 on registers, 1876: 50 in attendance
124	Mrs. Warmington's	(Ladies)	35 on registers, 1876
148	Mr. Spears's	(Boys)	34 on registers, 1877: 26 in attendance
101	Mrs. Rigby's	(Ladies)	16 on registers, 1876: 15 in attendance
133	Mrs. Morris's	(Mixed)	8 on registers, 1876: 6 in attendance

St. John's Road

34	Miss Fletcher's	(Ladies)	No information
50	Miss Andrews's	(Ladies)	38 on registers, 1873: 28 in attendance
41	Mrs. Drake's	(Ladies)	No information

Canal Street

8	Mrs. Clarke's	(?)	16 pupils in 1877

The reason such information survives reflects the policy of the Bootle School Board to legitimate these establishments, so that they might count them in the overall accommodation figures for the borough required by Whitehall. It therefore had necessarily to take a generally rose-coloured view of the quality of the provision, but at the same time strengthen its case by listing, visiting and evaluating the schools it cited. Thus at Mrs. Clarke's in Berry Street, 18 children were found in one room, and the lady categorised as unfitted to teach.[28] Another Mrs. Clarke (or could it have been the same one?) set up the school at 8, Canal Street which took 16 pupils, all under six years of age, at the time of the visitation of the School Board in 1877. Space just about met Departmental regulations, and only reading, writing and spelling were taught. Mrs Clarke was in effect accepted as a child-minder, a widow of advancing years with no other means of livelihood. The Board recommended that it should not 'interfere with her'.[29]

TABLE 3

Private Adventure Schools in Enumeration Districts 5, 6 and 7, 1870s

Johnstone Street

| 10 | Mrs. Ryan | (Mixed) | 40 on registers, 1872: closed by 1873 |

Derby Road

| 291 | Mr. Worthington | (Boys) | 10 on registers, 1876: closed that year |
| 248 | Misses Lloyd | (Ladies) | No information, 1872; moved to Berry Street by 1876? |

Princes' Terrace

| 18 | Mrs. Robb | (Mixed) | 30 on registers, 1876: 27 in attendance |

Howe Street

| 4 | Mrs. Evans | (Mixed) | 35 on registers, 1876: 30 in attendance |

The private adventure schools in the heart of the dockland slum were even more suspect, and only the above have left traces in the records. The Board paid special attention to the establishments of this area. In 1872 the Visitor reported that Mrs. Ryan had 40 children crowded into one very small room in Johnstone Street (Fig. 9.5).[30] In 1875, in nearby Princes' Terrace, Mrs. Robb's school was described as 'fairly efficient' but with sanitary arrangements 'in need of improvement'.[31] By early 1877, the school was found to be 'slightly over-crowded'. But Mrs. Robb was 'vigilant over attendance', even though probably not capable of obtaining a teacher's certificate.[32]

It was, however, Mrs. Evans's establishment in Howe Street (Fig. 9.5) which excited the greatest disapproval. In 1875 the Board was told she was not a person fit to teach, and that her school could not be regarded as efficient.[33] But she was still there in 1877, when the Visitor found 33 children, ranging in age from four to 13 years, in a room capable of accommodating 20 at most. It was suggested by the Board that she should not be allowed to take children over seven years of age.[34] In 1879 it resolved that parents of children above this age should be summonsed if they continued to use this school. Mrs. Evans complained about the frequent visits and the interference from officials. The Visitor reported non-cooperation. The Board took the case seriously enough to list the addresses of Mrs. Evans's intake, which is mapped on Fig. 9.5.[35]

Thus the Bootle School Board found it necessary to mask its own inactivity in provision by making full use of the places offered by private adventure schools on its official schedules of accommodation, even though it was well aware of the sub-standard conditions and lack of efficiency in most of these establishments. It is equally clear that the local communities recognised them as useful social facilities, in part in their child-minding function, and in part as a means of evading the more intense attendance surveillance that took place in the public elementary sector.

THE PUBLIC ELEMENTARY SECTOR

The two elementary schools bearing the brunt of the difficult social conditions in south-west Bootle were St. John's, a National School opened in 1868, and St. Alexander's, a Catholic school which moved in 1872 from a temporary home off Derby Road to a large three-storeyed building in St. John's Road, just beyond the Bootle boundary in Kirkdale (Plate 9). Children from this area also attended St. Mary's National School, the oldest in Bootle, and also St. Paul's Schools in Kirkdale. The intake of the voluntary sector did not respect the municipal boundary.

The social intake of both schools was concentrated in SEGs IV and V, though that of St. John's in these categories was reduced from 86% in the early 1870s to 74% in the early 1890s, as a result of the building of an underpass under the railway which allowed the school to tap a growing and more respectable working-class suburb further inland. But it remained a dockland slum school. Its Catholic counterpart took two-thirds of its intake from Bootle. By the turn of the century, the proportion was about 60%, of which 22% came from Enumeration Districts 5, 6 and 7, and about 18% from District 4. Eighty per cent of the children were in families in SEG V. No other Bootle school was socially so homogeneous.

St. Alexander's (Plate 9) was a tall, gaunt brick building, of mammoth scale for a church school at this time. Extensions made it finally capable of accommodating over 1,400 children. Boys, girls and infants each occupied a different floor. The back of the playground edged on to the railway line.

St. John's schools were built to a quite different type of plan, with accommodation in the first stage for 278 boys and 278 girls, and 214 infants (Fig. 9.6). The girls' accommodation was all on one floor, with a large schoolroom 60 feet long and 20 feet wide, and three further classrooms. The boys' schoolroom, of the same size, was similarly designed to take 120 children. Its small classroom was on the ground floor, with two others on the first floor above the girls' classrooms. The Boys' 'offices' were in their separate playground by their separate entrance. Those of the girls lay at the back of their playground. The partitioned infants' schoolroom, accommodating 170 children, ran along Brasenose Road. There was a separate 'babies' room, very small, but designed to take 44 children. The girls' playground adjoined the churchyard of St. John's.

Fig. 9.6. Plan of St. John's School, Bootle

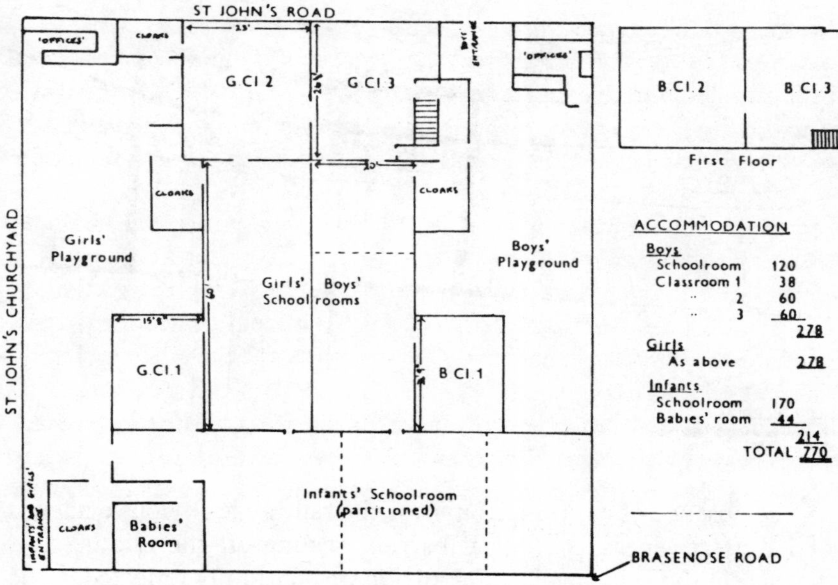

One of the ubiquitous features of Victorian street life was the daily journeys of children to and from school (Plate 6). In the dockland slum, the presence of two schools of different denominations in close proximity, at a time when religious rivalry was rife, led to lively and even violent exchanges when the children of the two schools came into contact, as the local geography made inevitable. Fig. 9.7 is an attempt to recreate the journeys of children of St. John's School in 1873, on the basis of information from the boys' admissions register. It makes the assumptions that those living in Camden Street and points south (Fig. 9.5) used the footbridge over the canal; and those from Emley Street and points north, Miller's bridge. Licence has also been taken in averaging out the numbers using the two entrances (Fig. 9.3a). Of course all the boys would have used the St. John's Road entrance to their playground (Fig. 9.6). The advantage of adopting this procedure is to create a more realistic impression of groups of children taking both routes to the schools.

Fig. 9.7. Bootle, St. John's School, 1873: Routes to School

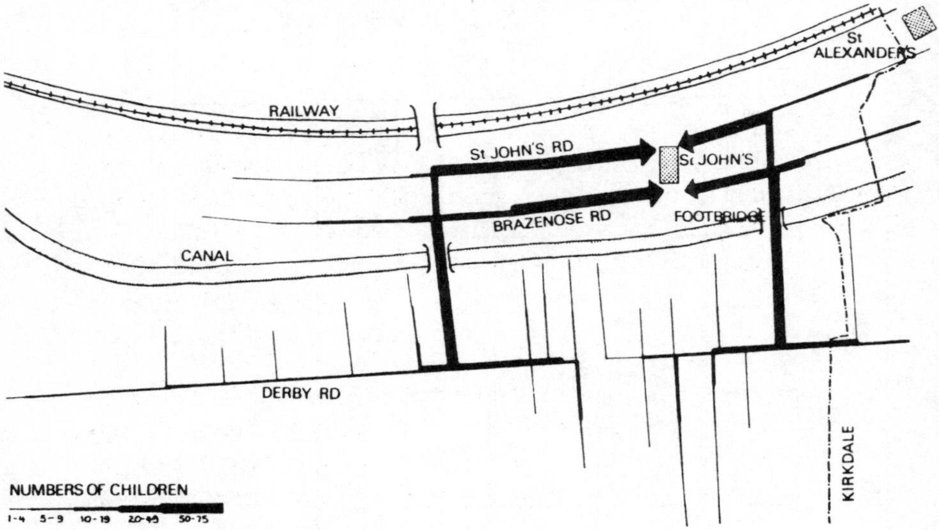

The absence of children from over the railway is obvious evidence of its effectiveness as a social barrier, sealing off the middle-class district on the eastern side. The divide was faithfully reflected in the intake of St. John's School. In the absence of admissions registers for St. Alexander's at the same period, the routes to school of its pupils cannot be mapped. But it is known that approximately two-thirds came from Bootle, so there must have been considerable scope for confrontation by the two groups of children, especially at pressure points such as Miller's Bridge and the footbridge (Fig. 9.7).

Street fighting resulted, and there is plenty of evidence of this in the school records. Thus in St. Alexander's Boys' School log book in 1872 it was recorded that ten or twelve boys were 'caned on the hand for

throwing stones at the boys of St. John's'. A representative of that
school had asked for the cooperation of St. Alexander's 'in attempting
to put an end to the disgraceful scenes daily occurring between the
children of both schools'.[36] In June a policeman was sent by railway officials, complaining of stones being thrown on the line.[37] By
September, the Headmaster was finding it necessary 'to superintend
in person the marching of children down St. John's Road'.[38] In
November, another dozen boys were punished for throwing stones at
the boys of St. John's.[39]

A further complaint was made in September 1876, certain boys
shouting and otherwise causing disturbance outside St. John's. On
the orders of the Priest, the Headmaster had fully investigated the
affray, 'and after denouncing such disgraceful conduct, punished the
ringleaders before the whole school'.[40] A quarter of a century later,
and this time seen from the St. John's viewpoint, it appears that
similar problems were present. Thus in March 1898 the Headmistress
complained of a 'dreadfully low attendance', but explained it as being
on St. Patrick's Day, on which 'many of the parents refuse to allow
their children to come for fear of accidents'.[41]

THE SCHOOLS AS SOCIAL WELFARE AGENCIES

In the heart of the dockland slum, both St. Alexander's and St. John's
churches took a major share of the responsibility for attending to the
needs of an endemically struggling population which periodically
lapsed into abject poverty. Poverty had both a short cycle, balancing
the weekly family budget, and long cycle aspect, the latter caused by
slumps in trade and lack of work at the docks or, from the 1890s,
strike. The schools, supported by the churches, attempted to maintain the health of the children in these times.

Thus in the severe winter of 1880–1, the Leeds and Liverpool Canal
froze over. In the frugally heated homes of the poor, the searching
cold made living conditions unbearable. A near-riot occurred in Bedford Place (Fig. 9.5) when a delivery of coal to the Mersey Woodwork-
ing Company came by cart rather than by canal. It was unloaded in
heaps in the street, which were 'quickly beset by starving people, who
could not be kept from filching the mineral'.[42] The Headmistress of
St. Alexander's Infants' School reported that owing to

continued frost and distress the attendance is very low. The children are continually supplied with food and clothes to keep them in school, kindly provided for them by the Reverend Manager and the Rev. W. Byrne.[43]

During the winter of 1885 the Bootle School Board was informed by the Visitor of St. Alexander's Schools that 135 children were going to school on two or three days of the week without breakfast. To cope with such problems, it was decided by St. John's to provide free dinners for those children whose parents were in receipt of fees from the Poor Law Guardians. The Headmaster of the boys' school commented on the improved physical appearance and increased capacity for school work which resulted from this provision. When asked if such dinners did not pauperise the recipients, it was pointed out that many of the children had lost one or both parents. Where destitution was caused by drunkenness and thriftlessness, 'why should the little ones be left to suffer?'. The Editor of the local newspaper could only plead: 'Our utilitarian and economic maxims all stand abashed at this question'.[44]

Again in 1890 free dinners were provided for Bootle children, starving because of a prolonged dock strike.[45] The strike similarly impinged on the running of the schools, as the Headmaster of St. Alexander's recorded:

There has been a strike ... The school pence is abnormally low, and the attendance not near so good as it should be for this time of year. The daily processions of the workmen induce many lads to play truant too.[46]

Another severe winter in 1895 led to both St. John's schools and the 'Bootle Temporary Relief Society' appealing for funds, the former to establish a soup kitchen, and the latter to distribute coal and food to 3,000 needy persons. Assessment of need was made by School Board officials and the police, and 500 children were daily served for several weeks with soup and bread.[47]

The mere fact of having to travel to school, down frequently unpaved, waterlogged or muddy streets, barely clothed and inadequately shod, together with lack of drying facilities in the schools, meant that bad weather took a heavy toll on attendance. Poor health was endemic even in good weather conditions and teachers prioritised welfare above educational needs. The local managers frequently gave permission for registers not to be taken or classes dismissed because of bad weather.

On Thursday afternoon a fearful downpour just as children were returning to school. The majority were drenched to the skin. Many of the poorer ones without hats and deplorable shoes. It would have been dangerous to allow them to stay in school, so sent them home.[48]

In a period of high staff as well as pupil mortality, and of disease ascribed to environmental rather than bacteriological factors, the weather was seen as a menacing external element, inhibiting the progress of schooling.

THE PROBLEMS OF ATTENDANCE

Several renowned truants have put in an appearance.[49]

As was noted in Chapter 8, the general strategy of the Bootle School Board in the first decade of its existence was to avoid building schools and to concentrate on enforcing attendance. Its earliest pronounce-ment took the form of what it saw as a rational appeal to the common sense of parents to avail themselves of the benefits of education and at the same time save ratepayers' money by ensuring that their children regularly attended the voluntary schools already provided.[50] Poor parents, claiming remission of fees from the School Board until 1876, when the responsibility passed to the Poor Law Guardians, were compelled to appear before one of its committees to make their cases. Fig. 9.3 indicates that the vast majority of such parents came from Enumeration Districts 5, 6 and 7, and most of these from the three poverty-stricken thoroughfares of Dundas Street, Lyons Street and Raleigh Street.

The incumbent of St. Paul's, Kirkdale (Fig. 9.3 (a)) was dismayed by this practice:

It will be perfectly useless to ask the parents to attend the Committee you speak of as they are completely indifferent as to the education of their children. If you would educate the little ones you must go to them and help their parents to send them to school ... Send visitors to their homes, give them no excuse, offer to pay ... I speak from long experience. I know the people.[51]

In this early period the new School Visitor made a survey of children in various parts of Bootle, and became acquainted at first hand with problems of squalor and child neglect. In March 1873 he reported that he had been to the homes of 100 children found on the streets and of 83 children reported by teachers for non-attendance.[52] The problems he faced were well publicised in the local press. Some parents were portrayed as powerless to influence their children, as in the case of

William Lockley, aged eleven, of William Henry Street, off Derby Road:

this boy is an incorrigible truant ... His nominal schoolmaster Mr. Gill avers that the boy is a perfect dunce and a discredit to his school. The parent declares he is quite unable to control him and therefore must submit to pay fines whenever they are imposed as has been done several times hitherto.[53]

The Visitor was faced with the triple constraints of uncooperative parents, the ease of escape from his attentions into private adventure schools, and unsympathetic magistrates. A case against James Reid, also of William Henry Street, was dismissed on the grounds that the burden of proof was on the Board to show that Mrs. Clarke's school in Berry Street, which he attended, was not efficient.[54] Many proprietors declined to afford information to the Visitor, who observed that this gave 'great scope for deception, of which I believe many parents avail themselves'.[55]

In its attempts to control the vagrant children of dockland, discussions on the School Board soon turned to the idea of a special school. By 1877 Liverpool had established an Industrial School for truant children, and Bootle, in a Memorial to Whitehall, quoted this as the most appropriate solution for it also, to deal with the children of parents 'of drunken and dissolute habits, to whom fine and imprisonment appear to have no terror'. But the burden of providing such a school was regarded as too great for a small Board. It sought funds from the national exchequer as a means of coping with 'the young arab classes' before they became the criminal classes.[56] The funds were not forthcoming and Bootle had to wait until 1895 for its Day Industrial School. Meanwhile, the Board had to pay for the accommodation of its 'incorrigibles' in Liverpool's truant establishments.

Head-teachers generally shared the Board's view that truancy and intermittent attendance were the besetting problems. 'Latecoming and irregularity are the bane of this school',[57] opined the Headmistress of St. Mary's, whose catchment area by 1891 had been overtaken by the northward growth of the Mersey docks. In January 1892 she noted some of the excuses for absence on a particular day: 'too late'; 'over-slept herself'; 'gone to town'; 'going to a party and had to have her head in curlpapers (not allowed in school) all day'.[58]

The weekly demand for school pence significantly reduced attendance, especially in times of distress. Thus in September 1874 the

Headmaster of St. Alexander's compared his fees with the previous year's and felt 'induced to pay more attention to this subject'.[59] The problem was still with him in 1886, when low fee income was ascribed to 'so great a number of the children's parents being unable to obtain employment'.[60] Again in 1890, the amount of fees dropped during a dock labour dispute, 'most of the children's fathers being among the strikers'.[61] The schools used various ploys to encourage the payment of fees. The Priest at St. Alexander's announced in 1880 that any child paying four weeks' pence in advance would receive five weeks' tuition for that amount.[62] On other occasions, the tactic switched from the carrot to the stick:

The master has made a list of regular truant players – about thirty of whom are in the senior department. It is a difficult thing to know what to do with these troublesome boys. The cane has been tried often enough and without effect. Many of them are so hardened that they will play truant the day after receiving a merciless beating from an angry parent. The master is trying the plan of compelling a boy to hold slates over his head for half an hour. It seems to be more dreaded than the cane, and is not attended with any inconvenient results.[63]

The School Board came under frequent criticism from the voluntary school head-teachers for not enforcing attendance with sufficient diligence. Each party defined the situation differently. The bureaucrat turned a blind eye where children were regularly putting in seven or eight attendances out of ten each week. The head-teachers resented what they interpreted as implicit support for parents playing the system. Relationships between the voluntary schools and the Board plummeted in the late 1880s and 1890s.

Thus in October 1890 the Headmaster of St. Alexander's complained about the 'great amount of laxity on the part of the Bootle School Board in allowing the children – incorrigible truants – to go at large in the way they do'.[64] Relations between the Headmistress of St. Mary's and the School Board Visitor broke down completely following a Board decision not to issue any more summonses owing to the physical state of her school. She accused the Visitor or being 'too feeble to do his work, so the attendance has to be attended to by our own staff'. The unfinished state of the school was merely an excuse seized upon by parents.[65] Continuing acrimony finally resulted in the Visitor complaining of discourteous treatment by the Headmistress, and requesting a replacement.[66] She retorted that she would only communicate with him in future in the presence of another person.[67]

Even the more conciliatory Headmistress of St. John's was unhappy with the Board's efforts, asking for more firmness in interpreting the partial and total exemption regulations. She complained also that some of the magistrates were 'quite satisfied with 60% attendance', as late as 1900.[68]

The board finally turned to building a Day Industrial School to accommodate its truant children. Opened in Marsh Lane in 1895, it was seen by many ratepayers as another expensive breach of the principle that parents should take responsibility for their own off-spring. An article in the *Bootle Times* in 1893 had attempted to clarify the objectives of such schools for an apparently sceptical readership:

The children we find in these schools are generally the poorest of the poor, whose objections to the daily confinement and accompanying teaching and industrial work must be much lessened by three good meals a day which are provided for them. The children receive no clothing, but are kept as clean as baths and soap and water can make them.[69]

But once the school was in operation, the Editor was critical of the transfer of responsibilities from parents to ratepayers:

It is ... necessary before children are committed to such institutions ... that every endeavour should be made to bring the parents to a sense of their responsibility ... The management of children is, perhaps, difficult, but why the poorer classes should be mastered by their offsprings more than any other section of the community is beyond us ... it is not unfrequent that a burly father, six feet in height, appears before the Bench and complains that he has no control over a puny piece of humanity.[70]

Reactions of the recipients to the system are less consistently recorded, and much of the information that has been passed down is fragmentary and circumstantial. On the basis of the contemporary stereotyping of slum-dwellers as likely to be more indigent, capricious and reckless parents than the norm, it would be expected that there would be a higher than usual proportion of non-scholars than scholars in the population; that there would be more claims for the remission of fees; that attendance levels in dockland schools would be poorer than elsewhere; that there would be more summonses for non-attendance; that there would be greater parental hostility to the agencies of enforcement, with strained relationships between parents and teachers and parents and School Board officials.

Taking the town as a whole, for each of the census years 1851, 1861 and 1871, statistically significant differences occurred in non-scholar/scholar ratios between the different socio-economic groupings, with

SEG V including a higher percentage of non-scholars than any other group. Similarly significant differences occurred between Enumeration Districts, but not wholly as expected. The highest ranking area in 1871 was District 4, with 73% scholars. Very much a social fringe district, it was heavily built up with a high percentage of respectable working-class people. The main middle-class area, District 3, also came out well, with 71% scholars. Districts 8 and 13, still with a residue of middle-class population, followed with 63.5% and 66.5% scholars respectively. On the other hand, Districts 10 and 11, lightly built up at the time, and less accessible to schools, had more non-scholars than scholars, with only 47.5% and 48.8% respectively (Fig. 9.2).

The lowest total, as the stereotyped view would have anticipated, was to be found in the dockland slum. It was in District 6, with only 41.4% designated as scholars. On the other hand, the most deprived area of all, District 7, dominated by the casual Irish labour force, produced a much higher figure of 57.4% as scholars. It might be surmised that in this case the power of the Catholic Church was a factor, at least functioning strongly enough to get its flock to register their children as scholars, if not at the same time to send them regularly to school. Additionally, the commodious new St. Alexander's Schools had been opened, which would have been likely to attract custom. But St. John's Schools had also not been open for very long, and had seemed not to have done as much to raise the scholar figures for the less Catholic dominated District 6. A further complication is that the actual recorded average attendance figures were better at St. John's than at St. Alexander's at the time, 66% at St. John's as against only 42% at St. Alexander's. Thus while it would be correct to assume that problems of attendance were indeed great among families in SEG V, there was much variation in response to school provision within the group.

The finding of school pence was a critical pressure on domestic budgets. To enrol children was not costly, but actual attendance was, especially a burden in times of trade recession. However ready parents might have been to send their children to school, more basic physical needs had often to take precedence over educational. What the authorities chose to condemn as indifference could logically be regarded by poor parents as getting the priorities right. The poverty factor emerges in the distribution of parents claiming remission of fees from the Bootle School Board between 1871 and 1876 (Fig. 9.8). Most claimants came from the dockland slum, and characteristically from the 'troublesome thoroughfares' of Dundas Street, Lyons Street and Raleigh Street.

While there were considerable variations in average attendance in the early 1870s, discrepancies were ironed out as the enforcement agencies made their presence felt. By 1900 even the most difficult schools were achieving averages of over 80%. In general the board schools achieved the better averages, ranging from 91.1% at Hawthorne Road to 87.4% at Bedford Road, as against a range of from 89% at Christ Church, to 80.6% at St. John's in the voluntary sector. The voluntary schools in the dockland area were behind the rest with, apart from St. John's, averages of 81% at St. Mary's, 83.3% at St. James's and 83.4% at St. Alexander's, showing that the Catholic schools were achieving somewhat higher averages than the Anglican at this time.

A similar pattern as for remission of fees emerges in the number of summonses for non-attendance. Again the highest figure was in the dockland zone of south-west Bootle, under constant scrutiny from police, officers of public health, and the school attendance officers. In these circumstances, tensions between the agents of enforcement and the local population were inevitable. The authorities were under continuing pressure to clean up the streets and expunge the image of 'Brutal Bootle'. A columnist of 1880 complained, for example, of the 'inefficient looking up of gutter children ... The advantage of an Education Act through which children run shockheaded and barefooted is not ... palpable'.[71] One of the School Board visitors was subject to public criticism in the *Bootle Times*, accused of preferring his office duties to those involving face to face contacts: 'it may be asked whether there are not some streets in Bootle which Mr. Porter would rather not visit'.[72]

To the dockland communities, however, there appeared a surfeit of visits and individuals, whether parents or proprietors of lodging houses or child-minding establishments, were prone to feel persecuted. On occasions they took the law into their own hands. Thus a Molyneux Street resident with a 12-year-old son earning 15/- per week during the day at the docks, and attending a private adventure school for two to three hours in the evening, resented notices being served upon him to cause his child to attend school, and pursued Mr. Porter along Derby Road 'using abusive and threatening language'.[73] Though assaults were not frequent, they continued to occur. A School

Fig. 9.8. Bootle, 1871–6: Parental Applications to Bootle School Board for Remission of Fees

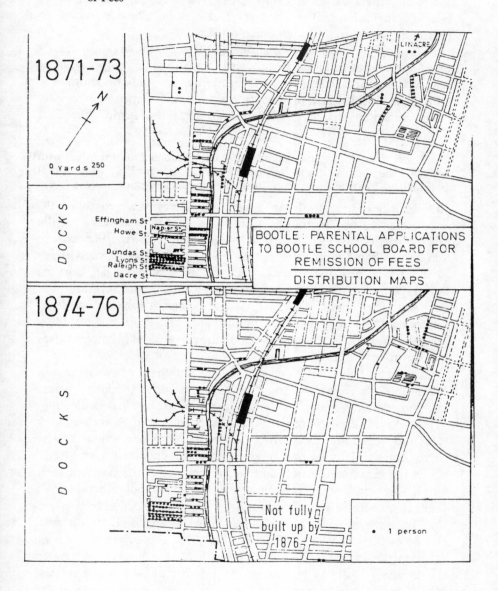

Board Visitor had a jug of beer thrown over him in Lyons Street in 1896, and then was struck on the head with the jug. At the court hearing, the defendant claimed she had neither 'chick nor child' to merit the attentions of attendance officers.[74]

Relations between parents and schools were similarly unpredictable, sometimes antagonistic towards and at others supportive of teachers' attempts to impose strict discipline. It was not uncommon to seek the help of the school to control recalcitrant offspring, especially over the attendance issue. In 1878, for example, the Headmaster of St. Alexander's reported:

Mr. James Roach of 54 Dundas Street came to the school this morning, with his son John (a truant) and begged the master to punish the boy. Moral 'suasion, having utterly failed, in this case, the master punished the boy.[75]

In February 1873 a pupil was reported as delivering a 'grossly insulting message' from his mother to his teacher, loudly enough for the other boys to hear. He was promptly sent home. The mother came in and denied having sent such a message. The boy later 'acknowledges in the presence of the whole school that he has told a lie, begs his teacher's pardon, and promises to be more humble and submissive'.[76] In a similar incident, a boy expelled for insubordination had been immediately brought back by his mother, and again on humbling himself before the whole school and in the presence of his mother, was allowed to re-enter.[77]

The picture was not always of confrontation or of pathetic submission, however. At least some teachers approached their diversified tasks in the slum school with considerable professional dedication. While those in aspiring middle-class fringe situations might well seek to exclude less desirable children, teachers in dockland schools had no such choice. They showed in some cases much care for childrens' needs for basic instruction and social welfare. Some devoted their whole working lives to service in this type of school. Thus in 1908 Janet Roe retired after 33 years at St. John's School. Miss McCarthy, the first assistant, and 21 years at the school, was made Headmistress, and Miss Gill, 21 years as 2nd assistant, her deputy. In her closing entry in the log book Miss Roe noted how deeply she appreciated the loyalty of 'all my assistants and how thankful I am that Miss McCarthy's splendid work has been recognised in her choice as my successor'.[78] It may be not without significance that in this difficult slum area an inspector's report of 1900 testified to this stable leadership:

The order, tone and general arrangements of the School are excellent while the teaching is, as hitherto, intelligent and effective in a remarkable degree.[79]

While it would be naïve to take this wholly at face value, such occurrences accumulate sufficiently to act as counsel against attempts to homogenize poor working-class communities and their schooling. The slum was but one of a number of different types of working-class milieu. It was and is only to the outsider, whether the contemporary middle-class observer or the latter-day middle-class historian, that the environment could or can appear as undifferentiated. It was of course the case that in this arena of limited choice 'biotic' forces functioned strongly, but these were not necessarily at the expense of group solidarity and neighbourly assistance, surely 'societal' forces in Park's terms. The slum was an appalling but intimate place, its people very human and 'like others', notwithstanding their external repute, with its own internal tendency to create a minutely-graded social status continuum.[80]

REFERENCES AND FOOTNOTES

1. *B.T.*, 25 July 1885.
2. Public Record Office, *Education File 16/162*, letter dated 17 Feb. 1872.
3. *National Society Files*, St. John's, Bootle, letter dated 6 Nov. 1886.
4. *Ibid.*, letter dated 19 June 1867.
5. For the detailed aggregate Enumeration District data in the sections on population and housing, I am indebted to Dr. C. Pooley of the University of Lancaster and Emeritus Professor R. Lawton of the University of Liverpool for their help.
6. See R. Lawton, 'The Population of Liverpool in the mid-Nineteenth Century', *Transactions of the Historic Society of Lancashire and Cheshire*, vol. 107 (1956), pp. 89–120.
7. *B.T.*, 1 Nov. 1890.
8. *B.T.*, 4 Oct. 1902.
9. *B.T.*, 15 Nov. 1890.
10. *B.T.*, 6 Aug. 1892.
11. *B.T.*, 18 Oct. 1890.
12. *B.T.*, 23 March 1878.
13. *B.T.*, 7 June 1902.
14. *B.T.*, advertisements of 13 Oct. 1883.
15. *B.T.*, advertisements of 14 July 1884.
16. *B.T.*, 18 Oct. 1884.
17. *B.T.*, 30 April 1881.
18. *B.T.*, 19 April 1879.
19. *Bootle Town Council Minutes*, 1902–3, p. 533.
20. *B.T.*, 18 Oct. 1890.
21. *B.T.*, 14 July 1888.
22. *Bootle School Board* (hereafter *B.S.B.*) *Minutes*, 19 Sept. 1872.

23. *B.T.*, 11 Jan. 1890.
24. *B.T.*, 28 April 1900.
25. *B.T.*, 4 Jan. 1902.
26. *B.T.*, 12 May 1888.
27. *B.T.*, 13 Oct. 1898.
28. *B.S.B. Minutes*, 12 Nov. 1875.
29. *Ibid.*, 9 Feb. 1877.
30. *Ibid.*, 17 Oct. 1872.
31. *Ibid.*, 12 Nov. 1875.
32. *Ibid.*, 9 Feb. 1877.
33. *Ibid.*, 12 Nov. 1875.
34. *Ibid.*, 9 Feb. 1877.
35. *Ibid.*, 19 Sept. 1879.
36. *St. Alexander's Boys' Log Book*, 15 March 1872.
37. *Ibid.*, 22 June 1872.
38. *Ibid.*, 5 Sept. 1872.
39. *Ibid.*, 22 Nov. 1872.
40. *Ibid.*, 7 Sept. 1876.
41. *St. John's Girls' Log Book*, 18 March 1899.
42. *B.T.*, 29 Jan. 1881.
43. *St. Alexander's Infants' Log Book*, 21 Jan. 1881.
44. *B.T.*, 24 Jan. 1885.
45. *B.T.*, 5 April 1890.
46. *St. Alexander's Boys' Log Book*, 11 March 1890.
47. *B.T.*, 23 Feb. 1895.
48. *St. John's Girls' Log Book*, 5 Oct. 1900.
49. *St. Alexander's Boys' Log Book*, 6 Oct. 1886.
50. See *B.S.B. Minutes*, 16 March 1871.
51. *B.S.B., Minutes of the School Fees Committee*, 19 Oct. 1871.
52. *B.S.B. Minutes*, 14 March 1873.
53. *B.S.B. Minutes*, 9 April 1875.
54. *B.S.B. Minutes*, 11 Feb. 1874.
55. *B.S.B. Minutes*, also 11 Feb. 1874.
56. *The Respectful Memorial of the Bootle-cum-Linacre School Board to Viscount Sandon, M.P., Vice-President of the Committee of the Privy Council on Education*, Dec. 1877.
57. *St. Mary's Girls' Log Book*, 21 Aug. 1891.
58. *Ibid.*, 4 Jan. 1892.
59. *St. Alexander's Boys' Log Book*, 22 Sept. 1874.
60. *Ibid.*, 15 Jan. 1886.
61. *St. Alexander's Girls' Log Book*, 14 March 1890.
62. *St. Alexander's Boys' Log Book*, 5 April 1880.
63. *Ibid.*, 9 Sept. 1875.
64. *Ibid.*, 20 Oct. 1890.
65. *St. Mary's Girls' School Log Book*, 25 Sept. 1894.
66. *Ibid.*, 25 April 1898.
67. *Ibid.*, 29 April 1898.
68. *St. John's Girls' Log Book*, 12 Oct. 1900.
69. *B.T.*, 18 Nov. 1893.
70. *B.T.*, 3 April 1897.
71. *B.T.*, 10 July 1800.
72. *B.T.*, 29 March 1879.
73. *B.T.*, 10 Dec. 1875.
74. *B.T.*, 23 May 1896.

75. *St. Alexander's Boys' Log Book*, 4 June 1878.
76. *Ibid.*, 13 Feb. 1873.
77. *Ibid.*, 10 Dec. 1872.
78. *St. John's Girls' Log Book*, 30 April 1908.
79. Quoted in *Ibid.*, 16 March 1900.
80. See, for example, R. Roberts, *The Classic Slum: Salford Life in the First Quarter of the Century* (Manchester, 1971).

CHAPTER TEN

'Two Sides of the Railway Tracks': Schooling and Communities in a Victorian Suburb: Birkdale

> Birkdale may be considered as the West End of
> Southport ... Strange to say, [it] is ahead of its larger
> sister town in having a school board, consisting of seven
> members, of whom one is lady. In spite of this separate
> rule, the two places practically count as one. The private
> schools are legion ... Birkdale especially teems with
> them, there being brass plates on more gates than one
> could count.[1] (Bryce Commission, 1896)

Though Southport and Birkdale were located less than 20 miles to the north, they had become the world that Bootle had lost by the last three decades of the nineteenth century. A columnist in the *Bootle Times* commented with some ambivalence on Southport's increasing popularity:

Among the retired and semi-retired people of Southport there are 'all sorts and conditions of men'. Rich merchants from Liverpool and Manchester, others from Bootle, including several from Merton Road and neighbourhood, wealthy widows ...; pretty little maidens who will some day inherit the fortunes which have been carefully gathered by their fond parents ...; struggling shopkeepers, in broken health, who have come here from every manufacturing town in Lancashire and Yorkshire with only half a living, hoping to make the other half by the aid of lodgers ... Visitors to Southport are not long here before they are struck with the predominance of the gentler sex ... There is comparatively little poverty or distress in Southport ...[2]

Southport's origins as a watering place dated back to the late eighteenth century. Early nineteenth century growth had been slow, the population increasing from 2,096 in 1801 to 7,774 in 1841. Two critical factors shaped its more precipitate late nineteenth-century expansion, culminating in a population of 48,046 by 1901.

The first was the coming of the railways, lines being opened to Liverpool in the 1840s and Manchester and south-east Lancashire in the 1850s. Southport immediately became a magnet for commuters, holiday-makers and day trippers. Following the opening of the Lancashire and Yorkshire railway (Plate 14), the local newspaper reported:

The week which ended Saturday June 2 was a memorable one for Southport. Never before within memory has the town witnessed so busy and bustling a scene as its streets presented during Whitweek. The railways from the manufacturing districts poured in their thousands daily, who flowed through the streets in one vast living stream, and swarmed on the wide expanse of shore like a newly-disturbed ant-hill.[3]

Over 40,000 came in that week via the Lancashire and Yorkshire and East Lancashire railways alone.[4] But the ant-hill metaphor was not calculated to appeal to local residents. The objective of resorts such as Southport was to become select residential towns, leaving Blackpool, with its Tower complex, Morecambe, with its Winter Gardens, and New Brighton, with its Tower and Recreation Company, to concentrate on the working masses of the Lancashire cotton, West Riding woollen, and Merseyside manufacturing districts respectively.[5] Southport was prone rather to extol its celebrated shopping boulevard, Lord Street (Plate 12).

Complementing this overriding policy was therefore the compatibility of the social pretensions of the resident community and the development intentions of local landowners and local authorities. In Southport, the dominant landowning families were the Heskeths and the Scarisbricks. Charles Hesketh in fact resolved that his estate in Southport should be developed as a select middle-class area, and implemented it by deploying restrictive covenants. Land was leased in relatively large plots enabling the growth of villa-type residential districts,[6] concentrated on Hesketh Park and Birkdale Park, on the north and south fringes of the developing town centre (Fig. 10.1). Though in conflict with the middle-class lessees and the local authority over their reluctance to provide new streets, sanitary improvements and other amenities, they were at one in their common interest in countering the influence of the day tripper:

Fig. 10.1 Southport and Birkdale, 1895–1900

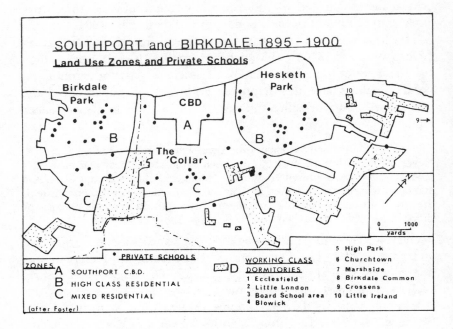

The commuting and retired middle classes had not escaped to their havens by the sea to be followed by hordes of the very class they had sought to segregate themselves from ... Political hatchets were buried as the landowners and the town's leaders presented a united front in the face of this common threat.[7]

To the south of this growing seaside town lay Birkdale, in the early nineteenth century a straggling collection of agricultural cottages, without the nucleus of a church or manor house. Its population had risen from a mere 360 in 1801 to 625 in 1851. Birkdale's late nineteenth-century growth, like that of Southport, was fashioned by the railway connection to Liverpool, together with the initiatives of the local landowner, Thomas Weld-Blundell.

In a petition to the House of Lords in 1847 in support of the plan for a Liverpool, Crosby and Southport railway, the local ratepayers argued

That if the proposed line of railway were opened, so that persons engaged in business in Liverpool could go to and fro at little expense of time and money, great numbers of them would reside at Southport during the summer and many would make it their permanent place of abode.[8]

So far as Birkdale was concerned, the ideal became reality with almost indecent haste. Following the opening of Birkdale Station (Fig. 10.2), Weld-Blundell offered land for building on leases of 99 years on Birkdale Park Estate, a planned garden suburb just beyond the southern boundary of Southport:

The township will be laid out under the superintendence of eminent surveyors and landscape gardeners ... We do not despair of shortly seeing the healthy locality covered with beautiful residences suitable for the habitation of the most respectable parties.[9]

A church, crucial to the success of any reputable suburb, was completed in 1857, and 'castles in the sand' grew round about it (Plate 14).[10] By the 1860s, the fortunes of Birkdale Park were assured, with 18 well laid out streets, as *Mannex's Directory* of mid-Lancashire testified:

Birkdale ... has made such rapid progress in buildings and population ... that it not only forms a most important suburb of Southport, but has actually the appearance and some of the characteristics of a separate town. The buildings are generally on a scale of grandeur and magnificence superior to those of Southport, and many of them are occupied by opulent merchants and manufacturers from Liverpool and Manchester, as well as by other wealthy and highly respected persons. The streets are asphalted, and laid out with much taste and elegance.[11]

Progress was even more rapid in the 1870s, when 700 building leases were granted, as against 228 in the 1860s. An arcaded shopping centre developed near the station and this, a Town Hall, a Carnegie Library, a huge Victorian hotel, its own Promenade, known as Rotten Row, and park, Victoria Park, gave Birkdale visible independence from Southport, and was symptomatic of a rivalry which made the final amalgamation of 1912, while inevitable, also contentious.

It is recorded that in Birkdale's early days inhabitants were distinguished as dwellers in the 'Heys', the inland side, or in the 'Hawes', the sandhills, and kept to their local division. The railway, when it came, ran very approximately along this divide, forming something of a physical boundary, with Birkdale Common to the east and Birkdale Park to the west.[12] Of the population of 1,100 in 1856, two 'classes' were identified, the 'agricultural' of Birkdale Common, and the 'suburban' of Birkdale Park, the former numbering 700, and the latter 400, albeit 'rapidly increasing'.[13] Even today, local estate agents draw attention to the higher prestige of residences on the 'Shoreside' of the railway.

Fig. 10.2. Birkdale Park, Private Schools, 1868
(Source: Johnson and Green's Directory)

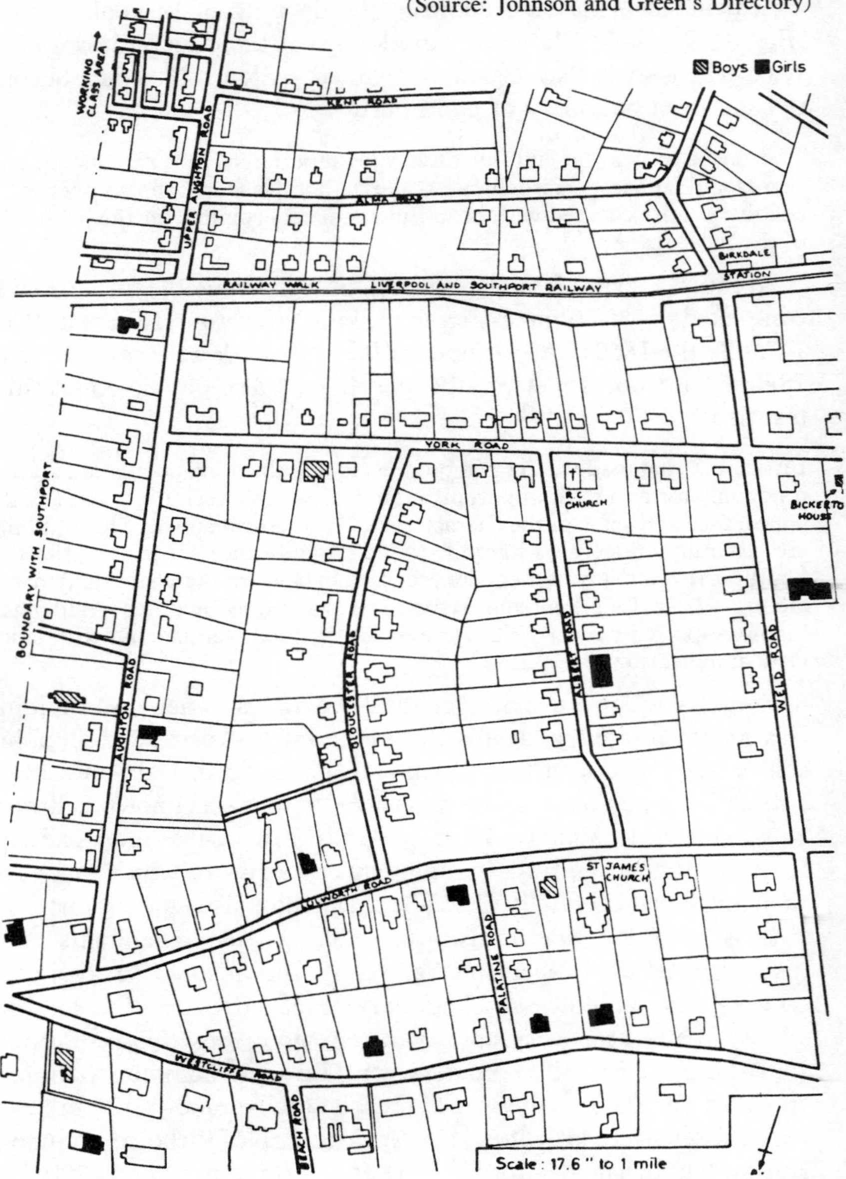

Johnson and Green's *Directory* of 1868 provided a clear outline of the divide, shown in Table 1.

TABLE 1

Heads of Household	West of Railway	East of Railway	Total
1. Professional classes (merchants, solicitors etc.)	84	16	100
2. Lower middle & working classes (including tradesmen, agricultural labourers etc.)	21	98	119
3. No occupation given (including retired, spinsters, others of private means)	88	82	170

Of the professional groups, 41 heads of household had their place of work in Liverpool, nine in Southport, seven in Manchester, five in Bolton and four in other Lancashire cotton towns. Of these 66, 58 lived in Birkdale Park. Another extract (see Table 2) provides details of residents in Westcliffe Road, one of the main thoroughfares of Birkdale Park (Fig. 10.2).

TABLE 2

(From Johnson and Green's *Directory* of 1868)

WESTCLIFFE ROAD
From Southport boundary to Weld Road

East Side
Westcliffe House. Crook, Mrs. M.
Westcliffe Villa. Berry, Mr. J.
Beach Cottage. Kemp, Mr. J.A.
Ayton Villa. Himmers, Mrs. A.
Westlands. Gregson, Jane & Hannah. *Ladies' School*
Mitchell, A. Cotton Manufacturer (Manchester)
Westcliffe Lodge. Dodson, W. Hosier (Liverpool)

—— Here is Palatine Road ——

Regenten House. Sissons, Sarah. *Ladies' School*
Netherwood. Hosker, Maria. *Ladies' School*
Letson, Mrs. M.P.

West Side
Beachfield. Fletcher, E. Cotton Manufacturer (Manchester)
Gaskell, H. Esq. J.P.

(Table 2 Continued)

Table 2 (continued)

Wyborne Gate, Sharp, Prudence. *Ladies' School*
Commercial College Webster, Rev. E. M.R.C.P. Principal.
Westcliffe Shatwell, W. Silk Manufacturer (Manchester)
Shatterthwaite, Miss M.A.
Westholme. Horsman, Mr. F.
Starr Hill. Smith, Mrs. C.
Morningside. Doke, W. Stockbroker (Liverpool)
Beach House. Froane, W. Merchant (Liverpool)

—— Here is Beach Road ——

Cleveland House. Himmers, W. Esq. J.P.
Helensholme. Chamberlain, G. Stockbroker (Liverpool)
Sandhurst. Banning, J.J. Esq. Solicitor (Liverpool)
Radford, S.C. Corn Merchant (Liverpool)
Birklands. Taylor, Mr. S.
The Warren. Burton, Mrs. Ellen.

On the other side of the railway tracks, however, the situation
changed. Following a transition zone of somewhat less prestigious
middle-class housing in the area south and east of Birkdale Station
(Fig. 10.3), which included Alma Road and Kent Road (Fig. 10.2),
working-class enclaves developed in the Ecclesfield district, overlapping the Southport boundary, and in the Birkdale Common area,
marked as 1, 3 and 8 on Fig. 10.1. Liddle indicates that in the
Southport part of Ecclesfield there was in 1862 no sanitation, no
drainage, no gas, no pavements and no footpaths. The parsimonious
policies of the Scarisbrick estate allowed no provision for such
amenities, which could not be compensated by private initiative in the
artisan areas of the town.[14]

By the late 1880s, though far from desperate by the standards of the
Bootle slums, this growing working-class zone was depicted locally as
a social problem area. Thus the Birkdale School Board made reference
to serious over-crowding in the Chatham Road district, where in
addition a notorious 'baby farming' scandal led to the establishment of
a local office by the N.S.P.C.C.[15] The social contrasts are illustrated
by the directory extract (Table 3) of Grove Street, on the Birkdale side
of the Ecclesfield working-class enclave.

Fig. 10.3. 'Two Sides of the Railway Tracks': Residential Variations in Birkdale in the
Early 1890s (6″ O.S. map extract)

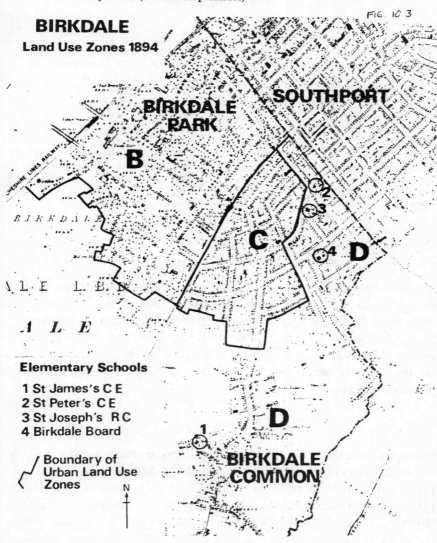

BIRKDALE
Land Use Zones 1894

FIG. 10 3

BIRKDALE PARK

SOUTHPORT

B

C   D

D

Elementary Schools

1 St James's C E
2 St Peter's C E
3 St Joseph's R C
4 Birkdale Board

Boundary of
Urban Land Use
Zones

N

BIRKDALE COMMON

TABLE 3

(From Johnson and Green's *Directory* of 1868)

GROVE STREET

From School St. to Shuttering Lane

Howard, R. labourer
Brookfield, J. labourer
Hosker, J. gardener
Rimmer, J. bath chair man
Burrowes, J. plumber
Rimmer, H. carter
Coulburn, P. cab driver
Wareing, J. gardener
Mackerell, W. gardener
Russell, J. painter
Dawber, J. coachman
Rosker, W. pointsman

Blair, Mary Ann, laundress
Draper, W. blacksmith
Buck, W. labourer
Timperley, J. gardener
Parkinson, T. miller
Rimmer, J. platelayer
Barton, R. gardener
Brown, R. labourer
Clare, W. cabinet maker
Durham, W. painter
Roberts, G. labourer
Bond, G. labourer
Turner, J. bricklayer

THE PROVISION OF SCHOOLING

As previously indicated, the population pyramid of Southport and Birkdale was unbalanced as compared with Bootle (Fig. 3.1), with a more aged population and a preponderance of females over males. Many of these were unmarried domestic servants, and spinsters and widows of private means. A high proportion of the population was middle-class. These factors dictated less publicly and more privately provided schooling.

THE PRIVATE SECTOR

Southport and Birkdale were therefore classic territory for the small but exclusive private school, and particularly the girls' school. From the opening of the first such school in Southport in 1813 by the Misses Wilson and Cowling, such establishments proliferated.[16] The advantages were obvious. The conditions needed for a successful resort and place of residence and retirement were those which favoured private school development. In the case of Southport and Birkdale there was access to many of the major industrial and commercial towns and cities of south Lancashire, an open coastal location, level topography, absence of industrialisation, and an existing reputation for cleanliness and good health. Robinson's *Descriptive History* of 1848 thus pointed out that the private and boarding schools had arisen with 'the notoriety of the town' while the salubrity of the air had 'a most beneficial effect upon the constitutions of the young folks'.[17]

The proprietors of the boarding schools were quick to seize upon such perceptions. Waterloo House School headed its advertisement 'Education at the Seaside', pointing out that the climate of Southport was 'mild, dry and bracing, rendering it, for young people especially, one of the healthiest places in the kingdom'.[18] Another proprietress brought her private school from Manchester to Southport, 'for the advantage of the purer air',[19] while the Manor House Commercial Schools in Wigan became the Commercial College in Birkdale Park.[20] Here Westlands School (Fig. 10.4) drew attention in its advertisement to its 'Extensive Grounds Facing the Sea', even though on the inland side of Westcliffe Road (Fig. 10.2).

Fig. 10.4. Advertisement for 'Westlands' School, Birkdale

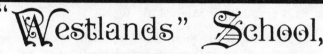

"**Westlands**" **School,**

BIRKDALE,

A First-class School for the Daughters of Gentlemen,

(Conducted for 20 years by Miss H. S. Cheetham.)

PRINCIPAL:—

MISS RAND, L.L.A., A. & M.C.P.

(Formerly Second Mistress in the Saltaire High School, and Lady Principal of the Princess Helena College).

EXTENSIVE GROUNDS FACING THE SEA.

Tennis Courts, Hockey and Archery Ground, Cycle Stable, Gymnasium, etc.

Cambridge Local and Associated Board Musical Examinations.

In such a setting, as Lewis Mumford suggested,

domesticity could flourish, forgetful of the exploitation upon which so much of it was based. Here individuality could prosper, oblivious to the pervasive regimentation beyond its curving roadways and naturalistic gardens.[21]

Thus the Manchester merchant, Bolton millowner or Liverpool broker might have indirect acquaintance with the social malaise and environmental blight of the industrial towns, but his wife, children and servants need not. If the family had a villa residence in Southport or Birkdale, the children could attend school daily in a similar environment. If the family continued to reside near the place of work, the child could be sent off to the seaside school as a boarder. To the search for environmental well-being was added that for social protection. As Joyce Pederson has described, for the small but exclusive school for girls (or for little boys) the most apposite milieu was the secluded and substantial private detached villa, in which a family atmosphere was given precedence over academic potential in attracting custom. Numbers of scholars were small, but of choice background.[22]

The majority of the early private schools of Southport and Birkdale conformed to this type. In 1853, for example, the local newspaper was used to advertise the fact that at Hope Cottage, Aughton Road, Birkdale Park (Fig. 10.2) Miss M. A. Walsh

purposes, at the close of the midsummer vacation, opening a school for a select number of young ladies, and begs leave to solicit patronage and support. The locality of her residence is particularly open, healthy, pleasant and genteel, and will be found a desirable situation for the improvement of health. Miss Walsh hopes by constant attention to accelerate the general improvement of young ladies entrusted to her care, and by her domestic arrangements promote their comfort.[23]

Similarly, Hannah Wallis, of whom we will hear more later, in opening her 'Friends' Preparatory School in Albert Road (Fig. 10.2) in 1861 informed

her friends that it is her intention to take a limited number of children to educate with her own family, in the usual branches of an English education. H.W. desires to unite the comforts of home with the necessary discipline of school; and while the utmost attention will be given to the mental and moral training of her pupils, it will be her endeavour to combine education with exercise and relaxation, as to promote the health and happiness of the children.

H.W. has taken a house in the healthiest part of this well-known and highly-esteemed watering place, within a short distance of the sea.

The terms were 30 guineas per annum, with French and Drawing two guineas extra. Three guineas per annum were charged for washing, and each pupil had to be provided with towels, dessert fork and spoon. A quarter's notice was required prior to the removal of a pupil.[24]

The schools were exceedingly various in type, however, leading Kitchener, an assistant commissioner of the Bryce Commission, to attempt a classification. His first category was the large establishment, probably with some boarders, carried on on public school lines. The second was the smaller establishment, for backward or delicate children, a mixture of the mental and physical sanatorium. The third was the preparatory school, preparing boys for the public schools. The fourth was the kindergarten of mixed boys and girls, and the fifth the school with no particular aim, which existed only because the lady's husband had died, or the gentleman's proper venture in life had failed. Kitchener concluded somewhat pejoratively that

almost anyone who sets up a school at a seaside place like Southport can get some pupils; there will always be well-meaning friends who will canvass for pupils to go to the new schools; in one case I was told the principal had not previously been a schoolmaster, but he had had an accident and lost his memory; so his friends set him up as a schoolmaster.[25]

Kitchener's classification seems to do less than justice to some well-provided schools for girls, which fit none of his five categories with exactitude. In these schools there were marked differences in curriculum and much less emphasis on the competitive ethic than the first category suggests. As his wife, a fellow-assistant commissioner observed, the stress in the girls' schools was rather on cultural activities, such as Music, French, and social accomplishments. The idea of a career education was anathema. '*My* pupils will never need to do anything' was one response received by Mrs. Kitchener.[26] There is, however, evidence that such assumptions were too sweeping to count as a balanced appraisal.

For the boys, more material considerations, such as modern facilities and preparation for mercantile and professional careers, as well as for a higher education were emphasised, as in an advertisement of 1857 labelled 'Strictly Private Education for the Sons of Noblemen and Gentlemen':

A clergyman long resident on the Continent, and now living at Birkdale Park, an Honours man of his University, and whose pupils have invariably been similarly distinguished, receives five Boarders and six Day Pupils whom his system of instruction will rapidly prepare for a successful College career. The course of instruction embraces the following subjects – Science, Mathematics, Algebra, Numbers and Logic, Languages: Hebrew, Greek,

Latin, French, German, Italian and English. The sciences and antient languages are so soundly taught as to assure that the pupil shall attain University Honours; the modern languages as accurately and expeditiously as they could be acquired on the Continent.[27]

The scepticism implicit in the Kitchener Report about the quality of some of the schools had long been a cause of concern locally, on the evidence of letters to the Editor and his leaders in the local newspaper, which complained variously of 'quackery', of 'charlatans' who had 'turned their attention to educating the young', and of the 'assumption of sham degrees'. The Editor condemned advertisements which reflected the self-important attitudes of principals, and described 'the home comforts' the youngsters were to enjoy 'like the flowery advertisements of an universal pill'.[28]

The high birth and death rate of many of the private schools, particularly in the early years of Birkdale Park, was no doubt in some instances an outcome of dubious quality and inefficient management. But as Pederson has observed, in the case of some of the small girls' schools, the principals may have been as much victims as villains. They were in an ambiguous position.[29] While purporting to be 'Ladies', they had to work for pay. Their livelihoods depended on their demonstration of linguistic and artistic accomplishments and mastery of social etiquette. Their economic prospects were, however, gloomy, for even successful principals of small schools could not expect to make a profit of more than, say, £300. Like governesses, they were in a subservient position. The whims of parents were a perennial threat. They treated the schools capriciously, withdrawing children without notice, complaining over fees, objecting to other children in the school, and interfering with the curriculum. Principals such as Hannah Wallis were clearly aware of the problem, and asked, as indicated in her original advert, for notice of removal.

Another uncertainty was the onset of social change in a particular area. While Southport and Birkdale were never subject to the intense ecological forces that beset large cities such as London and Liverpool, resulting in flights of respectable population from blighted central areas to the suburbs, and indeed were the beneficiaries of such change in broader terms, at the micro-level there were detailed problems. In Southport, for example, extension of the shopping and commercial core ate into an area of town houses and small private schools. As a result, the Misses Hobbs's school in Hoghton Street and Misses

Magnall's in Lord Street moved out to Waterloo Road and Weld Road respectively, both in Birkdale Park.

Local directories usefully reveal the life-spans of individual private schools. Robinson's *Directory* in 1848 listed 21 privately run day and boarding schools in Southport and Birkdale, of which one only had survived from 1831. Mannex's *Directory* of 1866 listed 45, but only 30 of these reappeared in a *Directory* of 1868. By this time, however, 26 new ones had been established, making 56 in all in that year. Of these, 21 survived to 1876. With 39 new ones, there were 60 private schools recorded in 1876. All but four of these were housed in private dwellings of various shapes and sizes. The turnover was reduced in the later years of the century, with the total number of private schools averaging about 50 in any one year.

Of those recorded in the 1868 *Directory* extract of Westcliffe Road, Westlands was the most permanent, though with changes of principals. Fig. 10.4 is an advertisement of this 'first-class school for the daughters of gentlemen'. It was recorded in directories between 1861 and 1901. Miss Sharp's Wyborne Gate was recorded in 1861 and 1871 directories, but Miss Sissons' Regenten House runs through to the early 1890s. 1871 seems to have been the peak year numerically for private ventures in Birkdale, when there were 18 such schools. Numbers declined to 17 in 1881, 14 in 1892 and ten in 1901. But those which had persisted were larger and more stable.

The census enumerators' returns[30] are informative about private schooling in recording details about the proprietors and their families, residential teaching staff, servants and, not least, pupils, though unfortunately only boarders. The returns for Birkdale thus refer, among others, to five of the schools in Westcliffe Road. At Westlands, June Gregson took 12 boarders in 1861, of whom ten were from Lancashire towns. She was helped by an assistant teacher and two servants. Born in Hull and aged 51 in 1871, Miss Gregson had by then been joined by a sister and two nieces who helped with the teaching. She employed three servants and accepted 15 boarders, of whom two came from Merseyside, six from the rest of Lancashire and seven from Yorkshire.

At Wyborne Gate, Prudence Sharp, a widow aged 79 in 1871, used four unmarried daughters, aged from 38 to 48, as teachers. The two servants of 1861 had been increased to three in 1871, and the number of boarders had grown from three to 16 over the same period. Of these

12 came from Lancashire towns. Sarah Sissons at Regenten House was similarly a widow assisted with the teaching in this case by one daughter. In 1871 she employed four servants and took 16 boarders, of whom only five were from Lancashire and nine from other parts of the British Isles. This was atypical, for most such schools relied on the industrial and commercial towns of northern England for their clientele.

Maria Hosker was the Principal of Netherwood, 23 Westcliffe Road. A spinster aged 35 in 1871, she employed Florence Watts, aged 22, as a 'governess' and two servants. She accepted eight boarders of whom six were from Lancashire. Next door at No. 24 Alicia Hayne and her sister Mary ran Dagfield (not mentioned in the 1868 Directory), employed one assistant mistress and five servants, and took 15 boarders of which nine came from Lancashire, four from Cheshire and two from Yorkshire.

Two striking features emerge from the returns. One offers some explanation of the female skew of the population of places like Birkdale. Of 102 persons recorded as residing in the five schools, all are female, and all are widows, spinsters or scholars. The other is the narrow age range of the 70 boarders residing in the five schools on census night, with 43 of the girls aged 14 to 16, only six over that age, and five 11 or less. It would seem at this stage the schools were largely offering some 'finish' to the domestic accomplishments of girls who presumably had previously attended private schools or even elementary schools of the more respectable type.

By 1903 there were in Southport and Birkdale 36 significant private schools, 12 girls', 13 boys', and 11 mixed. Of these, 21 were taking more than five boarders. The home area of 260 of the 541 boarders was recorded in a Lancashire County Council Survey of 1903.[31] Of these, 196 came from northern England, mostly the manufacturing districts of Lancashire and Yorkshire. The schools were characteristically located in the high status districts of Hesketh Park and Birkdale Park, with 46% of boarders in the former and 53% in the latter. In the schools of the 'collar' round the town centre less than 15% of the pupils were boarders. They included, however, some highly respectable schools of the 'proprietary' type, two of which later became the local authority 'split-site' girls' grammar school. Fees in general were significantly higher in the schools of Hesketh Park and Birkdale Park (Fig. 10.1).

Of the private schools the largest were Brentwood, with 120 girls and the University School, with 99 boys, both in Hesketh Park. The largest in Birkdale Park were Wintersdorf, with 82 girls, Bickerton House, 78 boys, and Brighthelmston, 71 girls (Plate 15). The girls' schools tended to have the higher proportion of boarders, 78 in the case of Brentwood, 52 at Wintersdorf and 45 at Brighthelmston, as against 40 and 17 respectively at two major boys' schools, University School and Bickerton House respectively. Birkdale Park had the larger concentration of girls' schools, 69% in comparison with 40% in Hesketh Park.

Some detail of the nature and provision of such schools can be abstracted from occasional surviving school prospectuses and records left by former pupils. Bickerton House was founded in the 1860s[32] and survived for more or less one hundred years before its buildings were demolished and the extensive site used for flat development. The school was the brain-child of Henry Mathwin, B.A., J.P., who was born in Kent in 1828 and moved to Lancashire in 1850, taking charge of elementary schools in Preston then in Bolton. He came to Southport in 1861, in which year, aged 32, he was running a boys' school at 52 Gloucester Road in Birkdale Park where resided also his mother, his wife and three young children aged eight, five and four. He accepted six boarders, all from East Lancashire towns. Later in this decade he erected a purpose-built school in York Road, in 'a wilderness and sandhills', which he named Bickerton House (Fig. 10.2). The first boys moved in in 1866 and the school was completed in 1869. It had primary and secondary departments and accepted both boarders and day boys.

The 1871 returns show Mathwin to have married again, and to have another young child. By this time his elder son, aged 18, was a student at Cambridge. He employed three resident unmarried masters, aged 37, 21 and 18, and four servants, including a nurse and cook. His 41 boarders were predominantly from the north-west, 13 from Merseyside, 19 from Lancashire, and two from Cheshire. More of the boarders were in the 13 to 16 age range with only four less than 13 and five over 16. By 1881, Mathwin's eldest son was 28, an M.A. and a master at the school. He continued to employ three resident masters, and now seven servants. Of 32 boarders recorded on census night, 25 were from northwest England and most of these from East Lancashire.

The school established an early reputation through successes in the Oxford then Cambridge Local Examinations. By 1903 it was preparing boys in its highest classes for University of London matriculation examinations. Mathwin, a staunch nonconformist, took his boarders regularly for Sunday worship at Trinity Wesleyan Church in Duke Street, just over the Southport border. He became a prominent figure on the Birkdale School Board. The subjects taught at Bickerton House included English, Arithmetic, Mathematics, Latin, French, German, Mechanics, Physics, Chemistry, Drawing, Shorthand, Wood-carving, Physiology and Music. Extra fees were charged for Music, Practical Chemistry and Wood-carving. The fees were £9. 9. 0 to £15. 15. 0 for day scholars and £52. 10. 0 to £63. 0. 0 for boarders. Three of the staff of six were graduates.[32]

The Principal of Brighthelmston girls' school, Hannah Wallis, was perhaps the most interesting educational personality in the area. As a widow with three children to support she had moved north from Brighton to found a school, previously mentioned, in Albert Road (Fig. 10.2). She used her two daughters, Mary and Margaret, aged 23 and 18, as teachers, and employed three others, including native-born teachers of German and French. Her 16 Quaker pupils came from a wider area than was the norm for Birkdale schools, half coming from other parts of England than the northern counties.

In 1876 an advert appeared in *The Friend* in which Hannah Wallis took pleasure

in informing her friends that she has REMOVED to a larger and more commodious house, which has been built expressly for her, and is adapted to the requirements of a High-class School.[33]

The school was until early this century purely a Quaker boarding establishment. It was one of only two buildings present in 1876 on Waterloo Road, a new thoroughfare pushing south into the sandhills from Lulworth Road (Fig. 10.2). A political activist, and strongly fired by a commitment to an education for girls beyond that of furnishing them with domestic and social skills, Hannah Wallis was a driving force in the establishment of 'Lectures for Ladies' in Southport in the early 1870s. These were forerunners of the University Extension lectures. Still in existence today, Brighthelmston was a more substantial enterprise than many such schools, taking advantage of a period of some emancipation of girls and women, a movement strongly supported by Hannah Wallis, and the introduction of Cambridge Local Examinations in the town in 1869. The girls of the school took the local examinations and attended the successful Lectures for Ladies, which were transferred from Southport to Birkdale Town Hall in 1876. According to the Census Enumerators' Returns for 1881, of which Table 4 is a one-page extract showing some of the boarders and servants, Hannah Wallis was still helped by her elder daughter, Mary, now aged 33, but her younger one, Margaret, is recorded as blind. There were four other resident teachers, a matron, and seven servants, together with 48 boarders. No doubt a result of national advertising in *The Friend*, the school attracted boarders from a wider catchment than Bickerton House, 21 coming from outside northwest England.

The curriculum of the school in 1888 included English Literature, Scripture, Geography, Science, Latin, French, German, Music, Drawing, Needlework and Philology. But whereas in Science at Bickerton House the boys studied Mechanics and Physics, here it was the 'softer' sciences: Botany and Geology. Reports of external examiners were published by the school in annual Reports. Unlike earlier stages, when the girls' schools gave priority to their social function, Brighthelmston was keen to establish its academic credentials, while maintaining a decent balance of activities. The Principals pointed out in their general remarks in a Report of 1888 that

more brilliant results might doubtless have been obtained at these examinations had more pressure been put on willing and eager students; but in the belief that examinations are only useful in so far as they represent the unhurried work of the whole year, gained in the regular school course, no amount of extra study is permitted which might, in any degree, overtax the physical powers.

By 1893, Sloyd, a Swedish system of manual training through woodwork, had been introduced, designed to help in the education of body and mind, the claim being that the hand was trained so that it might be the instrument of the will; the sense of sight to give the power of judging size and form; while patience and accuracy were cultivated as necessary to good work of any kind. The girls also played cricket (Plate 16) and other sports, and some took horse-riding lessons. Another unusual venture was the establishment of a teacher training class. The 'student teachers' wrote out abstracts of Fichte's lectures on teaching and studied the lives of great educational reformers, such as Rousseau, Arnold, Pestalozzi and

TABLE 4

Section from Census Enumerators' Returns, 1881, on Brighthelmston School

Froebel. They also received instruction on the development of the brain and the nervous system. They gave lessons to junior forms in the school, and their teaching methods were discussed and criticised by other students. The aims of the class were expounded by one of its organisers:

We try in this class to make it the aim of the would-be teachers to follow in the steps of the greatest of all teachers, who said of His mission "I am come that they might have life, and that they may have it more abundantly", to help them to understand that a teacher's office is not merely or principally to instruct the child, but to educate her, to draw out and train all her faculties so that none may be wasted, and thereby to widen her life and increase her powers.[34]

Thus Brighthelmston had moved unashamedly into vocational work for its girls. The school was a long-term success. By 1903 it was taking pupils to 21 years of age, in eight classes, preparing the highest classes for Cambridge Higher Local and Oxford Local Senior examinations, though it must be said that on the evidence of the 1902 results the numbers entered at these levels were small. The subjects being studied at this stage were English, Arithmetic, Mathematics, Latin, Greek, French, German, Botany, Nature Study, Drawing, Political Economy, Physiology, Scripture, Drill, Woodcarving, Needlework, Cookery and Singing. Extra fees were charged for Music, Singing, Advanced Drawing, Painting and Cookery. Fees ranged from £9. 9. 0 to £22. 10. 0 for day scholars and were £68. 5. 0 for boarders. There were 15 teachers, eight part-time, three of the latter being males. The school's 45 boarders included 22 from Lancashire and Yorkshire, six from Ireland and four from overseas.[35]

There was also a handful of private schools in the Birkdale part of the 'collar' round Southport town centre (Fig. 10.1). These were mostly day schools, smaller in size than the more prestigious establishments of Birkdale Park. They were located along or near the line of the tram route down Liverpool Road which ran to Birkdale Station and on towards Southport. In 1901 there were six schools in this area. They included Scarisbrick College with 44 day boys, Birkdale Grammar School with 25 day boys and six boarders, and Dinorwic High School with 21 mixed pupils.[36] All were relatively cheap by Birkdale Park standards, and were supported by aspiring local lower-middle-class parents. Some of the schools had serious academic pretensions but, to cater no doubt for the whole range of parental criteria, others were 'cut-price' versions of superior boarding schools, with a limited curriculum but some social selectivity. For some of the principals, schools of this type were test-beds for taking over more ambitious establishments.

As was noted in Bootle (Chapter 9), nineteenth-century working-class areas also spawned a range of private schools.[37] Between 1861 and 1891 eight private schools rose and fell in the working-class enclaves of Birkdale Common and Ecclesfield, none surviving for more than a decade. They were all on a small scale, held in private semi-detached houses, taking children who would otherwise have attended local elementary schools. In Birkdale it would seem they were used by parents who preferred the slightly more select intake, or because for the time being there were no accessible elementary school places available.

Thus for Southport and Birkdale Foster's recent classification of private schools is more applicable than Kitchener's somewhat off-hand effort of the 1890s. The classification is hierarchical, and all the categories included are below the major public school level.[38]

Group 1: the 'superior' schools, taking boarders, larger and better appointed than the norm, with graduates on the staff, relatively high fees, sometimes purpose-built accommodation, and a degree of permanency. Many of Birkdale Park's later schools were in this category, and particularly Wintersdorf, Brighthelmston and Bickerton House.

Group 2: the larger and more reputable schools of the 'Collar', including proprietary schools, in which most of the children were day pupils, travelling perhaps a small distance by tram or local train, and training pupils, in the case of boys at any rate, for clerical occupations. In Birkdale these included the group on the inland side of the railway tracks: Scarisbrick College, Birkdale Grammar School and Dinorwic High School.

Group 3: Foster describes these as 'middle schools' in the prestige sense, the cut-price versions of superior-type schools, mostly for girls, and often described as 'ladies schools'. But these were smaller and less durable than their larger sisters, taking in a wide range of age but offering a limited curriculum. They were particularly frequent in the early years of development of private schooling in Southport and Birkdale. Some of the schools of Birkdale Park would be marginal between Group 3 and Group 1 and some Group 3 schools may have risen to the Group 1 category. There were a number of such schools on either side of Birkdale Station.

Group 4: the less reputable, quasi-elementary small and impermanent day schools, found in the working-class dormitories of Southport and Birkdale. They had clearly filled an accommodation gap in some of these parts of Birkdale, for along the boundary zone with Southport serious elementary accommodation problems arose in the 1880s.

THE PUBLIC ELEMENTARY SECTOR

Mr. Shepherd, proceeding, said they had good ground for delaying the erection of a new school and it was unjust on the part of the Education Department to try and force the hands of the Board in that matter. They knew quite as much about the accommodation in the district as the Department. Dr. Cooper had told him that 100 more children could be accommodated in St. Peter's School, and he (Mr. Shepherd) knew for a fact that there was room for 100 more in St. James's School. For that reason he thought the Board should be allowed sufficient time to go into matters more fully.[39] (*School Board Chronicle*, 11 April 1891)

The organ of rate-aided education, the *School Board Chronicle*, devoted a disproportionate amount of the space it allotted to reports from the school boards to one of the smaller representatives, Birkdale. In comparison with Southport, Birkdale, though if anything more wealthy, was less well-placed so far as the provision of elementary education was concerned. By the time of the 1870 Education Act, Southport was one of the Lancashire towns (see Chapter 6) which had been helped by an early start in the provision of elementary schools by voluntary effort, and had maintained an excess of supply of accommodation over demand. Despite some problems created by the 'free places' issue in the 1890s, it avoided the need to establish a school board. Birkdale did not.

As we have seen, Birkdale's growth spurt came later, after the coming of the railway in the 1850s. Unlike Southport, where in the early stages there had been some mixture of social groups, and the generation of an ethos which took some responsibility for providing

Fig. 10.5. Southport and Birkdale Ecclesiastical Parishes and Schools, 1895 (after Foster)

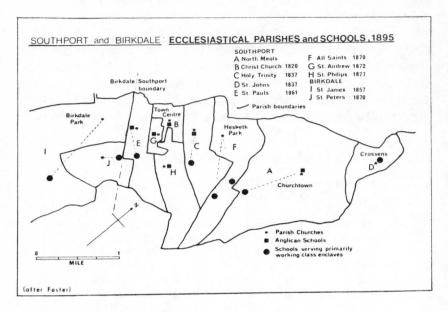

for poorer neighbours, Birkdale's middle-class population came in from outside. The social outlines were more clearly marked out. It was more difficult to develop, especially in the youthful stage of growth, a municipal spirit.

In one way, however, Birkdale aped Southport. The early churches of Southport, as at North Meols (Churchtown), Crossens, Christ Church and Holy Trinity (Fig. 10.5) had erected schools hard by the church. In these areas early development was socially relatively mixed. As the town grew, however, territorial segregation became more marked, and socially differentiated areas the pattern (see Fig. 10.1). At one social extreme, Hesketh Park and Birkdale Park became the most prestigious residential districts, while towards the outskirts working-class enclaves developed round existing agricultural settlements, as at Crossens and Birkdale Common, or grew from scratch. These were areas without sufficient resources to provide elementary education, but also those in which it was most needed. The response of the voluntary agencies was for a church in a middle-class zone to provide for a relatively distant working-class dormitory. Thus in Southport for example, St. Cuthbert's at Churchtown and All Saint's

in the Hesketh Park area provided three schools in the rapidly growing High Park–Blowick enclave, Holy Trinity in Little London, and
St. Paul's in Ecclesfield (Fig. 10.1). Birkdale's churches also followed
this principle. In 1857, St. James's established a school on Birkdale
Common, approximately one mile away, and St. Peter's, in a middle-
class fringe zone, for the Ecclesfield part of Birkdale. Similarly St.
Joseph's R.C. Church in Birkdale Park erected a school for the
Catholic children of the Ecclesfield area (Fig. 10.6), a clause in its
deeds in fact preventing it from building a school adjacent to the
church site.

Fig. 10.6. Educational provision on the Birkdale–Southport Boundary, 1883
            (after Foster)

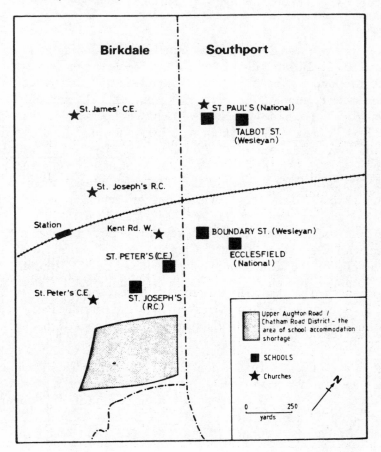

In Birkdale, however, this activity had failed to meet the needs of the rapidly growing working-class district round Upper Aughton Road and Chatham Street (Fig. 10.6), referred to by the Education Department as 'New Birkdale'. Here Birkdale had relied on the children being able to travel to schools in Southport. By the 1880s a major accommodation shortage had developed. There is little doubt that the inhabitants of Birkdale Park regarded the area not only as socially suspect, but also as distant from their concerns. Without the intensity of social problems which would have been recognised as diagnostic by a Bootle slum-dweller, through Birkdale eyes the district had rapidly acquired something of a similar reputation:

Chatham Road, Stamford Road, Kew Road, Broome Road, etc., – where most of our children come from – are inhabited by people in the poorest of circumstances ... in a great measure migratory ... moving in search of work ...[40]

Foster's research demonstrates something of the exaggeration contained in this Birkdale Board School Log Book comment, in that in 1895 the intake of its Infants' section included 63% of the children from socio-economic group III, 19% from SEG IV, and only 17% from SEG V. Even the Catholic St. Joseph's School had less than 40% in SEGs IV and V. The school with by far the highest proportion in the lower socio-economic groups was St. James's on Birkdale Common, with 30% from SEG IV, many being children of gardeners, and 38% from SEG V, mainly agricultural labourers.[41] But perceptions are relative, and the view that the board schools took the major share of socially deprived children was widely held.

As the working-class population grew, St. James's managed to keep pace with need at its Birkdale Common school and stave off the attentions of the Education Department, as did St. Joseph's for the Catholic children near the Southport boundary. St. Peter's was less successful. Lacking dynamic leadership, it would seem that the escalation of the accommodation problem in 'New Birkdale' had not been appreciated. The local HMI found a deficiency of 450 places in this parish in 1883, and no efforts being contemplated to plug the gap.

A First Notice to form a School Board in Birkdale had in fact been made over ten years previously, but the threat had been averted by voluntary effort. On this occasion, Birkdale found itself summarily confronted by a Final Notice and three months to form a School Board. St. Peter's was unable to supply the need. Kent Road Wesleyan

Church, which had recently closed a small school in Boundary Street (Fig. 10.6) refused to open its schoolroom in Kent Road, not wishing to compete with the reputable Talbot Road Wesleyan School in Southport, which many Birkdale children attended. Time ran out quickly, and the order for a School Board was issued on 24 August 1883.[42]

THE BIRKDALE SCHOOL BOARD

The first Birkdale School Board was formed, without an election, in September 1883, holding its initial meeting the following month. The Board had seven members, and these in the first instance were all middle class, four of them living in Birkdale Park. One of the group was Henry Mathwin, the Principal of Bickerton House private school. The majority was overwhelmingly voluntaryist in allegiance, a compact of Anglican and Roman Catholic interests, opposed by a Nonconformist minority.

The Board built its only school, for 490 pupils, in Bury Road in the heart of the 'New Birkdale' area in 1886 (Fig. 10.6), and appears not to have been particularly enthused by its own achievement. The local newspaper interpreted its mood as negative: 'The quieter they could have the opening the better', despite more radical members of the Board wanting a public ceremony.[43] The Board was correct in assuming that building schools was an expensive part of its responsibility. As Fig. 10.7 illustrates, major surges in expenditure were occasioned by the capital charges involved in building and extending schools, as happened in 1885/6, and 1892/3. The actual burden on the rates was relatively small, however, though approaching five pence in the £ by the late 1890s (see Fig. 6.4).

In the early years there appeared some doubt as to how large the Board School should be. The Education Department accepted the Board's estimate that 490 places would suffice, but the most radical member, William Warburton, renewing the mode of conflict he had engaged in some years earlier with voluntaryist opponents on the Salford School Board (see Chapter 6), claimed that 750 places were required, although he would have accepted 600 as a compromise. The sufficiency of places was brief, and by the late 1880s a serious deficiency was apparent. Again the response was too tardy. The Birkdale School Board was about to face the discomfiture of having grant withheld by the Education Department.

Fig. 10.7. School Board Income and Expenditure, Birkdale, 1885–1894

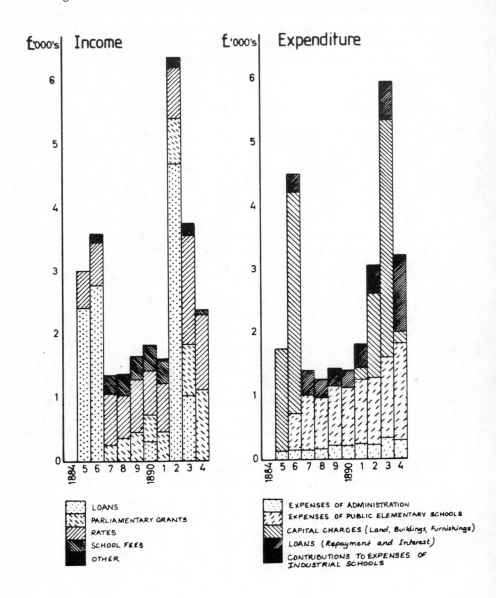

£'000's Income

£'000's Expenditure

LOANS
PARLIAMENTARY GRANTS
RATES
SCHOOL FEES
OTHER

EXPENSES OF ADMINISTRATION
EXPENSES OF PUBLIC ELEMENTARY SCHOOLS
CAPITAL CHARGES (Land, Buildings, Furnishings)
LOANS (Repayment and Interest)
CONTRIBUTIONS TO EXPENSES OF
INDUSTRIAL SCHOOLS

Conservative members of the Board strove to maximise accommodation provision in the voluntary sector to avert the need to extend the
Board School. Their nonconformist opponents objected to the claim
that a joiner's shop and old saw mill at St. Joseph's were 'certified for
school purposes' even though they had not been subject to inspection.
Under the pressure of this charge of 'massaging' the evidence, the
Chairman was forced to redesignate them as 'extra' rather than 'certified' accommodation. Mathwin further accused the Board of attempting to force non-Catholic children into a Catholic school.[44]

The Board's next tactic was to try to exclude Southport children
from Birkdale schools by demanding higher fee payments, amount-
ing to fourpence for infants, sixpence for Standards I to IV, and
ninepence above Standard IV. Mathwin condemned this ploy as a
'monstrous proposition' seeing such a 'protective tariff' as unique:

It appeared to him that the Board were smitten with paralysis, and if not at
present they would some day be the laughing stock of the country ... It was
humiliating and disappointing to him to be mixed up with a Board which
appeared to him to be doing nothing to supply the educational wants of the
district.[45]

The *School Board Chronicle* drew attention to a report in the *Southport Guardian* from the Rev. J. Hirst Hollowell of the Northern
Counties Education League, which accused the 'Evangelical Church-
men' on the Board of doing their utmost to break the law, violating
parental rights of conscience and retarding education:

The pressure on the Board School is so great that, when I visited the school,
little children were doing their sums kneeling on the floor, remaining in this
position a long time, because there were no desks, and no space to put desks.

In the event, the Education Department regarded the fees proposed
for Southport children as needlessly high, but did allow threepence,
fourpence and sevenpence as a compromise.[46] The more serious
rebuff was to follow. At a specially called meeting on 20 March 1891
the Clerk to the Board read the following letter from the Education
Department:

Their Lordships have had under consideration the report of H.M. Inspector
of the above-named school [the Board School]. I am directed to point out
that in spite of the warning given last year the average attendance of your
mixed school has been allowed to exceed the amount of the recognised
accommodation. H.M. Inspector reports that nothing has been done as yet to
add to the accommodation. I am to desire you to furnish my Lords with an

explanation of your failure to take measures for supplying the deficiency. I am to inform you that the grant to your school cannot in the meantime be paid.

While one of the voluntaryist members deplored the injustice of this procedure (see reference 39), Mathwin referred again to his sense of humiliation in belonging to a body that had received an 'unmistakable snub' from the Department, placing it in 'a very undignified position'. The Chairman, in concluding the debate, unashamedly supported the course the Board had followed, however, arguing that the position of the majority had never been absolutely to oppose the provision of further accommodation. Its intention had

simply been to deal honourably and honestly with the Denominational schools, to refrain from undue competition with those schools, and to allow them a proper opportunity for development.

The fact that the Board was being 'hurried a little in their progress' could in no sense be interpreted as a humiliation.

At the next meeting, there occurred another bitter dispute between Mathwin and voluntaryist members of the Board, Mathwin being accused of acting underhandedly by 'talking to the Inspectors' about accommodation, the letter from the Education Department being interpreted as the outcome. The Board had to bow to the inevitable, however, and finance a school extension. The Chairman, Dr. Newsham, laid the blame for the Department's intervention squarely on the managers of the voluntary schools. The Board had given them the opportunity for providing for the educational wants of the district and they had failed to take it. He accepted Mathwin's resolution to increase accommodation at the Board School on land recently purchased, and asked for unanimous support. In fact the voluntaryist vote split, and the motion was carried by five votes to two.[47]

Conflict was reawakened in 1892 over the free places issue. Stirred into action by a nonconformist pressure group, first 57 parents petitioned the Education Department, stating their desire to enjoy free education in public elementary schools, and complaining that there was insufficient accommodation available without payment of fees. At a special meeting of the School Board on 15 November 1892, the voluntaryist group argued that the memorials 'were not exactly the spontaneous declaration of the parents of the children' and demanded that the School Attendance Officer check the *bona fide* nature of the signatures. The Chairman reiterated that he saw it as the Board's duty to take an overview of elementary provision in Birkdale which meant protecting the interests of the voluntary schools as well as the Board School. The Nonconformist group insisted on the right of parents to claim free places.[48]

A further petition to the Education Department followed, signed by 259 families. Of these 104 parents, covering 167 children, were in a position of claiming but not receiving free places. Of these, six were at St. James's, 33 at St. Peter's, 116 at the Board School, and none at St. Joseph's. Not for the first time, serious confrontation was generated by an accusation from a Nonconformist member that the School Attendance Officer had exerted improper pressure on parents in checking the petitions.

A perennial reaction of a minority group to being constantly out-voted on what they saw as cardinal issues of principle, was to air their grievances in the local press, a procedure regarded as provocative by the majority, who thought all the debates should be conducted on the floor of the School Board. Thus a letter from William Warburton to the *Southport Visiter* (sic) in 1888, complaining over the Board's parsimony in allowing the Headmaster of the Board School to award prizes for good attendance, in not remitting fees for needy children, and refusing a request for a rise in salary from the Headmaster, asked the Editor, by giving publicity, to 'help to shame this Board out of its puerile and disreputable mode of procedure'.[49]

Similarly, unpleasant relationships between Nonconformist members of the Board and staff at the Board School followed a demand from Kate Ryley who, in the eyes of the majority, had taken on the mantle of Warburton as *agent provocateur*, that a punishment book be kept at the Board School. She wrote to the press, complaining of cruelty at the school. The Headmaster responded in kind, publicly branding her as a 'brawling woman'. While the Board objected to an employee writing thus to the press, in this case it admitted mitigating circumstances.[50] The acrimony worsened, and when the opportunity arose through unfavourable inspectors' reports in the late 1890s to dismiss the Headmaster, Arthur Mortimer, it was seen by his supporters on the Board as 'paying off old scores'. It marked the start of the official involvement of the National Union of Teachers in Birkdale's affairs in the Birkdale tenure case of 1898–1900.[51]

CONCLUSION

Though small in scale, Birkdale none the less encountered many
of the cross-currents which characterised late nineteenth-century
educational development in England, and in particular in its suburban districts, much neglected in the historiography of education.
It experienced a wide range if not the full intensity of ecological
forces and socio-economic changes which, as we have seen, dictated
socially graded educational responses, and subtly but relentlessly
fixed inequality into the system. The social divides were in Birkdale,
as elsewhere, mediated through residential segregation into exclusive
and secluded private schools for the affluent, in Birkdale Park; into
less prestigious establishments which catered equally faithfully for the
perceived needs of more humble but aspiring parents on the other side
of the railway tracks; and into the grudging and meagre provision for
more proletarian working-class groups in Birkdale's 'East End', seen
stereotypically as meriting the most limited curriculum consistent
with the codes and not likely to be appreciative even of that. Thus the
disposition of its Headmaster of the Board School, on the evidence of
his log books, suggests as negative an image of the working-class
parents of his catchment area[52] as that of the local élites with whom he
was otherwise so often in dispute. Neither seemed aware of the
relativities: that Birkdale's 'troublesome thoroughfares' were of a
lesser order of magnitude than those of Bootle and similar slum
environments. But the perception was enough to shape the attitude.

The spread of inspected elementary education came late to Birkdale, and the more sophisticated provision offered by some progressive urban boards never arrived. Unlike its neighbour Southport,
Birkdale's suburban development and population spurt came late,
and within the School Board period, into which Birkdale was dragged
protesting when its voluntary agencies were found wanting. A School
Board was regarded as an alien, proletarian and anti-religious
imposition, lowering the tone of the place as compared with its rival,
Southport, disposed to remind Birkdale of its indignity. The story
of Birkdale's response is testimony to a widespread element in educational development in this period, whereby school boards were in
effect taken over by their opponents, as we have seen in certain Lancashire towns and cities (Chapter 6). Here local elites were able to
translate their idiosyncratic and sometimes anachronistic definitions

into decisions which trimmed the quality and quantity of educational provision for their districts. The permissive legislation of the time was exploited and even flouted, although, as we have noted in Bootle (Chapter 8), the central authority was prepared to hold the line if the local body strayed too far beyond the bounds of legitimacy.

Birkdale illustrates particularly well the uneasy balance between rate and voluntary aided schooling in an area already attuned to another dual system, in which parents had the choice of small privately run establishments or respectable publicly supported voluntary schools. It demonstrates also the paradox of a situation in which certain large urban boards propelled mass education forwards, raising standards of accommodation (Plate 3), demanding more highly qualified teachers, extending the curriculum as far as the codes would allow, and beyond them in the case of the higher grade schools, adding to the variety of provision in the elementary sector, and pioneering a public scholarship system; while others similarly formally constituted were almost Luddite in their response to the notion of educational improvement. Birkdale's was clearly placed towards the reactionary end of the spectrum. Among those most discernibly zealous for educational advance in the township were two private school principals, Hannah Wallis and Henry Mathwin, the latter reacting angrily, as an authentic nonconformist voice in the educational debate, against the stone-walling of his church colleagues. Finally the unsubtle confrontations and machinations of would-be reformist members of the Board inflamed the many internal and external disputes it experienced and ensured that Birkdale cut a poor figure in the educational arena.

The fact that Birkdale was part of a larger urban entity, while remaining administratively separate, was undoubtedly to its disadvantage. It was over-reliant on Southport's older-established school provision. Here there had been time for the voluntary sector to evolve a socially-graded public system, which included prestige elementary schools at Holy Trinity (Church of England) and Talbot Street (Wesleyan), and later higher grade schools associated with St. Andrew's (girls) and Christ Church (boys) in the town centre. Birkdale's public sector requirement was easily interpreted as plugging the gaps at the level of the lowest social common denominator: the education of the poor.

As noted in Chapter 6, the Inspectorate had increasingly complained of sub-standard provision in Lancashire's voluntary sector during the School Board period. Birkdale conformed to such judgements. In general its church school managers assumed a low profile in the educational debate, leaving their supporters on the School Board to defend their position. Enthusiasm for raising standards of provision was muted. Inspectors drew attention to the poor academic achievement at St. James's School on Birkdale Common, for example. In 1886 no merit grants were paid 'in view of the weakness and unintelligence of the instruction'. The managers reacted to the rebuff by replacing uncertificated with certificated teachers. But not for long. The grant steadied at about 18/-, 2/- less than that received at the oft-criticised Board School.[53]

The coexistence of regressive, early nineteenth-century type, attitudes to educational growth with the generally more expansive thinking which characterised the School Board period, a response in large measure to the build-up of pressures from tertiary society for a more responsive and variegated school system, impels reflection on the extent to which local autonomy and the voluntaryist spirit have been to the profit or loss of educational development in England and Wales. For unequal national provision and thereby unequal access and opportunity have been paralleled for over two centuries by these peculiarities which would appear, though by no means the only, certainly connected factors. The strictures implicit in the opening quotation remain applicable a century and a half later, for while the increments to the educational aggregate both in quality and quantity have been immense, the work of schooling the people is far from fully accomplished 'from the want of equality in the distribution'.[54]

REFERENCES AND FOOTNOTES

1. *Bryce Commission*, Vol. 6 (1896), p. 349.
2. *B.T.*, 17 Nov. 1888.
3. *Southport Visiter* (hereafter *S.V.*), 7 June 1855.
4. F. A. Bailey, *A History of Southport* (Southport, 1955), pp. 158–9.
5. H. Perkin, 'The "Social Tone" of Victorian Seaside Resorts in the North-West', *Northern History*, Vol. 11 (1976), pp. 180–94.
6. J. Liddle, 'Estate Management and Land Reform Politics: the Hesketh and Scarisbrick Families and the Making of Southport, 1842–1914', in D. Cannadine (ed.), *Patricians, Power and Politics in Nineteenth-century Towns* (Leicester, 1982), pp. 143–4.
7. *Ibid.*, p. 148.
8. Quoted in Bailey, *op. cit.* (1955), p. 155.
9. *Ibid.*, p. 198.

10. See J. Liddle, ' "Castles in the Sand": the Urban Development of Southport, 1792–1910' (unpublished University of Lancaster Ph.D. thesis, forthcoming).
11. Quoted in Bailey, *op. cit.* (1955), p. 200.
12. Rev. W. T. Bulpit, *Notes on Southport and District* (Southport, 1908), pp. 38–9.
13. Bailey, *op. cit.* (1955), p. 199.
14. Liddle, *op. cit* (1982), pp. 144–5.
15. See H. J. Foster, 'The Influence of Socio-Economic, Spatial and Demographic Factors on the Development of Schooling in a Nineteenth-century Residential Town' (unpublished University of Liverpool M.Ed. thesis, 1976), p. 183.
16. W. E. Marsden, 'The Development of the Educational Facilities of Southport, 1825–1944' (unpublished University of Sheffield M.A. thesis, 1959), p. 106.
17. F. Robinson, *A Descriptive History of the Popular Watering-place of Southport in the Parish of North Meols on the Western Coast of Lancashire* (London/Southport, 1848), p. 73.
18. *S.V.*, 3 March 1859.
19. *S.V.*, 8 July 1853.
20. *S.V.*, 15 June 1866.
21. L. Mumford, *The Culture of Cities* (London, 1938), p. 215.
22. J. S. Pederson, 'Schoolmistresses and Headmistresses: Elites and Education in Nineteenth-century England', *The Journal of British Studies*, Vol. 15 (1975), pp. 138–47.
23. *S.V.*, 8 July 1853.
24. *The Friend*, Seventh Month 1 (1861), p. 192. I am grateful to Mr. A. J. Usher for this reference.
25. *Bryce Commission*, Vol. 6 (1895), pp. 224–5.
26. *Ibid.*, p. 297.
27. *S.V.*, 6 Aug. 1857.
28. *S.V.*, 4 Aug. 1876.
29. Pederson, *op. cit.* (1975), pp. 138–46.
30. P.R.O., Rt 9/2759 (1861 returns) and Rt 10/3872 (1871 returns).
31. The details are recorded in a Lancashire County Council publication, *Particulars with Respect to Secondary Day Schools, Central Classes for Pupil Teachers and Evening Schools and Classes within the Administrative County of Lancaster* (Preston, 1903).
32. A manuscript account of this school, in the Southport Public Library, is contained in E. Glasgow, *Historical Notes on Bickerton House School*.
33. *The Friend*, Eighth Month 1 (1876), p. 4.
34. *Brighthelmston School Reports*, 1888, pp. 16–17; and 1893, pp. 31–2.
35. Lancashire County Council, *op. cit* (1903), p. 12.
36. Information taken from H. J. Foster, 'Variation in the Provision of Secondary Education in the late Nineteenth-Century: a Regional Study' (forthcoming University of Liverpool Ph.D. thesis, to which this chapter is heavily indebted).
37. For a study of working class private schools, see P. Gardner, *The Lost Elementary Schools of Victorian England: the People's Education* (London, 1984).
38. See Foster, *op. cit.*, forthcoming.
39. *School Board Chronicle* (hereafter S.B.C.) 11 April 1891.
40. *Birkdale Board School Log Book*, 29 March 1888.
41. Foster, *op. cit.* (1976), pp. 185–6.
42. *Ibid.*, pp. 188–95.
43. *S.V.*, 13 March 1886.
44. *S.B.C.*, 8 Nov. 1890.
45. *S.B.C.*, 23 Aug. 1890.

46. *S.B.C.*, 8 Nov. 1890.
47. *S.B.C.*, 11 April 1891.
48. *S.B.C.*, 3 Dec. 1892.
49. *S.V.*, 19 May 1888.
50. *S.V.*, 2 Sept. 1893.
51. See R. S. Betts, 'The Birkdale School Board Tenure Case, 1898–1900', *Journal of Educational Administration and History*, Vol. 17 (1985), pp. 39–47.
52. See *Birkdale Board School Log Book*, 29 Nov. 1887.
53. H. J. Foster, *op. cit.* (1976), pp. 209–10.
54. 'Popular Education in England', *The British Quarterly Review*, Vol. 8 (1846), p. 480.

Index